Bandiet

*Seven Years in a
South African Prison*

HUGH LEWIN

LONDON
HEINEMANN
IBADAN · NAIROBI · EXETER (NH)

Heinemann Educational Books Ltd
22 Bedford Square, London WC1B 3HH
PMB 5205, Ibadan · PO Box 45314, Nairobi

EDINBURGH MELBOURNE AUCKLAND
HONG KONG SINGAPORE KUALA LUMPUR
NEW DELHI KINGSTON PORT OF SPAIN

Heinemann Educational Books Inc.
4 Front Street, Exeter, New Hampshire 03833, USA

ISBN 0 435 90251 2

© Hugh Lewin 1974
First published by Barrie & Jenkins 1974
First published in African Writers Series 1981

*For Bram Fischer
and all other political prisoners inside South African jails;
for Jock Strachan (who made things so much better inside)
and for others like him, out of jail
but still restricted inside South Africa*

Set in Monotype Plantin
Made and printed in Great Britain by
Richard Clay (The Chaucer Press) Ltd.,
Bungay, Suffolk

Contents

Bandiet

an Afrikaans word meaning *convict*. No longer in official use because considered derogatory. Unofficially – i.e. in common use throughout South African jails – a prisoner is called a *bandiet*. Plural *bandiete*.

Warders are known, among bandiete, as *boere* – singular *boer*. The term is generic for all warders, whatever language they speak, and has little to do with historical antagonisms. *Boere* dislike being called *boere*.

Boop means prison. Origins doubtful, but probably 'booby-hatch' contracted to 'boob' – and always pronounced boop.

1 Arrest and Interrogation

Accused No. 2 states:

'My lord, I am twenty-four years old.

'I was born in Lydenburg, in the Eastern Transvaal, where my father was the Anglican parish priest. When I was one, my father was transferred to Irene, near Pretoria, where he became parish priest and chaplain to the Irene Homes.

'When I was eight, I was sent as a boarder to St John's College, an Anglican private school in Johannesburg. I matriculated there in 1956, then stayed on at school for a post-matric year in preparation for my studies at university.

'I wanted to become a priest, and arrangements were made for me to go first to Rhodes University and then to a theological college in England.

'I completed my B.A. at Rhodes University, Grahamstown, in 1960 but I felt then that I was not yet equipped to face the rigours and demands of the priesthood, so I postponed my trip to England. My father, my lord, was a gentle and loving man with whom I had a close and warm relationship until he died, aged eighty, in 1963. He brought me up to believe that all men, rich or poor, should be respected and loved as creatures of God. I have always believed, and still do believe, that all men are equal in the eyes of God: This belief was a strong factor in my decision to commit sabotage.

'During my last years at school I spent a number of Sundays as a guest of Father Trevor Huddleston and the other fathers of the Community of the Resurrection, in Sophiatown. Here, for the first time, I was brought into direct contact with the poverty and suffering of the African community that lived there. I listened to their conversations and heard them speak about their frustrations, caused by the laws which prevented them from improving their lot, and about their hatred, especially for the pass laws which disrupted their lives.

'In the white community, my father was a poor man. But by comparison with the Africans whose homes I went to, he seemed very wealthy. This difference between whites and blacks set the laws which governed them against the whole Christian teaching which was the basis of my life.

'As I grew older I began to believe that this negation was the fault of the whites who governed the country. I also began to believe that those who accepted the situation shared the responsibility with those who governed. I began to feel guilty of being white and I felt a powerful need to do something myself which could alter the situation.

'At university I joined organizations which were non-racial in character, and I became a member of the Liberal Party which then advocated a non-racial policy. I worked hard at these activities in the hope that I would be able to do something to change a way of life which white South Africans seem to regard as traditional. After university I continued to do what I could to focus attention on the laws which I felt prevented Africans from living a full and proper life. But my efforts seemed puny and hopeless. It seemed that nothing would awaken the whites. At about this time I was approached by a friend who asked me to become a member of the "National Committee for Liberation", a secret sabotage group. My lord, I was terrified. Instinctively I was opposed to any form of violence and I knew that I was not suitable to the active role I was being asked to play. In spite of this, I decided to join.

'Two factors in particular influenced me in making this decision. I was told that the N.C.L. was a small group, consisting largely of young people, who wanted to make a demonstration of their protest, in the hope that by such demonstrations attention would be focused on the living conditions of the blacks. My previous attempt to do this had been completely ineffective. I thought that sabotage might shock the whites into an awareness of the conditions under which the blacks were living and, in due time, change the system.

'Secondly, I was told that the sabotage would be committed

only against installations such as pylons, which were to be selected in a way which would ensure that the explosions would not endanger human life. The motive was to shock, not to injure. This, perhaps wrongly, I was able to reconcile with my conscience. So, with some trepidation, I joined the organization. I was a member of the N.C.L. – later called the ARM, African Resistance Movement – for about eighteen months. Our efforts were disorganized, our actions were sporadic. During that time I personally participated in three acts of sabotage. Another five acts were committed by other members of the organization, but there were no changes and it seemed that what we were doing was futile. I was filled with doubts, and even thought of leaving my own South Africa. But always I came back to the sense of guilt and the feeling that I was part of a problem which I could not escape from by running away. So I stayed in the organization and remained a member until my arrest.

'I know, my lord, that I must go to jail for what I have done. I know too that what I have said is not likely to lighten my sentence, but I have felt a need to explain myself not only to your lordship but also to those people who by their love and loyalty have shown their trust in me. I thank your lordship for granting me that opportunity.'

I made that statement from the dock in the trial in November 1964 when four of us were charged in Pretoria under the Sabotage Act. With me were Fred Prager, a widower in his late fifties, formerly married to one of the founders of the N.C.L.; Baruch Hirson, forty-three-year-old physics lecturer, an actual founder of the N.C.L.; and Raymond Eisenstein, economics journalist, three years older than me. Fred got off. The other three of us changed our pleas to guilty in the face of incontrovertible evidence against us. We knew that the Sabotage Act carried a mandatory minimum sentence of five years. Baruch got nine years. Raymond and I got seven years each.

By the time we were sentenced we had already been in jail for five months, three months in solitary detention, two months awaiting trial.

Now I have finished my seven and a half years in prison for

sabotage. Being a political prisoner, I got no remission. I served the full seven-year sentence. I was twenty-four when I went in. I flew out of South Africa on my thirty-second birthday, having been given four days after my release in which to leave the country or be put under twenty-four-hour house arrest.

Now I have finished my seven and a half years as a bandiet and I am not sorry. I am glad it's finished. I am also glad that I have been through it. Just as, at my trial, I could not apologize for the actions which had got me into the box, so too now I cannot regret that this has happened to me.

I can claim neither uniqueness nor courage. What happened to me could happen to anybody and it will, I am sure, happen to a lot more people. That will be good: it was only as a prisoner – as a bandiet in a South African jail – that I could begin to realize what life is like for most South Africans. I am white. I had to go inside to know what it's like to be black. I also spent eight months among ordinary criminals in a maximum security jail. The hanging jail. I think that any person, in any society, should know what it is like to live in a hanging jail.

That is why I write these things. Yet I hesitate to write anything about what I have experienced – not because it worries me, nor because I think it unimportant, but because it may give satisfaction to men like Aucamp and Swanepoel. They are the sort of men who wield power in South Africa today and they are men who like hearing about themselves.

Aucamp was the man responsible for the treatment of political prisoners. 'I don't care,' he once said, 'if people overseas know I'm in charge. I'm big enough to take it.' Aucamp will like to know that people outside South Africa know he was in charge of the politicals. That, he will think, is fame. (His other claim to fame was being manager of the Pretoria Prison rugby football club.)

Swanepoel will also like hearing about himself. Swanepoel was Chief Interrogator of the South African Security Police. He was the man who was in charge of interrogating political detainees. While Swanepoel was in charge of interrogating detainees, at least nineteen people died in detention.

I know Swanepoel will laugh when he reads that. I know he

will laugh when he reads that I say that, a fortnight after I first
met him, he swore he would kill me. Swanepoel will get satisfaction from that, knowing that someone is writing about him
and describing the fear he generates in the people he is interrogating.

But I must write this in spite of Aucamp and Swanepoel and
their pleasure – because they are not the only people who are
South Africans and they are the least important of the people I
met during seven years as a bandiet. I must write this because of
men like Bram Fischer, former Q.C., now political bandiet for
life. And Denis Goldberg, engineer, sentenced to life imprisonment at the age of thirty-one. And Dave Kitson, sentenced to
twenty years. And the others in Pretoria. And the others, worse off
because they are not white, on Robben Island. All bandiete, with
a long time ahead of them as bandiete, because they believe in a
decent society and were prepared to act on their belief.

I never thought that I would be in a position to do this. I never
thought that I would go to jail. I was white, living in the nice
easy white society, and even when I started to do most un-white
sorts of things, like blowing up pylons, it was possible to slip back
into the white suburban ways which provided a useful screen
against detection – and a screen against unwholesome reality. For
so long it had always happened to *them*, the blacks, and had never
directly affected us, the whites, never in an inescapable way. It
would never happen to me, I thought.

The sabotage organization I joined was a small multi-racial
group made up largely of people who were not widely known as
being politically active. By the time I was approached to join the
group in November 1962 – then still called the National Committee for Liberation – the organizational structure had been
fixed for a couple of years, centring around a dozen or so activists
in Johannesburg and a slightly larger group in Cape Town. There
was also a handful of people in Port Elizabeth and Durban. I
doubt if there were ever more than fifty people actively involved.
What I saw of the structure (not much) suggested an informal
rather than rigid hierarchy, reflecting the ideologically imprecise
nature of the N.C.L.: the orientation was, broadly, socialist,
ranging from some members who were dissident communists

15

through to those of us who had been members of the Liberal Party and who had become disenchanted with the Liberals' insistence on passive non-violent protest.

The group seemed bound together by a desire for action and by some initial successes, particularly a large haul of dynamite from a coal-mine store and a spectacular toppling of power pylons near Johannesburg. We were amateurs and it is easy, looking back now, to ridicule the group, to think of it solely as a small group attempting sabotage activities as a counterpart to the larger and more widespread activities of *Umkhonto we Sizwe* (Spear of the Nation), the military arm of the African National Congress. But even in the relatively short time I was a member, the N.C.L. – or, as we called it after the Rivonia trial, the ARM, African Resistance Movement – achieved fair success in terms of the group's objectives: there were at least half a dozen sabotage attacks on pylons, railway signal cables or power standards. These attacks were, on two occasions, coordinated between Johannesburg and Cape Town, giving the appearance of a larger organization than was actually the case. In addition, there were Africans involved in our group in Johannesburg and it was thus possible – in fact necessary, because of the apartheid society – to hit targets both in white and black areas. We would meet, train and construct our equipment together, then work apart. The results again gave the impression of a larger organization than actually existed.

And the N.C.L./ARM – despite itself – spawned the one cataclysmic act of South African sabotage: the petrol bomb placed in the crowded concourse of Johannesburg Station on 24 July 1964 by John Harris. That station bomb – which killed one and severely injured others, and led to John Harris being hanged – was an ironic end to ARM activities: it shattered the ARM policy of avoiding harm to people, and it happened a fortnight *after* the ARM had effectively ceased to exist. When John's bomb went off, most of the ARM members were either out of the country, or in detention.

The beginning of the end was on 4 July 1964 when the police carried out raids throughout the country, searching the homes of many Left sympathizers or assumed sympathizers. Among others, they picked up several members of Umkhonto who had managed to evade the earlier net which had resulted in the Rivonia trial. Also, by chance almost, they picked up 'Mark' in Cape Town. He had been president of the national union of students and he was an active member of the Liberal Party. He was raided along with many other similar people – all of them possible sympathizers of underground sabotage groups, among whose papers might have been some tenuous references which could lead to more tangible links. Unhidden in Mark's flat, they found virtually the entire history of the N.C.L. displayed in documents carefully kept by him. The police (so they admitted later, when using the documents as effective levers for interrogation) were most surprised at their sudden discovery.

At the time, those of us in Johannesburg knew only that Mark had been detained. There were suggestions in the papers that others had been held too. Four days after his arrest – towards midnight on 8 July 1964 – one of our Johannesburg group whom I knew only as 'Kate' contacted me and indicated that there was an emergency. I went out to meet Kate and 'Herbert', her husband, and found them already packed and ready to set off by motorbike for the border. They reported that 'Luke' had arrived from Cape Town having dodged the Special Branch there; that he reported that Mark was talking; and that the balloon was up. We must go, quickly. Out. The two of them on their motorbike were fine because they had a British passport and could make it across the border into Bechuanaland. But Luke had no papers. He would have to go with 'Diane', the woman who had originally recruited me and with whom I had searched out a safe route into Swaziland. They had left Luke waiting near their cottage, so I drove back there, picked him up in my car, then headed out to Diane's place, a fair distance out of town. We woke her at about two in the morning and told her, with her two kids asleep, that it was time to go.

A cool girl, Diane. She was up immediately, busy with useful things like coffee and biscuits – and did any of us have enough spare cash? She would leave with Luke and her kids at five; Kate and Herbert could leave at six. What was I going to do? We needed ready cash and I said I would return to town quickly and pick up what I could collect from friends. Time enough when I got back to decide finally what I would do. Immediately there was the need for cash, and the need to phone another friend to come and lock up Diane's house once we'd all left, and the need to find someone to phone Herbert's boss in the morning to say he was sick and so give them an extra few hours to reach the border properly, and the need for someone to phone 'Tom' and tell him to leave.

All the things to do immediately – which conveniently prevented me making the decision I had never thought I would have to make: whether to go or stay. I didn't want to decide. There were enough things, as we drank Diane's coffee at 2.30 in the morning, enough to keep us talking and planning without my deciding what I didn't want to decide. There was, for instance, Mark. Luke was adamant: he was talking, and talking a great deal; the Branch had been only a step behind Luke at every turn; he had escaped from Cape Town by a combination of luck and ridiculous daring. Mark was talking and talking fast – and nobody was in a better position to talk about the N.C.L. than Mark. He had, over a couple of years and through very hard work, established himself as national organizing secretary. He had tremendous energy and enthusiasm. He had also made a point always of insisting more than most on the constant need for security; all records and documents should be destroyed immediately they were done with, and nobody should press to know the actual identity of members of the organization. But Mark in fact knew more members of the organization than any of us. And he had, it seemed – in contravention of his own rules – become archivist.

Driving back to town in search of the cash we should have had permanently ready, I tried to come to terms with the fact of Mark talking. He was the one who had drawn up a long document on the effects of detention, on the effects of interrogation and how best to withstand the attempts of the interrogators to make you talk. Four days since he had been arrested, and now he was talking.

My concern wasn't that he had drawn up the document on

interrogation. It was that he was a close friend. He had been best man at my wedding – confirmation of a friendship stretching back over not many years but years of frequent contact and lively comradeship. He had been largely responsible for my recruitment to the N.C.L. If he was talking, the first person he would talk about in Johannesburg was me. But could he betray so close a friend?

Everybody talks, said Diane that night when she was being so practical and getting everybody organized to get out. Nobody doesn't talk, and talk about everything. She said she had just read an article by a team of psychologists studying the whole question, and everybody talks, she said. If they get you, you'll talk, some time you'll talk.

By the time I got back to her place after trying fruitlessly to raise some cash – it must have been about 5 a.m. by then – Diane had gone, taking her kids and Luke, heading for the Swaziland border by the route she and I had discovered months before, where you didn't need a passport. If I had gone that way, I felt, I would have been making myself a prisoner inside Swaziland, unable to get out anywhere. (Dennis Brutus had tried to get out that way only a year before and he had ended up on Robben Island, with a bullet in his gut.)

If I was to go at all it would be with Kate and Herbert, via the Bechuanaland (Botswana) border. We discussed the possibility: ditch their bike and take my car, let me off before the border to walk across while they went through with their passports. It would have been easy. It would have been the natural thing to do in terms of my thoughts during the previous few months: that we were achieving nothing and that, with my marriage on the rocks and my personal life in a mess, the place for me was outside somewhere else starting a new life in something else. But when it came to trying to decide that early morning – about 5.30 on the morning of 9 July 1964 – I couldn't decide. I felt nothing dramatic in the sense of choosing between freedom and imprisonment. I felt merely that I didn't want to leave. I know I was influenced by a distinct feeling of loyalty to Mark, a sort of double-think which accepted that he was talking but which made me want to think that he wouldn't talk about me, so made me want to stay behind to see whether this was so or not – a feeling that someone, especially me, should stay behind to be with him if everybody else was leaving. Perhaps, by then, I was too tired to decide anything. All I know is that I did not want to leave.

Then Herbert reminded me that it would help if someone phoned his boss and said he was sick that morning. And someone must phone Tom. I stayed to do the phoning.

I'm not sorry, after all, that I did.

I left Kate and Herbert at Diane's place, resting before they set off for the border. It was already near sunrise, there seemed little point in returning home for sleep and there was time still before I went to work to contact John Harris again. John was the friend whom Herbert and I had contacted earlier in case we were picked up. Our arrangement had been that John (who had thus far played a very minor role in the organization) would take over from us and continue working with Diane. That *had* been the arrangement, but now Diane was on her way out, Herbert was on his way out, and I wanted to let John know the latest. I woke them about six and I remember lying on their bed while Anne fed the baby and I felt tired and sleepy, explaining what had happened during the night, about Luke's arrival and about Mark and his talking and the fact that I didn't want to leave and that Diane was leaving. Diane was leaving and that, it seemed, put an end to any previous plans we had made about continuing things. We discussed the possibility of John getting in touch with my flat-mate, 'Ernest' – who had also become peripherally involved – but we discussed nothing definite about anything that could be done. Nothing at that time of the day and at that stage of collapse seemed possible – only the fact that everyone else had gone, that it was light again and that it might help if I took two pep pills with the coffee Anne made.

Then I drove back to my flat, shaved, changed for work and drove to the office, feeling very tired and wondering what would happen. Ernest was away on holiday which meant, as he was also a sub-editor with me on the newspaper *Post*, that I had more work than usual to do that Thursday morning. I also had some urgent phone calls to make: I phoned Herbert's boss to say he was ill that day (an interesting call for me because it had involved my having to learn Herbert's real name for the first time and I found it odd replying to him by a totally strange name after knowing him familiarly for so long as 'Herbert'). I tried to phone 'Tom', the person I had worked with a great deal and got to know as Raymond Eisenstein, a financial reporter with French/Polish origins. If I could contact him I knew he could contact 'Eric' – the other person I had met often but whom I did not know personally. Tom and Eric had to be warned. I couldn't get Tom/Raymond and left a message for him to phone me. I also phoned Jill, the girl-friend whom I'd left the previous evening with a joking request that, if I were picked up, she would look after me while I was inside. Of course, she had said, laughing, not knowing that I was serious. I wondered, speaking to Jill that morning, whether I would speak to her again.

Tom had not phoned back – it was still fairly early, about 10.30 – when I looked across the office and saw two men in raincoats talking to the secretary at the main door. She nodded towards me and they came. I don't remember their faces at all. I don't remember whether they had hats even. I remember only that they had raincoats, not overcoats, and they said was I Lewin and would I come with them. I said I was very busy, could I finish what I was doing? No, they said, please come now. So I went across to the editor's office – they followed quickly – and opened the door and said I've got to go, I'm sorry – and he looked up, terrified I thought, his eyes large and disowning, nodding and shaking his head and seeming to need to be comforted. I didn't feel like comforting him. I thought perhaps he would try comforting *me* but I didn't want that either because I didn't want to feel that I needed to be comforted. There were the two men in their raincoats and there was me, going with them, and I didn't have time or energy to think what it was that I was feeling. Come, they said, and I took my coat and nodded to the assistant editor and smiled at the secretary and went downstairs to their car, sitting between them, looking up at the building and noticing for the first time that there was a huge dirty ugly plate-glass window on the ground floor which was filled with posters I had never seen before. Then the secretary came running out of the building and asked for the keys to my car, in case they needed to move it, and I was struck by her sense of practicality. She smiled and waved as we drove off. I felt cramped, sitting between them on the front seat of the car, not talking.

They drove straight to my flat where there was another car, full of Special Branch men in raincoats, with a tall large man in charge, with a face like a bloodhound and a scraggy voice. Was I Lewin? Was this my flat? Yes, and would you like to come in? Would you all like some tea? – which gave me something to do while they pawed through the books and the files and letters and filing-cabinet, muttering to each other and saying nothing to me, drinking my tea and watching that I didn't wander on to the balcony or slip into the kitchen. Polite, in a surly sort of way. I had expected it too long to be angry – and I knew there was nothing for them to find that could be incriminating. I felt strong, knowing the innocence of the contents of my flat. They took a couple of things: a banned book by Patrick Duncan, a file of notes I was preparing for a Liberal Party document on Rule by Intimidation in South Africa, and a chart of figures from my newspaper giving letter-counts for different sizes of type. They took me to the Greys, Special Branch headquarters, which I had visited only once before when negotiating press passes for some of our African reporters. They had hardly talked to me at the flat, only a few remarks from the tall scraggy senior officer with ears and jowls like a bloodhound. They spoke little on the way to the Greys and there even less. Just Come – In here, into an empty office at the top of the building, with not many people actively in sight in any of the other offices, and not much attention being paid to me by anybody. I was left in the office with a young officer in civvies. We chatted perfunctorily, me asking him about his training, how long in service, did he like it, where was he stationed? He replied, briefly, and we sat looking at each other, waiting. I felt relaxed. Tired too. Nobody seemed in much of a hurry about anything.

Then a new tall man with a distinct air of authority came in. 'Kom/Come,' he said, and led me into another office down the passage.

There I met Captain Swanepoel. I had already heard of him

through a number of stories which had come to our paper in the preceding months (some of them were published) arising out of the interrogation of detainees and the accusations of assaults and torture by the police. Swanepoel had been widely referred to as the chief interrogator and one witness had testified about being aggressively questioned by a man with the neck and shoulders of a bull and a bright red face, Mr Swanepoel.

I was taken into the office down the passage and presented to a man sitting behind a large desk: a man with a boozy red face, the neck and shoulders of a bull, and sharp eyes. Captain Swanepoel, reading from a sheaf of papers, and shouting up at me. 'We know, Lewin, that you are a member of the regional High Command . . .' (and suddenly my initial terror faded, because we had never used such terminology and had no High Command as such, and I found myself almost smiling at the growling man) 'of the ARM, once called the N.C.L. . . .' (I stopped wanting to smile) '. . . and we know *all* about you and you're going to tell us *all* about you . . .' – the a-l-l drawn out into a roll – '. . . and all about everybody else in the ARM and the N.C.L.'

My mouth felt dry. 'I would like' – it came in a gulp – 'to see my lawyer first.'

Swanepoel laughed. Looking round at his attendant lieutenants, his cheeks swelling round and red, he closed his eyes and laughed. 'A lawyer! This, man, is 90-days and you'll never see a lawyer. And you'll talk.'

I said – dry-mouthed, feeling lonely – that I wanted a lawyer and that I disapproved of the 90-day detention law. Swanepoel laughed a second time and didn't need to look around to muster more loud laughs from the rest of them. 'This is 90-days' – he was shouting again – 'and you'll talk!' Waving a sheaf of papers at me as I was pulled away from the table by two of the lieutenants and led out of the office. I got to know these two well: Lieutenants Viktor and van der Merwe, always together with me, working as a pair, never apart. They took me off in their car (always a coupé, with me pushed into the back while they sat in front guarding the doors) and booked me into a police cell at Jeppe police station where a young police sergeant complained that they hadn't room there for detainees and that they hadn't

time to look after them. The Special Branch lieutenants laughed
and pushed me towards my first sight of a real cell – brown dark
walls and a black floor and a heavy grid over the barred window,
with a pile of dark felt mats on the floor and a seeping four-
gallon tin in the corner. Then, without a pause: 'Kom, nou gaan
jy praat/Come, now you're going to talk.' And they led me off,
back to the car, into the back, off again to the Greys.

It was late afternoon, on 9 July 1964. I was tired and beginning
to regret my coffee-only breakfast. They offered me nothing to
eat. They took me back to the Greys and up to the sixth floor,
into an office at the end of the passage: a room large enough to
take three desks pushed together, and an assortment of office
chairs, and two windows with thin tatty calico curtains which van
der Merwe pulled across the windows, barely keeping out the
disappearing sun.

'Stand,' they said, 'stand there' – and pointed to the open
floor in front of a steel-filing cabinet. Four of them at the start:
Lieutenant Viktor, Lieutenant van der Merwe, another lieutenant with no teeth, and their captain, Swanepoel. Swanepoel
came in last, when I was already perched on my spot in front of
the cabinet. He brought with him a picnic basket, a nice wicker
basket with thermos and packaged sandwiches and fresh fruit.
Plus the sheaf of papers I had seen before. He was businesslike,
with his picnic basket, not shouting now, rubbing his pudgy
hands and smiling – right, let's go. Viktor and van der Merwe
paced round me, long loping paces round and round, round the
desk and up to me – talk, you're going to talk – then away, then
back, around and around, while I stood on my spot.

There was no question of leaving my spot, no question of
sitting down. Once I moved backwards towards the cabinet,
slowly edging backwards till I could feel the relief of the steel,
cold against my back. They waited a brief moment then shouted,
pounced forward – stand there! – and drew a small circle with
chalk on the floor, away from the steel support. I couldn't think
at all of sitting down, now with the four of them there (and two
more reinforcements during the night), high up above the
distant almost soundless traffic, four then six of them. I felt very
alone and small and weak, unbrave. No idea ever of trying to sit

down and provoking their rage. Only the long intense concentration on muscles in legs and ankles, straining, wanting to burst and crack, and a tense ache beginning in the ankles and creeping up the legs, thighs, digging into my back and shoulders. If only I could lean forward, creak out of the upright standing standing and release the ache, stop the pain. But all I could do was ease from one leg to the other, rocking slowly, gently, trying to think the pain away, to concentrate on the legs and the ankles and thighs, feel them straining to burst; trying to think away the voices pressing in, persistent – you're going to talk, talk – gnawing into the pain, stalking round and round, and the window opposite with its tatty small curtain (who could have thought to put such a stupid piece of curtain up in the window?) faded and the sun went and the lights below shot up in flickers, and the voices kept pressing in, pressing persistent nagging nagging. I thought at first to keep absolutely silent, beyond giving my name and address and repeating my demand for a lawyer. They laughed and taunted: We know *all* about you – and they began telling me *all* about myself, precisely so. It was eerie. They knew all about my involvement in the N.C.L.: they knew when I joined and what I did; they knew about the meetings I had attended in Cape Town (including one I had forgotten about); and they knew a considerable amount about my private life, my marriage, my divorce, my newspaper work. They knew it all. 'Why stay silent when the others are talking?' taunted Swanepoel. 'Look how they're talking. You're on your own now, aren't you? On your own. All for one now, hey. Why shut up when they don't? All for one.'

I denied it all. They laughed. I asked again for a lawyer and they laughed. Dipping into his picnic basket, Swanepoel laughed and read from the papers in front of him. We know it all, he said – and he seemed indeed to know it all, all about me. His papers were telex messages and they could have come only from Cape Town – only from Mark. Only Mark could have known the details about me that Swanepoel was repeating, rolling them over his tongue and laughing up at me: 'We know *a-l-l* about you, Lewin.' Mark was talking. We'd known he was talking the night before. I had known it all along and I had wondered whether he would talk about me, his closest friend in Johannesburg. Now I knew: he was talking and he was telling them all about me. Diane was right, I thought, standing there on my spot: everybody talks in the end. I wasn't surprised. I don't remember, at that stage, feeling even angry about it. He was talking and the first person he'd talk about in Johannesburg was me. That was natural, of course. I felt tired, and the knowledge that he was talking added to the tiredness, seemed to add a physical weight, pressing down on my ankles and legs. I felt no mental strain, no emotional pain because he was talking: only an added physical strain.

What mattered was the ache stretching across my back and my legs and ankles. That was what mattered. So it didn't matter, it seemed, answered the simple obvious questions about myself. They knew all about me and my involvement. Well, I wouldn't admit to the involvement but what was the point of keeping silent on the obvious things. If I kept quiet it would seem I was admitting my guilt. So when Viktor stalked around me for what seemed the hundredth time (the window opposite was dark, the street noises hushed – I reckoned it was nearing midnight) and asked: 'How old are you?' I replied 'Twenty-four.'

He went easily on: 'Where at school?'

'St John's, Johannesburg.'

'University?'

'Rhodes, Grahamstown.'

'Is that where you joined N.U.S.A.S. [National Union of South African Students]?'

'Yes, of course.'

'Is that where you met Mark?'

No, enough, I must stay silent – and my silence itself was an admission.

Swanepoel said: 'You can't stop there – we know you know Mark' – and, of course, he was right. What was the point of denying knowing the man who everybody knew had been best man at my wedding?

So – 'Yes, I know him and I met him while I was at Rhodes University.' 'Seen him lately?' 'Occasionally.' 'On ARM business, hey?'

Dangerous again, so silence, admissive silence.

Swanepoel laughed: '*He* says the last time you saw him was recently and that *was* on ARM business.'

'He's a liar,' I say, and they all laugh and flutter the sheafs of telexes at me.

'It's all here, all here, so why not tell us straight away? You're going to talk sometime – we've got lots of time – so why make it difficult for yourself? Talk now and make it easier for yourself, easier for us too. We've got *all* the time in the world,' said Swanepoel, pouring a steaming cup of coffee from his flask.

He sat there, sipping the cup of coffee, about sixteen hours since I drank my last cup of coffee, and his sips sent the aches in my legs tearing round to my stomach, desperate for a sip of coffee, and a smoke, aching for nourishment, for a moment's relief, aching.

'Have some coffee,' said Swanepoel and I was given a cup – not allowed out of my chalk circle, but given a cup of coffee and with it a cigarette, and my whole body seemed to respond, stroked warm and comfortable, and the menace seemed to slip away as the ache began to leave the stomach and the smoke seeped down giving strength to my legs and ankles, pushing up into my back and easing the strain.

'Who's Tom? Who's Eric?'

It's dangerous to be lulled into their net. Viktor took away the coffee cup as I finished the smoke. 'Who,' he snapped, 'is Tom? Who's Eric?'

I'd been dreading that. It had seemed not to matter so much with Mark telling them about me, just a matter of him and me, old friends, involving nobody else. Ever since I'd been picked up I'd been trying to work out how long the others would need to make it across the border: Diane and Luke on their way to Swaziland, that wouldn't need much, but Kate and Herbert on their motorbike, much longer, a whole day, perhaps longer. So I had to hold out for that at least. But there were also the others who hadn't gone and whom I hadn't contacted – Tom, whom I knew, and Eric whom I didn't know. I didn't want to talk of them. I'd hoped they wouldn't come up at all. But now, after the midnight coffee and the smoke, they snapped: 'Who's Tom and Eric?'

'I don't know,' I said, feeling afraid because I was lying and feeling tired, slipping, yet feeling secure too because I didn't actually know Eric – the one successful piece of security gave me support, lifting itself into my back and making it easier to stand in front of Viktor, stalking around and around, with the window completely dark now and silent – two or three hours after midnight it must have been. Viktor and van der Merwe kept up their stalking and prowling, while Swanepoel sat sipping coffee from his picnic basket, or sleeping, seeming to sleep, leaning his head forward on his arms, thick arms with pudgy fingers, and the toothless man staying silent in the background, watching, or getting up occasionally to leave the room and return with more sheets of telex. More sheets of telex from Cape Town for Swanepoel – and for me, more questions and more questions about me and Mark and Tom – *who's* Tom? – and many others – *who's* Eric?

About three hours after midnight above the quiet streets and the room wasn't a room any more, not a room with chairs and desks and a couple of windows. It was a world with four faces, sometimes six, a world that was a void, moving around and around, swimming with faces and sheafs of paper, a talking pressing world where I was no longer standing because there was no need to stand because my legs were fixed into a solid mass of concrete covering my ankles and holding me up, pressing up into my back and forcing my shoulders forward, forcing my head to burst open burst open, under the weight of a huge sheet driving the ceiling down, and down, heavy into the floor . . .

'Wakker!/Wake up!' Viktor standing in front of me, shouting, prodding his finger into my chest: 'You can't stand there and sleep. Don't try this sleeping with your eyes open. You must talk, talk. Sing like a canary, like a canary, sing!'

Oh God couldn't they leave me to sleep, even standing-up sleep? To get a break from the pressing down, holding out and feeling too tired to hold out any longer. Will they have got across the borders yet? Is it time yet, is it time yet? They know everything about me and it's so unimportant, I'm so unimportant, thank God, it doesn't matter now. Won't they leave me alone, leave me alone?

'Come on now' – Swanepoel again – 'come on, man, talk. You're going to talk sometime so why not now? Save yourself the trouble. Save us the trouble.' He talked quietly, soothingly. 'You'll talk, like them all, because you want to talk. Don't think we'll beat you up, like you keep saying in the papers. That's not our way. You'll stand there and talk because you want to talk. We've had people here begging us to beat them up, begging us to force their confessions out. But we won't do that. You'll talk.'

Then the toothless man came into the room with a new telex which he gave, smiling, to Swanepoel. Swanepoel laughed and looked up: 'We know,' he said, 'who Tom and Eric are. Now he's told us. He's singing like a canary, see. Come on now, you sing too birdie.'

It was then, I think – a couple of hours before dawn – that I knew I was going to break. When Mark told them the identity of Tom and Eric, then I realized I would talk. For the first time I felt he had betrayed me: to talk was nothing, everybody talked, but he had tried to trick me, tried to make me seem responsible for giving away Tom and Eric. I knew well enough that he had known their identities all along, but had revealed only their pseudonyms. Why had he not spoken of them too, right from the start? Why only me? Why wait for at least twelve hours after giving my name to reveal their names? I was in the hands of the Branch, being cajoled, pressed, pressured into talking, tricked with coffee, threatened; and now I was up against him too, my former friend. I felt tricked. I was cornered, with nowhere to turn. How could I hold out any longer? I was tired, too tired even to feel anger now, too tired to care, too tired to think of anything except the effort of not falling down, in a daze of pain stretching across my back and shoulders – with a faint light beginning to play on the curtain opposite, lighting the window with dawn.

I knew I would crack then. Diane had been right. Everybody talks in the end. Swanepoel's picnic basket, the loneliness of the room on the top floor, the telexes – I couldn't hold out against them, not now with Mark against me too. There was nobody left in the world but them and me, in the room with the tatty curtain over the window and the traffic beginning far below. Nobody else in the world.

'If you don't talk soon,' said Swanepoel, 'we'll leave you. We'll put you in a cell and leave you there for ever. You'll cry for us to come but we'll leave you, alone there, for ever.' If they left me alone there would be nobody left in the world at all, nobody to talk to. I would be standing alone in the concrete of pain in the back and shoulders with my head pressed down under the pain, wanting food wanting sleep wanting to drink wanting to stop.

Wanting to talk.

I wanted to talk. They were the only people I knew now in all the world and I wanted to talk to them. I wanted to ease off the load and tell them what they wanted to hear. It wouldn't matter because they knew most things already, but they said they wanted to hear it all from me myself. That didn't matter. Nothing mattered any more. It was all over now, all over, with everybody gone (the others must have had time by now to get across) and those that weren't gone they knew about now anyway. Nothing mattered any more except that it would be so nice to stop, to sit and to talk. So nice not to feel so tired. So nice not to care, not to have to care about anything at all.

Van der Merwe stood suddenly in front of me, angry and menacing, the enemy. 'Come on now,' he said sharply, 'we've played with you long enough now. Come on, no more playing.'

I was afraid. I felt lost in the face of his hostility, something terrifying and new which I was not prepared for. Was he going to attack me? Beat me up? I was frightened, looking around for support. There was Viktor, standing next to van der Merwe but smiling, friendly, nodding and saying, protectively: 'Come on, man, talk. Come on – fuck you – talk, man.'

And I said: 'Fuck you too, O K I'll talk.'

And I sat down.

It was such sweet relief. So exquisitely easy to sit down with my head between my knees, rubbing my ankles. There was a cup of coffee for me, hot still from the thermos, and a smoke. Life seemed to slip back into my body as I leant forward on my arms at the desk, pushed myself up to drink the coffee, then leant forward again on my arms and told van der Merwe what he wanted to know. I told the whole pent-up story that they wanted to have in writing: the story of my recruitment by Diane, of how I met Tom who is Raymond Eisenstein, and Eric whom I still don't know, and others, and of how we planned and acted, and where I had taken part in whatever acts of sabotage – the pylons, railway signal cables, railway standards. Van der Merwe wrote earnestly in longhand and I watched him, slowly telling him what I thought then was the whole story, not thinking much about how it would seem but trying vaguely to shift things to the people I hoped were by now across the borders into safety, feeling too tired to feel remorse. Feeling only that the others knew Mark had talked and that therefore they would know it would be difficult for me not to talk, difficult for them not to talk because, anyway, it was finished, finished.

Van der Merwe sat writing, with me beside him. Two foolscap pages he filled with just the two of us in the room, the others having left with the picnic basket. They returned later, spruced up with shaves and clean suits, efficiently clean and ready for more – and now hardly noticing me, on a chair in the corner, too tired to care or to sleep.

The picnic was over. I was the debris, swept away soon to the police cell at Jeppe, left in a crumpled mess on the mats on the floor, to sleep.

I spent more than two weeks in the police lock-up at Jeppe. They were the first two weeks of my time inside, but I remember little about them. I remember being dumped there after my first day and night at the Greys – and I remember vividly what happened, a fortnight later, when I was taken back to the Greys for my second interrogation by the Special Branch.

But the time between is vague and misty. I was bemused by the sudden new world I was in. During that first day and night they had not only broken me, they had changed me. They had taken me from my world, cut me off from anything that could prop me up as a part of my world, and made me a part of their world. I felt too scared, too alone, too ashamed to fight the change. I was now part of their world and there was nothing I could do to change that. It was easier to do nothing, not to worry, easier to accept that all was finished, easier to feel uninvolved and dependent – numb, cold like the winter outside.

I was a detainee under the 90-day law which meant I was allowed access to nothing: no papers or visits, no lawyer, nothing to read (except a Bible), no writing materials, nothing. The cell too had nothing in it: just the mats on the floor and a pile of filthy blankets, and the leaking, open bucket in the corner. The police, who resented the arrogant instructions left by the Special Branch, had no time to look after me: time only to rush in briefly with cold food, three times a day, but no time ever to give me exercise, and little time to take me to the police barracks for a bath. I was a detainee and a nuisance. For fourteen days, I slept and ate, thought about nothing, dazed, and had nobody to talk to except three bumbling and fairly amiable detectives (seconded to the Special Branch to help process the numerous detainees) who visited me four times to get further details from me of the actual sabotage attempts in which I had taken part.

There was nobody else to talk to – except one Saturday night when a drunk was thrown into the empty cell next to me. I heard him coughing, puking, then he shouted to me: 'How you doing, mate?'

I danced to my door, shouting through the eyehole: 'Fine, man, and you?'

'Fine, man, yeah, they're getting my lawyer.'

'Why you here?'

'Pinched me for booze and breaking a flat.'

'That's bad.'

'Yeah, bad. And you?'

'Oh, me, sabotage.'

He was silent a moment, then said softly: 'Oh man, oh man, that's bad, man, that's a bad pinch, man.'

He said no more that night, and was gone the next morning.

On 24 July 1964, in the evening, I was taken back to the Greys by Lieutenants van der Merwe and Viktor. I remember that I had already eaten my supper, served usually before sunset, and had been playing a game of pat-ball against the wall of the cell with a pair of rolled-up socks. The cell-door opened suddenly and there was van der Merwe, looking angry, oddly morose and unresponsive, with Viktor in the car. 'Kom/Come,' he said. They wouldn't talk as we drove towards the Greys, through streets, I remember clearly, glistening with rain in the evening lights. We passed a newspaper poster – 'French Warned Against Fighting' – my first glimpse of anything to do with news for a fortnight. What fight, I wondered – then remembered the real Johannesburg world that had already become so far away, the world in which there was a touring French rugby team who would be playing a test match the next day.

Viktor and van der Merwe refused to discuss even that, as we drove past the turn to the Greys and drove instead down Eloff Street, down towards the railway station. Van der Merwe swung round and swore at me: 'Now you'll see your life dream come true' – and he bumped the car into the kerb in De Villiers Street, next to the entrance to the station.

'Kom/Come' – and they frogmarched me into the station and on to the interior concourse with its series of boxed-off stairway entrances leading down to the platforms.

'Look there,' said van der Merwe, pulling at my elbow and pointing at one of the entrances. I wasn't sure what he wanted me to look at. There were ropes tied across one of the entrances and cordoning off a large area around which stood a number of people, silently staring towards the platform entrance. Van der Merwe pulled me through the ropes and seemed to be pointing towards the entrance. I looked and could see only that the steel structure over the entrance seemed bent and twisted, and that there was a deal of broken glass around. And a uniformed cop standing by. Also standing near the cop – and this did interest me – was someone I recognized, John Stewart, a reporter on the *Rand Daily Mail*. His was the first friendly face I had seen since my detention fourteen days before and I smiled, pleased to see that he had seen me and had obviously recognized me.

Van der Merwe saw him too and began pulling me away, back to the car, and I went with him, being pulled by the sleeve of my coat, while I tried to hang back, nodding at John Stewart and trying to prolong the pleasure of a familiar face. Van der Merwe, pulling me by the sleeve towards the car, said:

'One of your bombs has just killed fourteen people there.'

I laughed. It was so ridiculous, so unthinkable. I had to laugh, as van der Merwe, furious – 'Your bomb!' – bundled me into the car. There was no silence this time from the two lieutenants as we drove back to the Greys. 'Fourteen people!' they shouted, 'your bomb! You're going to talk tonight. No jokes tonight Lewin. You'll shit yourself tonight. Fourteen people. Tonight you'll die.' Van der Merwe stopped the car in front of the Greys: 'Tonight, Lewin, I'm going to kill you.'

I believed him, but I felt detached. Nothing he had told me about the station bomb, nothing I had seen there, bore any relation to me. We had never planned such an attack. We had specifically planned *against* such an attack. I could think of nobody left outside – if there were still people outside – who could have planted such a bomb. Nothing they shouted at me was real. Nothing they said about me was real. They were talking about somebody else. It wasn't me they were shouting at. It wasn't me at all. It was happening to somebody else, not me. It was somebody else they were taking out of the car in front of the Greys; somebody else being walked, dragged, to the lift and up to the sixth floor and down the corridor into the room at the end with tatty curtains over the windows; somebody else being made to stand where I had stood before.

They stood me where I had stood before on the spot in front of the cabinet. Van der Merwe cursed me as he went round the room pulling closed the curtains across the windows (what was the point, I thought, closing curtains in a room so high up, and such useless curtains) and shouting at me: 'You're going to talk, you're going to die, tonight we'll kill you.'

Van der Merwe came back to me on the spot, straight to me. He pulled off my glasses and threw them on to the table behind him, and began hitting me: hard cupped fists, hissing through his teeth, hard fists to the head and face, mainly around the eyes and ears, beating beating while I screamed and pleaded. All I could think of was to scream, scream like one of our African reporters had said scream when you're arrested and they start beating you up, just scream because that pleases them and takes your mind off it too. Van der Merwe hit me and I screamed. I found myself down on the floor in the far right-hand corner of the room with van der Merwe standing over me, kicking, not hard, as I grabbed his leg and pleaded and screamed. He shouted at me: 'What sort of a soldier are you now? Where's your big talk now?' – and he gave hard kicks till I was back on the spot again in front of the steel cabinet, seeing double through one eye, double van der Merwe swinging his fists at my head and Viktor standing beside him watching. And then I saw only van der Merwe, as if down a long hazy tunnel with hissing teeth and fists at the end of it, slamming at me again, down on the floor next to a steel plate with scraps of food in it. Double plates of food and double pairs of legs as I struggled to get up to my spot again, surprised to hear through the haze van der Merwe saying: 'God, hy's fiks/he's fit.' I was back on my spot again, facing a tunnel full of fists and screams and hissing. A hand pushed through into the tunnel, holding back the fists, holding out a cigarette towards me, and a match. 'Have a smoke,' said Viktor.

I cannot say how long it had lasted. Possibly only a few minutes. Even less perhaps. But long enough to feel it would be the end, thinking: This is it and this is what it'll be like and I wonder if I'll actually know when it's over. Detached, never fully able to fix the body on the floor as me, not feeling hurt by the blows because it wasn't me they were hitting; somebody else with my body and my eyes beginning to cloud over, my ears beginning to ring, my head to hammer. But me screaming screaming that I didn't know anything about it and offering two scraps of information which I'd withheld before and which I hoped might stop the beating: the fact that I thought I knew where the rest of the dynamite was stored; and the name of a friend, John Harris. Viktor nodded – they'd already heard of him next door.

Next door, my former flat-mate, Ernest, was being inter-rogated. He had been detained the previous day. Four months later, he was the prime witness in the case in which John Harris was charged – and convicted – of planting the bomb in the station, killing one and seriously injuring two others. Five months after the case, John Harris was executed at Central Prison, Pretoria.

When I mentioned his name at the Greys on the night of the station bomb itself, Viktor nodded, unimpressed, and busied himself rather with what interested him more: details of the dynamite and where it had been stored. Van der Merwe left off threatening me and the two of them made to leave the office. 'God help you,' said Viktor, 'if we don't find anything.' They left me, sitting down with a smoke, one eye nearly closed, the other aching – watched by a series of strange-looking Branch men, all of them cursing, most of them drunk. One, whom they called Hokkie, sat down at the desk in front of me, growling, thick bull neck and bristling blond hair, growling: 'Jy's a Jood vokken Jood/You're a Jew fucking Jew' – and then suddenly screaming that I must get up, stand up on that spot there. He came round the desk towards me, his fist raised at shoulder height, the biggest fist I have ever seen, stinking of brandy and shouting 'Jood Jood vanaand is jy dood dood/Jew Jew you'll die tonight' – pushing me back against the cabinet with his fists: 'I'm going to kill you Jew I'm going to push my fist through your face Jood dood Jood.' Pushing me back against the steel, but never actually hitting me, a huge fist at my throat, threatening.

Then suddenly Hokkie was gone and the room began to fill with other, more senior men. Van der Merwe and Viktor were there again, and Swanepoel. I hadn't seen Swanepoel that night. Swanepoel came in with the rest, looking thunderous, the boss-man, I thought. But he was quiet with the rest, standing up and aside as a tall, elegant gent came in, with steel-rimmed glasses and a smart suit, looking like a smooth English businessman, and speaking smooth elegant English. I recognized him: Brigadier van den Bergh, head of the Security Police, henchman and former detention camp colleague of Vorster. Surprisingly smooth. He was polite and quiet: the man they were looking for, he said, had fair hair, was of medium height, and had used a timer of exceptional accuracy. He had phoned the papers to say a bomb would go off at 4.33 p.m. and at 4.33 the bomb had gone off. All they wanted, said the brigadier, was his name. They hoped I would cooperate. I explained – through my one closed eye and the other seeing double, seeing two smooth English-looking businessmen – I explained that I had, to the best of my ability, cooperated. But I doubted if I could help much because I knew nobody fitting the description (John Harris was almost bald) and we had opposed such activities. He nodded, said 'Thank you' and turned to leave, hands in pockets, bowing slightly to the attendant lieutenants. He stopped at the door, looked round at me with a slight smile, and said 'I hope that by the morning you will have decided to give us the name of the man.' Brigadier van den Bergh smiled and retired to his office just down the corridor. That was about 11 p.m., a long time till morning.

Five months later, when my assault charge against van der Merwe was brought to court, van der Merwe's counsel – while cross-examining me – informed the court that, if necessary, the head of the Security Police, Brigadier van den Bergh himself, would be prepared to testify on van der Merwe's behalf, that he was at the Greys throughout the night of 24 July and that he, van den Bergh, knew exactly what was going on in the building that night and that nobody was assaulted by any member of his force. He would testify to that under oath.

On the night itself, he had hardly left the beating-up room for his office just down the corridor when Swanepoel stormed at me: 'You may think you've convinced the brigadier but you haven't convinced me. If I catch you out in *one* lie tonight, Lewin, I'll kill you.'

Then Swanepoel left too and the room was almost quiet. I sat on a chair in the corner, watched by two Pretoria Branchmen. 'Don't think,' they said, 'you'll be protected by the papers and Jews overseas – you'll be shot dead there, just like that, shot dead while trying to escape ha-ha. You people just wait,' they said, 'just wait till we take over this country properly, wait till we get rid of softies like Vorster. Yes, Vorster's soft, he listens too much to outsiders. Then you'll see. Wag maar/Just wait. You bloody journalists. When *we* take over there'll be only two newspapers: the *Government Gazette* and the *Police Gazette*.'

At one stage the door opened and they brought in Raymond Eisenstein – Tom, also detained a fortnight before – his face puffy and red, bruises around the eyes. 'You know each other,' they said. We looked at each other and said nothing. They dragged him out again, into the passage, and I heard the one man (whom I met in Pretoria later, named van der Vyver) scream: 'Staan op Jood/Stand up Jew' – and there was a scuffle, with the sounds of thuds and hits.

Those were common sounds at the Greys that night. Doors slamming, thuds and screams, shouts, thuds, screams. At about midnight I heard distinct movements in the office immediately above us: bangings and scrapings, as if furniture was being moved across the floor, dragged and pushed, thumps on the floor shaking the ceiling of our office; then silence; then more thumps and scrapings. The two Branchmen looked at each other and at me smiling, nodding knowingly and smiling, as the noise above continued, seemingly endlessly, then stopped. Shortly afterwards the door of our room opened and a man came in, looking for the towel hanging behind the door. He needed it to wipe his hands; his fists were full of blood, particularly the right fist, the one with a large ring on, messy with blood.

'Daardie Harris,' he said, 'that Harris – another one who said he wouldn't talk without a lawyer.' Wiping the blood off his fist, and laughing. The other two laughed too. The man with the ring – he was Erasmus – went out again. He left the towel on its hook behind the door, dirtier now than before.

'You see,' said the Branchmen to me, 'you mustn't cause trouble.'

The building seemed quieter. No more bangings, no screams. Then Swanepoel stuck his head around the door – the first time I had seen him since his threat to kill me earlier. He looked pleased with himself. He ignored me but told my mentors to get ready to take me back to the police station. 'Om te rus,' he said, mildly, 'to rest.' He nodded to the others: 'Ons het hom/ We've got the man.'

That was about 1 a.m. By then, John Harris – 'the man' in the room above us – had a broken jaw.

Soon afterwards I was bundled into a car by the Branchmen. In the car already were two Africans, their faces bruised, and with handcuffs on their wrists. I knew one of them, 'Peter', one of the men I had occasionally met at discussion groups and who was said to have a group of supporters in the black townships.

'You know each other, don't you?' said one of the Branchmen laughing. I looked up at Peter and he nodded at me slightly, and said 'No' to the Branchman. It was a cold night, and cold in the car outside, but both Peter and the other man in handcuffs, whom I didn't know, were sweating. Their faces were bruised and glistening with sweat. It had been a bad night for everybody. Peter and his companion were dropped off first at two separate police stations, then I was delivered to Jeppe. It was about 3.30 a.m. in the charge office: there were a couple of the Jeppe cops on duty who had seen me often before during the previous two weeks. They looked surprised when I was brought in by the Branch, but they said nothing as they took me to the cell. Within three hours I was collected again by the Branch – stiff, aching and unseeing – to check addresses with them, and only then could I return to the cell-mats on the floor, to sleep, sleep.

The following morning – Sunday, after the Friday night – two young cops opened the cell with breakfast and offered to take me for a bath. I went, hobbling, and for the first time in days saw myself in the mirror: an unrecognizable face, with the left eye closed by a large blue egg beneath it, the right eye bruised, blood on both eyeballs and a large swelling behind my right ear. I stood in front of the mirror and stared, with the cops, at the sight, not helped by unwashed blood and three days' stubble. We laughed together about it, then they produced some aspirins for me and asked who'd done the beating-up. The following morning I was collected by Erasmus and another Branchman – Erasmus the man who had beaten up John Harris. They took me from the police cell at Jeppe and drove me to Pretoria, to prison. Erasmus had a bruised right eye. I asked him about it and he said he'd got it playing rugby on Saturday afternoon. I hoped he was lying about that – and I hoped it hurt.

2 Solitary

Local Prison stands huge and ugly on the road as you come into Pretoria from Johannesburg. It could only be a prison. We used, as kids, to pass it on the way into town and joke about it. That was where, said our mothers, we'd end up if we didn't behave. That was where, according to our jokes, you could have people committed for being insane and gain a mythical half-crown as reward.

The two Branchmen who delivered me to Local were not concerned with half-crowns. They knocked at the massive front doors, a peep-glass opened and shut, and a small door within the doors let us in. They took me to an office at the end of a corridor – a reception room with two old, benign-looking prison officers seated behind large ledgers. One of the benign old men looked at me, then said to the Branch: 'Why bother to bring this lot? You should shoot them all.'

The four of them started to natter together, leaving me to stand alone in the corner. Which was fine because I was busy trying to extract a pencil from my overcoat pocket and slip it into my sock – without appearing to do anything other than scratch my leg. They ignored me, so I slipped a ballpoint into the other sock and waited, feeling pleased with myself for not having been spotted.

I was expecting to be searched by the warders but the Branch left (nodding to the warders, looking at me) and one of the benign-looking warders grabbed keys from his table and said 'Kom.' We headed, I supposed, towards the cells, but the men gave no signs of bothering to search me and I became increasingly relieved. Through three sets of locked grills, which he opened himself, then we stopped at a fourth grill, a sort of steel concertina-gate. He rattled the gate and shouted down the corridor: 'Dankie, blankes/Thank you, whites.' From the gloom at the end of the corridor came another warder, with a uniform shirt and three stripes, and a different set of keys. He smiled at the elder warder, opened his grill and said 'Kom.' I went down that corridor with him and, as we walked, my earlier relief faded. The corridor, and the silent man with three stripes on his sleeve, seemed for the first time to mean prison. And when he took me into his office at the end of the corridor and said 'Strip', I realized I was there, really there.

Walking into prison is like walking into a butcher's fridge, empty. It is cold – no curtains, no carpets, no heaters, nothing decorative, nothing unnecessary, just this long dull corridor like in a sleazy passenger liner, with heavy blind doors, impersonal – and all very solid. Essentials only. You are stripped of everything inessential. You are stripped bare and given back only what they think is necessary. They strip you at the beginning and they go on stripping you, endlessly, to ensure that you have only what they think is necessary. You are stripped bare of everything that you can call your own, constantly stripped bare of anything that you make your own; you are stripped bare in an endless process of peeling off your protective covering and leaving you naked. So they can watch you. So that you, like the corridor, are without decoration, without covering, with nothing behind which to hide, with nothing they can't see into and watch.

'Strip,' said the man with three stripes on his arm. He was alone in his office – it was actually a cell – with a young warder with no stripes on his arm. There were wooden racks around the office walls, filled with piles of prison clothes. There was a large wooden box on which they sat and a lectern-type desk with a ledger on it.

The man with the three stripes was du Preez – the man who, for the next four years, was to make our lives hell. Barney John du Preez, Head-Warder du Preez, whom, because I saw his stripes and didn't know better, I called 'Sarge'. He looked at me through half-closed eyes, and said 'Strip.'

So I started to strip, article by article, thinking only of the pencil in my one sock and the ballpoint in the other. I could feel them pressing against my legs as I tried to steady my bag on the floor between my legs. Du Preez took my overcoat and began to go through the pockets. 'What's this?' – he held up the tiny set of cards I'd made from a toothpaste box, carefully wrapped in cord pulled from the police-cell blanket.

'A pack of cards,' I said, brightly.

'What for?' – absolutely deadpan, du Preez, with infinite patience it seemed.

'To play with,' I said. 'There's not much to do in a cell, you know.'

He took the cards, undid the cord, dropped the cord in the waste-box in front of him and slowly scattered the cards into the box too. He held out his hand for my jacket, then my tie, then my shirt, then my vest – carefully, with each article, holding it up with one hand and feeling down through it, and again, thoroughly, slowly – and then passing the clothes to the young warder who stacked them on the box out of my reach.

Before undoing my trousers I handed over the bag and stood watching while he emptied it. Maybe, I thought, I can slip the pencil in among the food boxes.

He took the towel, held it up and let it drop. The toothpaste tube got squeezed, the end of the shaving-brush was opened, each razor-blade packet was opened and left open, the new piece of soap taken out of its wrapping and the wrapping thrown away, and the box of paper napkins . . . Suddenly I remembered: I'd been so concerned with the pencil and the ballpoint that I'd forgotten the paper napkins and the diary I'd kept in the police cell, every day from the day I'd managed to swipe a ballpoint from the charge-office. Maybe he wouldn't notice the diary – maybe he'd flip through the napkins and pass on. He took the napkins out of their box and, one by one, started dropping them into the waste-box in front of him.

'What's this?' – he found the diary soon enough.

'Just a diary,' I said, quite casually, I thought.

'What for?' – with a slight note of annoyance.

I began, 'Because there's not much to do . . .' but I looked at du Preez and shrugged. My first acquiescence to his authority perhaps – or my first acceptance of reality. He took the diaried napkins, folded them neatly and tucked them into the ledger on his lectern.

Still the pencil and the ballpoint. After the discovery of the diary, I decided to surrender, so lent down, took off my shoes and one sock and handed over the pencil as if I'd found it on the floor. He took the pencil, inscrutable still, and threw it into the waste-box.

That annoyed me, so I kept the ballpoint-sock on and gave him, instead, first my trousers, then underpants and only finally the last sock, with the ballpoint now held with one cocked finger, hopefully hidden in my palm. He held up the trousers, shook and felt them, then the underpants, then the sock. 'Arms out, legs apart.' You feel very naked like that, standing in that cell at the end of the long corridor, facing du Preez and the young warder, as they look at you, up and down, with no comment.

And me with a ballpoint clutched stupidly in one naked hand, my whole existence seeming to hang in balance, dependent on the impossible task of hiding that ballpoint up against my skin. 'Give,' said du Preez, with a note of tired expectancy in his voice. He added more aggressively: 'Don't try and be funny, hey!' – and the ballpoint, last symbol of my independence, joined the pencil and the playing cards in the waste-box.

Du Preez picked up my now empty bag and slowly dropped back into it the few precious items which had passed scrutiny. I stood watching, waiting for my clothes. Finally they too came, thrown across at me by the young, silent warder – and it was he who then led me out of the cell-office with a single 'Kom.' Down the corridor again, past the long series of doors. I thought we would be going into another section, through another set of grilles, each marking off their corridors. I was sure we would move on into another section, because this corridor seemed so silent and unoccupied, dead. My stripping had taken a long time but throughout there had been no interruptions, no sounds at all from that section. So even when the warder opened a cell-door near the end of the corridor, I imagined it was a temporary move.

I sincerely hoped it *was* a temporary move. The cell was

rather like an up-ended shoe-box: about a door-and-a-half wide
(just wide enough to take a sleeping-mat) and about seven paces
long, but with a ceiling at least twelve feet high (the light socket
well out of reach even when standing on a table). High in the
wall opposite the door was a window casement, a cumbersome
sort of affair with two rows of small panes below and three rows
above, empty of panes. The wind swept through the openings and
out the other side of the cell, out of the large gap under the door
and out of the mesh-covered, barred opening high up next to the
door. The wind, in Pretoria during winter – and particularly the
winter of 1964 – was cold. It accentuated the fact that there was
nothing else in the cell: just the walls, the floor, the ceiling with
its light far up, and the open casement – and a semi-circular step
in the corner next to the door. I sat on the step hugging my overcoat around me and looked at what I took to be the temporary
cell, and felt a sudden concern for the people who, I thought,
might once have had to stay a long time in that small windy box.
Buys (he was the young warder) opened the cell-door and
pushed in a sort of enamel bucket, with a lid fitting into its rim.
He pointed to the step I'd been sitting on and then to the bucket.
And left, again locking the door. I was learning, so put the bucket
on to the step. But I still wondered why he should want to put
that in here and when he would collect me to take me to my
proper cell.

Then he opened the door again, wider this time, and beckoned
to me. I hurried out, ready to leave, and there saw him pointing
at a small table and a wooden stool, four folded blankets and a
roll of felt. He pointed at them, then pointed back into the cell.
My cell.

I carried in my furniture and my bedding, and Buys completed the picture with a small enamel bowl. 'Water,' he said,
putting it down on top of my pot in the corner. Before I could
get an explanation of his ambiguous statement, he slammed the
door locked again. So there – within the space of 13 ft $\times$ 7 ft – I
had my complete house: bathroom in the corner on the step,
dining-room/lounge in the centre and, when I moved the
dining-room/lounge slightly towards the door, enough space to
lay down my bedroom. The bed consisted of two half-inch-

thick felt mats, rolled out directly on the polished floor, and the four dark grey blankets. Mats and blankets had to be kept rolled throughout the day – no secret sleeping allowed. I had scarcely finished setting out my house when the door burst open again – Buys: 'Exercise.' In my innocence – having spent the previous fortnight in the police-cells at Jeppe without once being taken out for exercise – I thanked him profusely and made to leave. 'Pot,' he said, pointing at the step. I grabbed pot and bowl and made to leave. 'Wash,' he said, pointing at my towel. At last I was ready.

The sight in the corridor amazed me. Three of those silent, seemingly empty cells were being opened and three other people were emerging, similarly bent, carrying pots and bowls. I was not alone. No communication was allowed by du Preez and his silent, staring minions, but I was not alone. Suddenly, after two weeks of absolute aloneness, the world seemed to open out again: there were sympathetic faces, at least two of whom I knew: Terry Bell and Geoff Lamb, young like me, and journalists too.

The exercise yard led directly off the corridors: a grim place, circumscribed and dull, bounded on three sides by the three-storied sides of the prison and on the fourth by a twenty-foot wall. It had a black slate floor with concrete gutters. In the centre was a low-walled construction with two open lavatories, a urinal, four cold showers, and a tap at the side with cold water.

Through the years spent in and around this grotesque centre-piece of our world at Local, we developed what was almost an affection for it. With its dominant cisterns and twisted shower tops rising above the side-walls, it sat solidly in the middle of the concrete; we called it: 'Potemkin'.

The drill at exercise-time was strictly controlled by du Preez, standing sternly in the centre of the yard, able to watch every-body at once. Each detainee had to walk up and down across one particular part of the yard – no talking, no communicating – while, one at a time, you emptied and cleaned your pot, filled your water-dixie and, if wanted, washed. There were never more than about five of us in the yard together – sometimes only three – so it was fairly simple for the warders to keep us all apart, with few possibilities of even passing each other at close quarters.

My initial eagerness to wash died as I walked into the icy openness of the yard and saw the cold-only showers. I put down my pot and, unused to the routine, looked around at the others. 'Shower,' said du Preez, pointing. 'No, thanks very much,' I replied, 'but I think I'll give it a miss this afternoon, thanks.' He pointed. 'I said shower' – and I showered, forgetting my embarrassment in the shock of that first cold shower outside in the winter yard. Inevitably too, I took so long showering and trying to get dry, that I missed the opportunity to smoke: one's cigarettes were kept in a carton which was brought to the yard only – none allowed in cells.

Du Preez made a personal inspection of each cell every supper-time (about four in the afternoon on weekdays – earlier at weekends): round the table, a look at all the walls, then out with 'Good-night.' He usually switched on the light (the switch, of course, outside the cell) before he left. It would be switched off again by the night warders at 8 p.m. – and on again the next morning at 5.30, to wake you up in time for inspection at 6 a.m.

I clearly remember my first night at Local. In the preceding two weeks I had neither spoken to nor seen any friends. In all ways, I felt battered. Now, suddenly, I was with other people again, in with other people in the same predicament as myself – and two people I knew, Geoff in a cell on my left and Terry in one farther up on my right.

Excited at these changed conditions, I was lying on my mat after my first supper and wondering if it would ever be possible to contact them, when I heard a distinct whisper from the corridor, and in English: 'Geoff, Geoff, did you see Hugh's face?' Why my face? Yes, of course, my face was in a mess, one eye still virtually closed and both heavily bruised. It needed two friends to remark on it: throughout the signing-in and the searching and the stripping during that day, the warders had said nothing, had not raised an eyebrow.

Terry was speaking in a loud whisper, recognizably Terry despite the heavy whisper-hiss which reverberated in the corridor. Geoff replied in the same way, clear and close. I rushed to the door of the cell and tried hailing them through the judas-hole. They heard me but not clearly. I hissed more loudly, a croak almost, frantically trying to cement this first contact. But the door seemed so thick and my whispers futile. I tried speaking aloud, a shout it seemed – and at once both Geoff and Terry urgently whispered me into silence, and then explained the simple solution: take the pot off the step, put the stool there instead, stand on the stool and speak through the meshed-over grid. So simple – and so beautiful, that first short conversation with them, straining on tiptoe on the stool and staring into the dim passage from which came their whispered replies, as I poured out an incoherent breathless account of the previous fortnight's experience and tried simultaneously to answer all their urgent questions about events and people and arrests and questionings.

Then keys sounded in a gate, horribly close. Quickly scramble off the stool, grab it, silently, and replace it by the table, just in time to seem to be wandering innocently round the cell as the judas opens and an unseen warder does his check.

It was a game, of course, an elaborate game of cat and mouse in which we, the mice, could do nothing more than exploit to the full whatever leeway we thought they, the cats, would allow. Any communication between detainees was forbidden and the Prisons Department, tending us on behalf of the Special Branch, carried out their duties with remarkable application (reaching what I suppose they would call heroic proportions in the case of men like du Preez). But it was impossible for them to have somebody in our corridor for twenty-four hours a day: there were up to fifteen of us detainees, kept separated in two long corridors, and there seemed to be only a small night staff. Furthermore, we assumed that they would find it in their interests to let slip the odd conversation between us, so long as they had access to it, presumably by way of tape-recordings. Ours was a game in which we as mice had very little, or nothing, on our side – but those brief conversations which we did manage to sneak in provided a life-saving outlet, a tangible means of support. Sometimes we talked for long minutes, till my legs began to ache with the strain of stretching up on the stool. Sometimes we were stopped almost at once, either by the sound of the keys or, frequently, by furious shouts from the end of the passage, shouts which first introduced me to the startling qualities of prison obscenities, reaching a level lower than any other I've met.

To talk to friends, however briefly, was to feel alive. The whole day – all the hours from wake-up at 5.30 till after the final lock-up at 4 in the afternoon – became focused on those brief minutes in the evening when there might be a chance to talk to the others. Sometimes it was impossible: during one long week, I counted the number of words I actually spoke aloud. Taking 'Good morning' and 'Good evening' as one word each, I reckoned that during that entire week I managed to speak ten whole words aloud, usually by way of greeting a warder – which meant, naturally, that I would have had less than ten words said back to me that week.

If you can't talk, you communicate by other means. During the conversation on my first night, Geoff excused himself for a while 'to tap to Jock'. There followed a seemingly endless series of taps: their method was the most obvious, and slowest – one tap for A, two for B, three for C . . . which meant forty-six taps alone for 'How' if you wanted to begin with a common greeting like 'HOW R U'. Far better, and much less laborious, was to use the grid system. But at the beginning we couldn't remember sufficiently Koestler's explanation of it in *Darkness at Noon*, nor was there any real need for us to tap to each other in that section. Geoff and I actually remarked one night at the sound which came regularly from upstairs, as if someone was learning to type and Terry explained, contemptuously, that that was people tapping, using the grid.

The grid involves dividing the alphabet into blocks of letters, say five per block (which was the grid we generally used): ABCDE/FGHIJ/KLMNO/ . . . and you tap first the block number then the place of the letter in that block. Thus B is./.. and E ./..... and G ../.. and M .../... and P ..../. and so on. It is surprising how quickly, when forced into it, you can become fairly proficient using this type of code. Some people used Morse, but the walls at Local were too thick to allow distinctions between soft (for dot) and hard (for dash). And not enough of us had been in the Signal Corps during the war, nor good Boy

Scouts. A variation on the grid-tapping came to my notice only indirectly. The cell-door unexpectedly burst open one morning and Buys demanded my mirror. I was busy shaving with it and said I needed it, only to be told gruffly to hand it over. I shaved thereafter using the murky reflection on the back of my spoon – and subsequently learnt that the cause of our deprivation was the discovery of a note from one upstairs detainee to another, reading 'Flash with mirror on wall opposite.' The tapping, like the talking and flashing, was strictly forbidden and we were often harangued about how gross a crime both were.

Although we were then only detainees – none of us having been brought to trial and convicted – we were nevertheless subject to prison punishment, which came, for most of us, soon enough. One evening, for instance, we had been whisper-talking for quite a time when an unfriendly voice from the passage right below us said: 'O K, that's enough for tonight' and the following morning those of us who had been talking were 'given meals', as the prison saying is: i.e. we were taken *off* meals, on that occasion for a whole day. Our private food parcels were removed early in the morning, and the cell thoroughly searched to ensure that we'd not secreted away the odd prune or sweet to see us through twenty-four hours' hunger.

This was probably the prime disadvantage of being detained in prison, as opposed to police cells: that we were subject to the paramilitary regime of the Prisons Department. The fuss and fluster of tensed backs, stamped feet and obsequious salutes filtered through to us in our sloppy unconcern by way of slammed doors, curses, threats and fumings, and childish, often petulant punishments. Under the circumstances, it was difficult to remain unconcerned or even unafraid. But it was nevertheless amusing – and if not always that, then at least useful in terms of training for the subsequent life as a prisoner – to watch the chain-reaction of official choler: a snapped comment from the commanding officer (a major) to the chief-warder about a smudge on a shining brass tap becomes (in the absence of the major) a growling complaint from the chief to the head-warder, which becomes (in the absence of the chief) an obscene scream from the head-warder to the poor warder supervising the cleaning of the section – and from there, there's only one person left to bear the brunt of the hysterical howl of the warder: me, bandiet.

To survive in a system like this, you must do two apparently contradictory things. On the one hand, you must accommodate to the system sufficiently for you to be able to ride with it and not be ground down by it. This, in itself, requires that you somehow maintain a balance between appearing to be acquiescent to the system and losing your self-respect in doing so. On the other hand, you must constantly fight the system, cheat it at every possible stage, and find as many ways as possible of beating it – which also requires that you maintain some balance between success and failure, for to be beaten too often is demoralizing.

You must, to survive prison, become a successful criminal. Only as a practising crook can you gain any comfort for yourself or retain any sense of personal dignity. It is this complete denial of normal social behaviour and accepted morality which makes prison so different from Outside – and it is this which, I think, makes it impossible for anyone Outside to imagine what it is like Inside without themselves actually experiencing prison life. Prison is a complete world, a life complete in itself, without reference to anything outside itself.

This was brought home to me most forcibly by my three months in solitary confinement, in detention – which, being at Pretoria Local, was prison life without *any* trappings. This was the stripping process at its most essential. Just a cell, with nothing in it; nothing that could give you any semblance of control – no light switch, no windows which you could open or close, no taps to turn on or off, no toilet to flush, no pictures, curtains, carpets, no phones, radios, newspapers, and no handle on the inside of the door. Just a cell, with four walls, a floor and a ceiling; the bare essentials of clothing, furniture and bedding, with a spoon to eat with (no knife, no fork), a Bible to read (no other books) and nothing on which to write nor anything with which to write. And no contact at all with Outside: no private visits, no letters, no personal messages. You can send dirty clothes out once a week, through the warders, and receive back a clean bundle, through the warders. You can receive food-parcels from outside, carefully searched and handed over by the warders. Your world is your cell and the cell-door, opened only by warders, and the short walk to the yard, watched always by warders. You are allowed to communicate with nobody – you do so at the risk of losing what little comfort you have: food and the two brief exercise periods. The warders too are warned to avoid any but the most essential contact.

This is a twenty-four-hour-a-day world, with no time off, no holidays, no break. So you have to find ways of beating the system.

I had lost my pencil and ballpoint at that first stripping by du Preez. I was consumed, for days after, with the desire to find a substitute. I had nothing to write on anyway, but I wanted to know I had the choice: that I could write if I wanted. So I searched the cell, everywhere, for a pin: in all the cracks and dents and hollows in the floor, in every corner and every join, in every lapel in my clothes, in every joint in the table, in the stool, and in every part of the passage-grating. There was no pin. So at every exercise in the yard, I paced slowly, deliberately, up and down across my portion of the slate, moving across fractionally each time, then returning to seek out (without appearing to do so) a pin from among the slates and cracks. Nothing. Not even an old matchstick.

Then – it must have been about the fourth day of my yard-search – I spied a pin, up against the wall, a little to the right of my territory. I tried to pass it when going for my second cigarette, but couldn't, so planned to walk there during exercise the following day. But that evening, before supper, I thought I heard the yard being washed (this was done regularly by the awaiting-trial prisoners). All that evening I waited, remembering the exact position of the pin, and again the next morning, waiting for first exercise and wondering whether the pin might have been washed away. When at last we were opened up I tried to hurry in front of Terry in the corridor so that I could get to the correct part of the yard to find the pin. I got to the correct part of the yard. The pin was gone. Two days later I saw another pin right in my line of walk. I stooped down, as if to tie a shoe-lace, and had my pin. I dropped it into a trouser pocket where it safely eluded the search which stopped us nearly every time we returned from the yard to our cells. That pin – which I used every day from then on to prick out a date in my cell – must by now be going rusty, hidden still in the grating high above the cell-door.

They allowed us to smoke only during exercise periods, long enough maybe for two smokes in the morning, one and a half in the afternoon. The cigarette packets were kept in a carton which the warder threw down in the centre of the yard, right in front of him. When you wanted a smoke you indicated it to him, he nodded and you came forward, took out your packet and one cigarette and went to him for a light. No matches were ever left lying around by the warders – by order. We discovered that it required not too difficult a sleight of hand to flick out two cigarettes at a time from the packet and to secrete one of these in your palm while getting the other lit by the warder. The extra smoke had then to be smuggled back into your cell, either tucked into your palm while you carried in your pot or left in a pocket (this method was the riskier of the two, dependent on the thoroughness of the warder when he searched you on the way back to the cell). Nothing is quite so frustrating as having a cigarette to smoke in your cell at night, but no matches. We had to devise ways of stealing matches – and not only matches but also 'slatch', the matchbox sides without which safety matches are virtually useless.

The problem was made more difficult by du Preez who made up for his lack of intelligence with a sort of dog cunning very akin to that of a good petty criminal. He specifically told his warders to throw their matches into the water in the gutters, and to keep their empty boxes until they could be thrown away outside. But there had to be a slip sometime, particularly as our yard was also used by the awaiting-trial prisoners, who were allowed to smoke freely and who one day left behind an empty matchbox. Terry managed to pocket it and smuggle it back to his cell. There he broke it up, then smuggled back into the yard two small pieces of the box sides which he dropped behind the wall of the toilets where Geoff and I, separately, could pick up one little piece each and smuggle that back into our cells.

Now all we needed was a match. I discovered a somewhat

dubious way of procuring matches, from the horse's mouth, as it were. Once when I asked du Preez to light my cigarette the match went out and du Preez, busily holding forth to another warder next to him, handed over the box to me. With a nonchalance bred solely by necessity, I took the box from him (he watched me all the while), took out two matches simultaneously, and managed to strike only one of them, hiding the second match in one hand while I handed back the box with the other. That night, lying on my mat after lights-out, I enjoyed the exquisite delights of a clandestine smoke. I now had to exploit this discovery, so the next day, as I leaned forward to get a light, I gently blew out the match he held alight for me. He looked down, cursed, and again handed over the box. Success! I had another free match, and another pleasant evening.

But my method was risky in the extreme and hardly reliable. Terry discovered – or rather created – a far more efficient and fruitful method, which depended, like any other successful prison smuggle, on the cooperation of an outside party. Our section was cleaned every morning by a number of white awaiting-trial prisoners, the 'stokkies', who were kept in the multiple cells further up the corridor. Each morning they cleaned outside our cells; swept and polished the floor, rubbed up all the brass fittings, and dusted everywhere. They were always accompanied by at least one warder. We could hear them from our cells, murmuring to each other, and occasionally passing remarks with the warders. In each of our cells was a strange square hole in the wall alongside the door, large enough to take an electric-light globe. In some cells, this was still the sole source of light, the opening into the cell being covered with a piece of heavy mesh, the opening into the corridor being closed off by a small wooden door. Each of these little light holes had to be dusted out each morning. Usually, if you were quick enough on the inside, you could see the hand and duster of the stokkie as he opened the small door to dust the light, and, in the background, the figure of the watching warder.

Terry one day stood at the hole in his wall and waited for the dusting stokkie. As the little door was opened, he made a noise like that of a match lighting. Immediately the door slammed closed. The next morning Terry waited again: when the door opened, he made no noise but held up his hands, indicating the one striking the other. Again the door slammed. The third day he tried again, with the striking noise. The slam was not so violent. And again on the fourth day. On the fifth day, the door opened, the hand and duster were thrust into the hole – and two matches were pushed hastily through the mesh. The next day, three matches. The next day – a week after.the initial refusal – a long thin envelope was flicked under Terry's door, clearly by one of the floor-polishers. It contained a handful of tobacco, a good week's supply of matches for us, and a replenishment of slatch. We were in the smoking business, for a week or so.

Windfalls like this were rare. Terry's friend slipped in one more packet – complete with note saying 'You don't like the govmint, nor do I, good luck' – but we did not hear from him again. Then Terry himself was released. I remained a solitary smoker while my supply of matches lasted, then I reconciled myself to exercise-only cigarettes. This did not matter too much because clandestine successes carried their own measure of risk: besides the regular searches in the yard, our cells were frequently ransacked too, and discovery of anything illicit meant more meals.

The cell searches – 'skuds' they were called, from the Afrikaans skud, to shake – were a diabolical extension of the stripping process. Cells had, as a general rule, to be meticulously neat: the table and stool just there in the centre, the mats rolled up with the folded blankets on top of them just there, your packet of food just there, clothes there, and the floor always well polished, walls and window sill well dusted. This regimen of cleaning had the advantage of passing a fair amount of time during the morning (everything had to be ready for the O.C.'s inspection before lunch) and it was, as prison chores go, a comparatively painless exercise. It nevertheless accentuated the fact that, with so few facilities around, it was very difficult to hide anything. A cigarette, for instance, becomes a remarkably conspicuous object when unrolled from a dull grey blanket.

Far worse than the humiliation of being caught with an illicit cigarette or found with a sweet while doing meals (the humiliation in some way lightened by the sheer farce of the authorities finding these offences so heinous), far worse than being humiliated in this way, was coming back to your cell after exercise to find it wrecked, torn apart: the table overturned, the stool knocked sideways, blankets and mats unfolded and unrolled, piled anywhere and anyhow across the cell floor, and your food bag spilled everywhere. That was the worst: the silent pent-up rage at being so impotent, so powerless, stripped down to nothing and discardable, like a crumpled piece of sweet paper in a corner. Rage, as du Preez, with mock and mocking care, stepped gingerly through the wreckage, tapping his walls, checking his windows and bars, and leaving with an over-the-shoulder 'Good night'. Not a good night. Not a lot of good nights. Not a good night as slowly you pick up the pieces of your rage and stack them, neatly folded like the blankets, into a whole again, ready again for more.

That is one thing you have to do: strike a balance between your beating the system and it beating you. The other is to learn how to accommodate to the system, so that you use the system to suit yourself.

In many ways, this is not a difficult thing to do – not because of any special qualities of ingenuity or guile or courage, but because the system carries you with it whether you like it or not. There's nothing else you can do. I remember well that first nasty moment when Buys pointed back into the cell and I realized it was my cell, permanently. There was nothing I could do about it: the door was locked on me, the walls were solid, the window was inaccessible. Clearly I couldn't get out. The encounter with du Preez had been long enough to indicate that there was little point in crying out or weeping. I could try testing the proverb by knocking my head against the wall – in fact, then and on many occasions thereafter, I slammed the wall with my fist. But it hurt, and made me think of more useful activities.

As for changing the immediate circumstance of my new existence, I could do absolutely nothing. I was there in that cell and that was that. Yet before I really had time, on that first day, to comprehend anything fully, the door had opened again and it was exercise time; and then, after being locked up for a while again, the door opened and supper was pushed in (a bowl of soup, a cup of coffee, and a chunk of bread); then the lights went off at 8 p.m. and on again at 5.30, followed by early-morning inspection (shouts, keys, with the door opened and slammed shut in a flurry of passing brass); then breakfast, pushed quickly through the door (a bowl of meilie-pap, a cup of black coffee, smaller chunk of bread); then a long wait till morning exercise; then lunch (the bowl again, usually with chopped meat and veg, and the chunk of bread on top); then another long wait till afternoon exercise; and the round began again.

Always the same routine, the same regular interruptions, the same regular pattern, day in, day out, week in, week out. What changes there were were secondary – like at weekends, when the programme was compressed so that the day staff could go off earlier: not pleasant for detainees because the warders used frequently to combine our exercise periods, giving us only one shorter time out, often just before supper which was served right after lunch, at about 2.30 in the afternoon – which meant long, long evenings. Outside these changes, the routine remained the same, predictable and regular.

It was eminently comforting. It provided a sure basis to life, a pattern against which to measure the unpredictable. It was a source of consolation to which you could return to find relief from the uncertainties and unwelcome pressures of being a political detainee, held incommunicado by the political police, unsure of any future, always uneasy at what the Branch might suddenly uncover and produce. The unexpected breaks in the routine were what caused concern. There would be an unusual clatter of keys down the corridor and you waited, listening to see whether they came near, listening and trying to judge who was being opened, and why. You learn most things in prison through the noises and changes in pattern of noise. When the clatter of keys died, so did your concern. Until your own cell-door burst open unexpectedly and du Preez said 'Kom'. That was bad, unwanted and threatening.

It would be the Branch, wanting clarification and information, never friendly, never giving any indication of when the uncertainty of detention would end. You return to your cell with relief, hoping you haven't missed exercise and the chance to see some of the others, hoping you haven't missed lunch and will still find your bowl inside the door on the floor, with congealed food and soggy bread.

It is not difficult therefore to accommodate to the system and let its rigidity become your own support. It took about a week, I suppose, to become accustomed to the routine and learn to distinguish the multitude of noises. So many different shouts – instructions (always shouted), greetings, requests; different gates and doors being opened and slammed shut (always slammed); and a variety of noises peculiar to Local – the kitchen boiler immediately opposite our cell-block which seemed to explode every hour, and be filled, with attendant clatter, every morning before the lights came on. In the evening, in the calm after the day staff left, a rising chant of songs which resounded through the whole prison, the chorus of black prisoners in their massed cells, and often at night, screams – sudden terrifying screams of some man in terror, seemingly far away in the unknown centres of the prison, followed sometimes by a distant shout, and silence.

There were the noises – and also, the smells. I'll never again smell silver or brass polish without immediately being back in the corridor at Local where every light fitting, every tap, every keyhole, every brass stud on every gate and door had to be polished every day, rubbed smooth in an endlessly futile exercise of time-spinning. And floor-polish: I'll always know the stench of the clear polish that was spread, every morning, on the already-bright length of the concrete corridor, and then polished off and rubbed and brought back to its former gleaming, slippery brightness; and the nastier black polish for cell floors, with its insidious smell of petty authority, insisting that each floor *had* to be polished every morning, and especially on Sundays in time for Inspection.

But above all, I can still smell – still *feel* almost – that overwhelming smell of Local, a smell which lingered during the days, began to build up during the long cell-nights and which then flooded through the whole prison in the early mornings with its attendant clatter of emptying toilet pots: the sweet sick smell of shit. There were no toilets in any of the cells at Local or, where we went later, at Central: only toilet pots. Some, for the whites, were enamel, with lids and sealing rims; others, for the blacks, were iron and uncleanable, and often without lids. At open-up every morning, cell doors throughout the prison let loose their stewed up stench as each toilet pot, cell by cell, was carried to the bathrooms at the end of each section and tipped into the drains. That was how the day began; with the clatter of pots and lids against the drains, letting loose a seeping pall of shit-smell to permeate the whole prison and hang heavily in the corridors as the cleaners ladled out the breakfast porridge. It was a smell that lingered on through the whole day's routine.

I learnt the routine – but also, while I slowly realized the need to lean on it, I learnt too that I must establish my own routine within the routine. It became important to have a sufficient number of different routine activities available from which to be able to choose each morning, to be able to feel that I was, in a small way, controlling my own day. The possibilities were not numerous. I could walk around the cell. I could do exercises. I could shave. I could read the Bible. I could sleep. Some of these activities were more rewarding than others: to shave with cold water and in the reflection of a spoon is hardly inspiring, and not very time-consuming; it is possible to sleep sitting on a stool, but to sleep too long during the day raised the possibility of lying awake too long at night; and it can become as endlessly tedious reading the Bible for hours on end as it can to walk round and round your cell.

The solution, I found, was to vary my routine as much as possible within the set times of the system's routine. I set myself tasks: walk so many miles each day, do so many press-ups each day, read so many chapters of the Bible . . . Between breakfast and first exercise there was time enough to shave, to walk two miles (I reckoned my thirteen paces around the cell covered about ten yards, so I did 176 circuits per mile, going first one way round the cell, then in reverse) and read maybe ten full chapters. I would walk a mile, then shave, then read a little, then walk again, then read till exercise. Or shave, then read, then walk, read again, and walk till exercise.

After exercise, it was the same till lunch: read a little, walk, read, then do physical jerks, and more reading. I discovered that late morning was a bad time for physical jerks in the cell: inspection once came while I was on my back, furiously bicycling, which embarrassed me and produced a bleat from du Preez for having my mat down on the floor during the day. So I brought forward the physical jerks to the earlier period before exercise – and in this way discovered that I could use 'bed-making' as yet another separate activity: I left my blankets unrolled while I did the press-ups and could thus spend quite some minutes after the exercises rolling the mats and beautifying the blankets.

Similarly after lunch. Similarly after supper. Here I discovered another refinement on time-stretching: I would set out to walk one mile round the cell, promising myself that at the end of it I could undo my bedroll to lie down and relax – but at the end of the mile I would suddenly decide to force myself to do another mile, and possibly even another. Or I would promise myself a drink of water at the end of the next half-mile, then force myself to wait till the full mile.

I wished for a chess mind that would enable me to play endless games in my head, leaving my body uncomplainingly idle. But I could never retain the image of the board and pricking out a tiny board on my table-top helped not at all. Instead I found stimulus in other ways. Each morning I began saying and singing myself through mass. Even without a prayer-book I found I could still remember a large number of the formal prayers, and most of the responses, from the communion service – and by constant repetition found that I could recall more and more hymns sung in my choirboy days at school; with the Bible readily at hand, I could easily substitute psalms for hymns, and passages from the Epistles for forgotten prayers. Having devised my own full service, I then instituted it as the major activity after breakfast and was able – by choosing long sections of the Bible as lessons or by repeating well-liked hymns – to reach first exercise without having to indulge in any of the other activities available. (I spared myself having to listen to my own sermons – which might well have taken me through till after exercise.)

The success of this self-service meant that I could postpone the physical jerks session until after supper, when there was no possibility of unwanted interruptions. I discovered another diversion. I started to produce my own Gilbert and Sullivan. I had acted in three productions at school, and two others at university, so my repertoire was limited, but again I found that by actually working at remembering words and tunes (all sung quietly to myself), I could gradually recall large sections of the operas – and what I couldn't recall I would fill in, embroidering a new libretto so as to arrive at the next known song without too strange an effect. This process (usually carried out while I wandered, not counting the miles, round and round the cell) consumed an agreeably large portion of the morning: I would plan an opera in the morning, delving to see what I remembered, and produce it in the evening, if possible with imagined movements, costumes, lighting and added effects. And compose a barbed critique of the night's production as an early-morning entertainment.

All this was fine for a while and was the sort of thing that kept the time passing, somehow measuring off the days, then weeks, edging slowly towards the end of the 90-days. Although we knew that some detainees had already been re-arrested and re-detained immediately after their first 90-day period, the 90-day mark still provided some sort of horizon, a goal. But it palls. The sheer boredom of living inescapably with yourself for hours and days on end has to be alleviated somehow. One way was to devise games.

My enjoyment of these games seemed to be dependent on their level of triviality: the more puerile they were the better. Take my skittles. I had begun to save the pips from a box of dates sent in one of my food parcels: at first so as to have something extraneous which I could leave lying around for du Preez to find, both to annoy him and to let him have something to distract him from other more important discoveries (like the slatch tucked under the table-top). When dry, the date-pips looked pleasantly grained and I used to roll some in my fingers shining them as I paced out the miles. Then I thought of skittles, chose the longest of the polished pips and set them up in rows on the end of my table, each skittle standing in a small blob of toffee, chewed soft – there at the end of the table they were ideal targets for the unpolished pip which I held upright under my forefinger at the other end of the table and flicked the length of the table, occasionally taking with it some of the pip-skittles, together with a number of toffee-blobs. The game seldom retained its attraction for long, but while it did so it was fascinatingly stupid – and led me on to choose six of the flattest date-pips which, when suitably marked by the never-failing pin, became a useful set of dice with which to while away any lingering pauses during a bad day or evening.

The Bible too could provide distraction as well as interest. I found it incredible, reading through from cover to cover as I did, three times in all, to discover how many catch-phrases of the English language in fact originate in the Authorised version. More important, in terms of frivolous games, I had never before realized how eventful the Bible really is, particularly the Old Testament. One of my games was to approach each episode from the point of view of a headline writer for a tabloid paper – immediately a vast source of blood-and-guts drama presents itself, with an endless flow of murder, arson, adultery, rape and scattered foreskins.

There were other diversions too, provided often by the prison itself. In the upstairs cells (where I was moved after about a month) the windows were slightly lower than in the downstairs ones. Whereas you needed to stand on a table downstairs to see out of the bottom of the window (into the hospital yard), a stool was sufficient upstairs. Du Preez furiously stopped anybody going anywhere near the windows with either table or stool, so a stool was safer, being more easily whipped back into position than a table. I stood long hours on that stool and soon realized that, discipline apart, du Preez had a point in trying to prevent us looking out.

Our windows overlooked a large yard bounded on the far side by a single-storied building which was being renovated inside by a squad of Prisons Department builders: two warders as supervisors, two white prisoners as bricklayers/plasterers, and about a dozen black prisoners doing most of the work, including bricklaying and plastering. This truly South African scene was enacted largely in the yard below us and continued through those August winter days, some of the coldest I had known. Up in my cell I wore most of my clothes, including the overcoat, most of the time. In the yard outside, the blacks used to arrive in their two-by-two team before the early morning shadows had disappeared: they wore short khaki shorts, khaki shirt and small khaki jerkin – no socks, no shoes, no jerseys. They would come out into the yard rubbing their heads and hopping, a perpetual jive to keep warm. They worked mainly in the yard, mixing concrete, sawing wood, carrying bricks; the whites stayed in the building, coming out only to yell an order or clobber some poor black bandiet over the head as he ducked past with a wheelbarrow. That was the daily entertainment: no black prisoner could go past without the help of a great white hand or boot. Completely genial and relaxed: no particular animosity from the white who hit, no responding sign of hurt from the black who was hit (maybe an occasional rubbed head and stumble – nothing more). It was an eerie comedy, which became deliberately vicious only once that I saw, when there was an unusually loud bellow from inside the building and an African came spinning out of the doorway into the yard, spiralling outwards and falling slumped on the concrete, followed by the boss-warder, furious and still shouting, his fists up. The prisoner recovered in time to scuttle off down the yard, just escaping the warder's boot. The warder shouted obscenities at him, shook his fist, then shrugged his shoulders, turned round and peed in the gutter.

The Special Branch themselves provided occasional, less entertaining, diversion. In my early weeks at Local, they were particularly attentive, coming to collect me at least once a week and taking me to their headquarters in Pretoria – the Kompol building, whose huge ancient walls, they assured me, had been built by Paul Kruger. Apart from this history lesson, there appeared to be little reason for their attention: they rarely questioned me, and then only perfunctorily, and usually left me in an office with a series of young Branchmen who sourly watched over me while cleaning their guns or picking their teeth. In the evening after the third of these footling outings – which had been particularly annoying because I had not been allowed even my normal exercise smoke, nor had I been able to steal either smokes or newspapers at Kompol – I overheard Terry and Geoff discussing their interview that day with the magistrate. I had by then been at Local for some three weeks but had still not seen a magistrate, although a weekly visit was required by the 90-day law. It seemed, we thought, that there might well be a link between my uneventful visits to Kompol and the visits to the jail of the magistrate – because of the state of my face. So the next morning I said 'Meneer!' loudly as the inspection swept past on its usually unstoppable way. They stopped and I asked when I would see the magistrate. They would see, they said.

Two days later the cell-door burst open unexpectedly – the hospital orderly: where were these eyes I had been complaining about? This was the first time the man had been near me in the three weeks since I reported to the doctor on my arrival at the prison. What eyes, I said, but he ignored me and started putting ointment into both my eyes, both of them still showing the bruised after-effects of Mr van de Merwe. The orderly, unbidden by me, returned every day that week, diligently tending the eyes and noting their recovery. The following week I saw the magistrate for the first time, and was not again taken to Kompol.

The magistrate sat behind the chief-warder's desk in one of the offices downstairs: he had two chief-warders beside him, a head-warder telling him who was coming to see him, and a couple of warders in the office too. It was a forbidding line-up for a detainee. Any complaints, he asked, without looking up. Yes, I said – and the whole room stiffened: I was assaulted by the Special Branch at the Greys about three weeks ago, and this is the first time I have had an opportunity of telling anybody who could do anything about it. How assaulted? – still not looking up. I was made to stand for a long time on one spot and I was subsequently assaulted with fists and beaten about the face – you can see the marks around and on my eyes still. He looked up, then continued writing. He would look into the matter, he said.

I didn't think he would and was surprised when, some days later, I was called to the front and presented to a man in plain-clothes – from the police, he said, and he understood I wanted to **lay a c**harge against the Special Branch. Oh, I said, I hadn't **thought** of it in those terms (it felt rather like being inside a cage, watched over by an angry lion and deliberately teasing the lion when there was no visible means of defence) – but yes, I had complained. He wanted a written statement, he said: did I have pencil and paper? I laughed. He asked the warder for paper and then – happiness! – handed me his propelling pencil. He would return that afternoon, he said: would I please write the statement in my cell? Was that all right, he asked me. Yes, sir, quite all right.

It was all right indeed: at last I had something to do out of the ordinary, and at last I was actually able to write again, with permission. Most important: propelling pencils have lengths of lead, and spare leads. I had by then learnt one of the fundamental laws of prison: you seldom get the same chance twice – grab whatever comes your way, at once. That afternoon I gave the man a two-page statement and returned to him his pencil. I doubt if he noticed that he had lost some spare leads.

The result of my complaint was interesting. Shortly before the end of my detention I was taken to the front offices to be interviewed by another policeman, this time an impressive-looking guy in uniform, with pips on his shoulder: Captain Somebody-or-other. From the C.I.D., he said, and they were going ahead with a prosecution against Lieutenant van der Merwe. Again I felt somewhat encaged, the more so about a week later when I was called again and there were Viktor and van der Merwe – come for my fingerprints, they said, and took them. All full of smiles, both of them, and then van der Merwe said, I hear you're charging me. I nodded. They laughed. That'll be nice, he said, when I'm convicted and you're convicted, they can lock us up in the same cell together. Wouldn't that be nice, hey? I was pleased I was going back to my cell.

I saw van der Merwe again only after our trial, when the case against him was finally brought in the Johannesburg magistrates' court (in December 1964, three weeks after I'd been sentenced). It was surprising that the case was brought at all by the police as a criminal charge against a Special Branch man. I was the main witness and, of course, I was the only prosecution witness of the actual assault so the result of the case was never in much doubt. The prosecutor was young, seemed to be not much on top of the case and was, understandably, a little reticent in putting it: he had to face one of the top Afrikaans advocates, defending a lieutenant of the Security Police, whose main witness was another Security man (Viktor) and who let it be known that he could, if necessary, also call the head of the Security Police (boss-man van den Bergh) to testify that there had been no foul play at the Greys that night. Van der Merwe's story was that, when they had shown me what had happened at the station, I was so shocked that I had rushed away and tried to climb back into their car too quickly, thus hitting my head against the door and injuring my face. The doctor testified to the effect that he could not definitely say that the bruises on my face were not caused by an action such as bumping into a car.

It was never clear why they brought the case against van der Merwe – or allowed it to be brought. One rumour, according to some lawyers, was that the captain who handled the case was one of a number of cops who disliked the Special Branch generally (we saw several indications of tension between cops and Branch) and hated van der Merwe particularly: van der Merwe had apparently been seconded to the Branch temporarily from the Murder and Robbery Squad, and was much disliked by those he worked with. I can understand that.

By the time he and Viktor came to take my fingerprints at Local, I had been in detention for some eighty days. I remember their visit not only for van der Merwe's reference to our sharing cells together but also because, by then, the whole solitary detention business was wearing thin for me. I must have been in a bad way: I remember actually welcoming their visit, welcoming the fact that I would have an opportunity to talk to somebody, even those two. Earlier I had had a visit from another set of Branchmen – a pleasanter crew, who let me sit near the fire in the office and who gave me a couple of cigarettes – and I remember beginning to feel desperate and saying: 'Charge me, please, charge me. I don't care what the sentence is – twenty years, twenty-five years, I don't care, as long as I know.' The indefiniteness was the worst part of it: nothing certain, no fixed point around which to structure your thoughts and actions, only an aimless vacuum of uncertainty and silence.

When van der Merwe and Viktor came to take fingerprints, the silence was about to end, for some of us. Of the fifteen or so of us who were detained at Local between July and October 1964, most were connected with the trial which began in Johannesburg early in the following year, when thirteen men and women were charged with being members of the banned Communist Party. Geoff and Terry, for instance, had been detained and questioned in connection with the case but were finally released, without being charged, after a couple of months. I knew only some of the faces which I saw walking around the exercise yard each day – people I had met socially outside or whom I had only heard of, and one person whom I had last seen on the night of the station bomb at the Greys, Raymond Eisenstein – 'Tom'. He had been brought to Pretoria on the same day as me but it was some days before we were taken to exercise together. His face still looked bruised and puffy from his handling by the Branch on that station night. We could never communicate at exercise, but when I was later moved upstairs, I found myself in a cell two away from Raymond and there was the chance then, occasionally, to whisper-talk in the evenings. We were the only members of the N.C.L. at Local and we had no way of discovering what would happen to us: the Branch left us both alone, apart from the infrequent and unproductive visits, and it was only when we were both, separately, called to see van der Merwe and Viktor for fingerprinting, that we thought perhaps the end was in sight.

On day eighty-four of detention, the end of solitary came: Raymond and I were summoned to the front office and told, by the more jovial of our Branchmen, that they were releasing us from 90-day detention but that, before we got any ideas about leaving, they were re-arresting us and holding us in custody on charges under the Sabotage Act. We would, they said, appear in court the following day.

That was the end of September and the changed status – from detainees to awaiting-trial prisoner – should immediately have allowed us access to lawyers, family, and the world. But it was Local and you don't, at Local, have phones available. I asked the warder as he took me back upstairs if I could now have my cigarettes in the cell, and whether he would please get me a newspaper. He laughed and slammed the door: I could wait another day.

Awaiting-trial was, in terms of what preceded and what followed, like Christmas. For two months we were beyond the beck and call of the Special Branch. We had access to lawyers, whenever they could find the time to visit us; we were allowed two personal visits every week; there was no limit to the number of letters we could write and receive; we could have books sent in; and we could order daily newspapers. And we could talk to each other, talk, actually *talk*, discuss what we wanted as we wanted, talk or not talk if we didn't want – talk, and feel human again. I can still see the look of polite amazement on the faces of our lawyers when we were led in for the first consultation, briefly before appearing in court for the first time, and when we bubbled at them with a stream of incoherent excitement, talking and feeling the joy of talking.

There were five of us at the start of the trial: Baruch Hirson, whom I had known only as Eric, a physics lecturer from Johannesburg; Fred Prager, whom I'd met socially, a professional photographer, well kept in his late fifties; Raymond Eisenstein, Tom, three years older than me and a financial journalist; Alex Cox, whom I had neither met nor heard of at the time we first went to court, a company director; and myself. Alex was released within days and left the country quickly. That left the four of us awaiting trial in the cells at Local. The commanding officer gave permission for three of us to share a single cell at night and for all of us to be locked up in it during the day to give us opportunity to discuss and prepare our case. When we were not in court or busy with our lawyers in an office downstairs, we were given two half-hour exercise periods a day and, but for one unnecessary occasion, were spared the annoyance of being skud.

Suddenly there seemed so much to do, so much to detract from the fact of living in a single cell cluttered with three bedrolls, three lots of clothes, three food-parcels, and three toilet pots – so much to read in newspapers and books, so much to tell the lawyers, so much to discuss – to live again. We first appeared in court on 1 October and were remanded until 11 November. The six weeks of preparation produced mixed feelings: of wanting to prolong the proceedings so as to maintain contact with the outside world, and wanting to get the whole business over quickly so as to begin our sentences as soon as possible and not prolong our time in prison. None of us really doubted that we would be convicted. There was too much evidence, too many witnesses against us. The main interest of the trial was to see how long the judge would give us, remembering that the minimum mandatory sentence under the Sabotage Act was five years. And we wanted to see who, of our former comrades, would actually give evidence against us. The cases against the members of the N.C.L. were separated and there was not – as there had been at the Rivonia trial and as the Branch once mentioned as a possibility for us too – one mass trial in Pretoria. Each group was charged and tried apart: a trial in Cape Town, another in Pietermaritzburg, another in Pretoria, and, also in Pretoria, the trial of John Harris on his own. John was kept at Local too, separated from everybody. His trial ended while we were awaiting-trial: in October 1964 he was condemned to death for the station bomb.

Having been able, out of detention, to follow most of the case, I wasn't surprised at the verdict, but the news of the sentence itself was the sort of news that can't be conceived. I remember comprehending it – that he would be hanged – and feeling sick; but it was too huge to be real, too close to be imagined. Easier, in the callousness of prison, to leave it, a numb presence somewhere outside my involvement – leave it and concentrate on the more immediate things: like the fact that the main witness against John Harris had been Ernest, my flat-mate and the man I had recruited to the N.C.L. to help in small ways. After giving evidence against John Harris – and effectively putting the rope round his neck – Ernest was allowed, for the first time, to see friends, and he sent a special message to me: he had agreed to give evidence against Harris but had always said he would refuse to give evidence against me.

That was some comfort, but Ernest was only one of a number of potential witnesses, prime among them, for me, being Mark, who had already done so much damage to all of us. Another was Rosemary Wentzel, Diane, who had been kidnapped by the Branch from Swaziland, then put under intolerable pressure to give evidence against us. As far as I was concerned, a combination of Mark and Diane against me would be absolutely conclusive – they had, after all, been the two people primarily responsible for recruiting me to the N.C.L. It was hardly necessary for Ernest's voice to be added and I was pleased to hear that he would refuse to give evidence against me – but I hoped too, after what he had done to John Harris, that he wouldn't be joined to our case if he did refuse to testify.

There were three other witnesses against us who affected us closely: three Africans, members of the group from its beginning, any one of them in a position to be charged along with the rest of us. But it seemed that the Special Branch wanted to make ours an all-white trial, hoping perhaps to avoid creating the impression of cooperation across the colour line. Or was it that they wanted to indicate a white–black conflict? In Cape Town, Eddie Daniels – a Coloured – was charged and sentenced alongside the other N.C.L. whites, but there he was the only non-white involved and for us in Pretoria, the blacks were kept apart and forced to give evidence. In addition, unlike the white witnesses, the blacks against us were forced to put across Special Branch lies: the whites could tell their stories with unencumbered straightforwardness, which made them very good witnesses (for the State); the blacks had to tell their stories, plus the embellishments wanted by the Branch, for instance to substantiate the idea of a non-existent mass movement.

The need to embellish immediately made them vulnerable to cross-examination – which was not, in the end, a bad thing for us, or rather for Fred Prager, because it was the evidence of the Africans which would largely account for his being found guilty or innocent, and they were made under cross-examination to look bumbling and self-contradictory. Fred got off. And I couldn't help remembering, watching them in the box with Swanepoel and the rest of the Branch sitting below them with the Prosecution, the night I had seen 'Peter' and the other African I didn't know at the Greys, where their faces had been puffed and bruised, and where they had been sweating on that very cold night. Remembering that, I couldn't completely blame them: in that system, they didn't have much of a chance.

I was waiting for the people who had been my friends. The early part of the case had been taken up with legal technicalities and argument, leaving those of us in the dock with the distinct feeling that the whole business was a vast game, played out among Judge, Prosecution and Defence, having much to do with incomprehensible and seemingly irrelevant jurisprudential niceties but having little to do with the suckers sitting in the dock. Then they brought in a nice old auntie who described what had happened one night when the pylons crossing the veld on their farm had gone boom and fallen down. Then – it was quite late in the afternoon, I remember – they said 'Call Ernest.'

If you're walking down a street and you unexpectedly bump into an old friend whom you've not seen for some time, your immediate reaction is to smile and greet him. As Ernest came into court, I felt myself wanting to smile and greet him; and I wondered how the judge would react when he refused to give evidence. Would they, I wondered, put him straight into the dock with us? Or would he be tried separately? Or maybe he'd go free without talking? He was sworn in as a witness and, with hardly a nudge from the Prosecution, he began to tell his story: speaking very fast and looking straight ahead, he told the full story, his story, my story, our story.

I didn't believe it at first. I sat watching Ernest; fascinated, not bothering (as we normally did) to take notes of what he was saying. I had not thought I would have to take notes. Ernest talked so fast that my advocate, Arthur Chaskalson, had to interrupt and ask the judge to slow him down so we could take down what he was saying. He left nothing out. He added nothing. When he had finished, the judge said the court would adjourn for the day and Ernest left the box and came down the court towards us, looking staringly back at me. I no longer felt I wanted to smile and greet him. I felt numb. In the cell under the court afterwards, the lawyers asked whether anything that he had said was substantially incorrect and whether we felt there was a chance of challenging him under cross-examination. No, we said, no chance. The following morning, the three of us – Baruch Hirson, Ray Eisenstein and myself – changed our pleas to guilty and the rest of the trial was taken up with the Prosecution trying to prove a case against Fred Prager.

Their attempt was of particular interest to me because it involved their calling Mark and Diane as witnesses. Mark we had already read about: he had been the main witness in the corresponding case in Cape Town; had been substantially responsible for getting Eddie Daniels fifteen years and Spike de Kellar ten years; and had, in the process, made a fair exhibition of himself in the box. He broke down and wept, blamed apartheid for his agony, and explained that he had decided to give evidence against his comrades because if he didn't he would go to jail himself for twenty years. We hoped he wouldn't weep for us too. In the event, we were spared that: there was not a great deal he could say about Fred and little point in saying much about the rest of us who'd already pleaded guilty so our lawyers decided not to attack him but rather use his testimony to support the mitigatory evidence we were leading.

Again, as Mark came into court, I felt an instinctive urge to greet him. I had had more warning that he was coming and I was under no misapprehension about what he would do in the box – but still, when I first saw him come in, I felt that, had he had time to look my way, I would have found myself smiling a greeting. Even knowing and experiencing what he had done, I could not prevent an involuntary nod of friendship. In fact, when we were led down to our cell under the court during the lunch-break, there he was just outside the cell-door, sitting having a smoke with his Branch mentors all round. As I reached him, he made as if to greet me and I felt myself, involuntarily, almost reaching out to greet him. But even as I did so, the Branch got up too to prevent it and that brought back the reality. I turned away, into the cell.

When Diane came in to testify, she was wearing a hat. I'd rarely seen her in a hat and the strangeness of it (it was a horrible Sunday-school-type hat) kept me occupied for quite a few moments, a pleasantly silly distraction which made it possible not to concentrate on the fact that she was the person who had originally recruited me and here she was, in the box, giving evidence.

Her evidence, as it happened, was meaningless in terms of affecting us adversely: by the time she came to testify, the three of us had already changed our pleas to guilty and it was only Fred Prager who was concerned. And by the time she came to testify, we had heard her story: of how she had escaped with Luke and her kids during that long night so long ago and of how she had been kidnapped from Swaziland and brought back to Pretoria. She had tried to bring a charge against the Branch for the kidnap but then, under pressure and the threat of losing her kids, had withdrawn the charge. It was never disclosed who had kidnapped her – but I remember Swanepoel, when he heard from me early that morning that she had gone to Swaziland, turning to Viktor and saying 'Let's go and get her.'

In the box, testifying against Fred, Diane looked strange in her hat. As she talked, I remembered the only other time I had seen her wearing a hat: a balaclava, like the balaclava I had worn too, when we went together to hit a pylon in the veld outside Nigel. And I noticed that, in the box, she said remarkably little about the pylons, remarkably little about anything that could harm any of us. Mark, on his way to freedom through the box, had tried to diminish his own role and attribute much of his activities to others. Diane, in the box, diminished the roles of others and increased her own. As she walked back from the box, on her way out, she looked across at me, as if pleadingly – and I couldn't help but nod slightly to her, and wink.

I wonder if she understood what that meant. I'm not sure that I did. It was a nod of recognition, and goodbye too. We had been friends. Mark, Ernest and Diane – all had been close friends of mine and we had been through things together which made for very close friendship and comradeship. That was over, done, and nothing could ever redeem the change. I sat in the dock and went off to be sentenced. They stood in the witness box and bought themselves a sort of freedom. Now – after my seven years inside – I am free and I am sure I have had the better part of it. I sat in the dock where there was plenty of room, lots more room in the dock for others with us four accused. They stood alone, in the box, where there was room only for one, like in a coffin.

On 30 November 1964, Fred Prager was found not guilty and released. It was a good sensation that, sitting in the dock next to him and hearing the judge say: You may go – and watching him go, dutifully down the steps to the cell in the hands of the Special Branch, furious at his having got off. (He was allowed home, then later put under twenty-four-hour house arrest.) The next day, 1 December 1964 (Raymond Eisenstein's twenty-eighth birthday and two days before my twenty-fifth) we went to court for sentence. We expected heavy sentences, similar to the fifteen and ten years which Daniels and de Kellar had got in Cape Town. The Branch, we heard, wanted even more for us: twenty years for Baruch and fifteen years each for Raymond and myself.

I think two things worked in our favour, getting us less than expected. The first was the mitigatory evidence brought on behalf of Raymond and myself. Nobody in court – except the prosecution, with the Branch sitting there with them – could remain impassive as Raymond's mother, speaking through a Polish interpreter, described how she had smuggled her young son out of the Warsaw ghetto in an orange sack while the Nazis burnt their home. That, I'm sure, had an effect – as did the appearance on my behalf of Sister Dorothy Raphael (who had worked with my father and who, as Dorothy Maud, had founded the Sophiatown mission in Johannesburg) and Daantjie Oosthuizen, my philosophy professor at university. His quiet testimony visibly infuriated the Branch: he could, he said, well understand what I had done because he too had become involved, while a student, in an underground organization involved in sabotage – he had been a member of the 'Ossewabrandwag', an extremist Afrikaner group dedicated to fighting the English. The second factor that got us shorter sentences than expected was, I'm equally sure, the address to the court by Arthur Chaskalson, which was well linked to the point made by Daantjie Oosthuizen.

Arthur Chaskalson traced the history of dissent in South Africa and outlined the many cases of people – mainly Afrikaners – tried in South Africa for subversion and sabotage, and the long history of leniency which characterized these trials. He pleaded that the judge pass a sentence on us which would not produce bitterness but which would give us a chance still to hope.

There was an additional point in our favour: we had a judge – Toss Bekker – who could, even within the strictures of the Sabotage Act, consider the arguments put to him and who could act independently, uninfluenced for instance by the sentences imposed by the Judge President of the Cape. 'The sentence which I am about to impose,' said Mr Bekker, 'is one which I cannot reduce any further. To do so would, in my opinion, render the law a mockery.'

Hirson, nine years' imprisonment. Lewin and Eisenstein, seven years' imprisonment.

At the end of each court session, we were led down a flight of steps to the cell below the court. Our way down was usually guarded by several Branchmen. One, in particular, always stood at the bottom of the stairs, a small pig of a man who looked as if he was trying to look like a Special Branch man: shifty, mean and ugly, with the effect heightened by his always wearing a pair of dark glasses. He was there again when we were led down the stairs for the last time, having just, as we saw it then, escaped from sentences of twenty or fifteen years. Raymond, normally rather phlegmatic and inscrutable, bounded down the stairs in front of me and flung his arms around Dark Glasses, dancing him round in an astonished circle and cheering: 'We have only seven years! Only seven years, ha-ha!' That was the last time, for a long time, that we felt quite so jubilant.

3 Full-time Bandiet

We were now, officially, bandiete – full prisoners, out of detention, finished with awaiting-trial, and ready to start our prison terms. Normally in South Africa, when a person is sentenced to imprisonment, he first spends some time 'under observation'. This process of observation is designed to prepare the prisoner for the sentence ahead and, by determining qualities such as intelligence and capability, set him on the course best suited to aid his eventual rehabilitation. The process is in the hands of warders with special training, commonly referred to as 'the psychos'. The Observation Block is commonly called 'the madhouse'.

But for us at Local Prison, Pretoria, there was no separate madhouse. Having been sentenced – and become bandiete, we returned to the same prison in the same way that we had done throughout our trial. We returned, in fact, straight to du Preez's little cell-office.

'Strip,' he said.

We took off our clothes and packed them, together with our watches, pens, pencils, writing-pads, books and remnants of the food-parcels – packed all the little things that made us private individuals, packed them into a suitcase for sending out. We took a last couple of puffs on our cigarettes, then handed the rest of the packets to the warders, who were watching with mild amusement these last rites of freedom. Du Preez handed us our new prison clothes: underpants, vest, khaki shirt, khaki longs, socks, shoes, short-sleeved jersey, corduroy jacket, brown felt hat. All prison uniform, brown and khaki (with one bright exception, a red handkerchief). The clothes felt strange, heavy and unfriendly.

We looked at each other and laughed. At once, stripped of our personal clothes, we looked like convicts. The memory of our smart suits and ties was immediately lost in the drab uniformity of the oversize, uncomfortable khaki. We had become bandiete. We laughed, awkwardly, and were led upstairs again, each now to an empty cell. We had a Bible, a spare set of clothes, and what were to be our towels: two small pieces of cloth, the size and consistency of tea-cloths. We would, said du Preez, be interviewed by the psychos, when they had time. The psychos would determine our grouping and explain our privileges. Everything depends on your grouping, said du Preez. Until the psychos come, no talking, absolutely no talking to anyone. It was a gloomy prospect, but when we went down for our first exercise, shuffling painfully in our new prison shoes, we found the yard filled, so it seemed, with large khaki convicts. Du Preez was there too, with several warders, shouting for silence, but where before, during detention, there had never been more than five of us in the yard at a time, now there were more than a dozen other bandiete bustling with toilet pots and water bowls, busily talking to each other and pointing interestedly at us, the new boys, silent and shy.

There were at least nine of us new boys: mostly N.C.L. members and all recently sentenced – half a dozen, mainly strangers to me, from Cape Town, plus two friends, Dave Evans and John Laredo from Durban. Du Preez screamed at us newies to stay apart and silent – we were set to walk round in a circle, one behind the other, snatching brief words of recognition through clenched teeth and, hopefully, unmoving lips.

It was like being in a prison movie. Gloomy guards, prisoners shuffling round in circles, the yard grim and colourless. The stereotypes were no less faceless and forbidding for being real. Somehow I thought it would be different. Somehow I thought that I would feel different as a convicted prisoner; that du Preez would act differently when one was convicted; that there would be some tangible change, possibly something dramatic, to mark the transition from detainee to prisoner.

There was nothing. No change, no drama. Just a further stripping down to a towel which was not large enough to go once round one's waist – and a silent walking around in circles. And an empty cell with a Bible. Nothing else, and now not even the possibility of a trial ahead, or a visit from the Special Branch, or the ending of detention.

Now there was only a void ahead – seven years, yes, but who can imagine seven years? How do you conjure up seven years ahead? It was as far ahead of me as were, behind, all my years out of school: three years at university, one year teaching, three years on four different newspapers; seven years, in three different cities, eight different flats or houses; seven years, twice the time of a marriage made and broken; seven years, of a whole life-time behind me. Seven years, ahead. Yet, I was lucky, having something definite, some finite horizon – seven years – unlike Denis Goldberg, with life, an indefinite, undefined life as a political. I was lucky to have something fixed. But I couldn't conceive it. I couldn't comprehend it. I could not, then, imagine serving so long in prison. I did not think that I *could* ever serve that long, that I could *survive* seven years. I did not see how anyone could survive seven years in prison.

But now I was not alone. I was one among a whole group of others, all of them political prisoners and many of them with sentences which made mine look, as they say in prison, like a parking ticket. We were, of course, whites only: apartheid applies as completely inside as it does outside, ensuring that blacks and whites – even if arrested and charged and sentenced together – are kept always separate. The black politicals are all on Robben Island off Cape Town, the whites in Pretoria. During my time inside, I met altogether twenty-six other white politicals: as a group we never, at any one time, reached more than twenty-one and, by the time I left at the end of 1971, there were only nine whites left (but still some 400 blacks on Robben Island).

A total of twenty-seven white political prisoners: twelve of us had been sentenced for sabotage, three under the Explosives Act, and the other twelve under the Suppression of Communism Act. We came together through fourteen different trials held in four different cities in South Africa over a period of four years. My seven-year sentence was about average, but still a 'parking ticket' because, above me on the time-scale, were two life sentences (Fischer and Goldberg), one 20 years (Kitson), one

15 years (Matthews), three 12 years (Tarshish, Schoon, Thoms), and one 9 (Hirson). Among those below me were $5\frac{3}{4}$ (Carneson), 5 (Evans, Heymann, Laredo, Schermbrucker, Weinberg), 4 (Arenstein), 3 (Strachan, Turok, Baker and Levy) and $2\frac{1}{2}$ (Ernst).

Sixteen of the twenty-seven admitted to being members of the Communist Party, with leanings to Moscow. Another one, a former expelled member of the Party, leant to Peking. He had one supporter and achieved one conversion. One other had been an avowed Trotsky-ite. Four of us had once been members of the Liberal Party, and had been expelled when it was learnt that we were members of a sabotage group. One other aspired to membership of the C.P. (Moscow).

Everybody was South African. All were South African-born except one born in Latvia, one Lithuania, one Poland, and one in England. Afrikaans was the home language of three and another three, when they arrived, spoke no Afrikaans at all. Everybody spoke English. Only two spoke Zulu and one Xhosa; two spoke fluent German, one fluent Polish and French, one claimed a knowledge of Italian and one remembered a little Russian. Four could read Hebrew.

The group included one Q.C., two attorneys, one artist, two engineers, three university lecturers, two teachers, a doctor, a professional photographer, two business secretaries, one accounts clerk, one businessman, one surveyor, one salesman, three students and four journalists. The average age was about forty-five.

Twelve of the group were Jews and were visited intermittently by a rabbi. Of the Gentiles, five were visited by a Roman Catholic priest, six by an Anglican priest, one by a Christian Science preacher – and two admitted to no religion at all. Of the twenty-seven, nineteen came to jail with university degrees, three from Afrikaans universities. Everybody studied in jail and, by the end of 1971, eleven further degrees had been obtained: three of them by people with no previous degrees.

There were at least ten bridge players, six of them fanatical. Twenty could play chess. Nineteen were fit and energetic enough to try our eventual brand of squash. We had twenty-two potential volleyball players. Two of the group exercised daily, running round the yard while the rest of us walked or sat talking.

We must have seemed an odd lot. We *were* an odd lot. It was not of our own choosing that we had been put together in such close quarters. Of the group, I had known only eight before going to jail: three of them fairly well (socially only) and three others not so well (socially only). Two I had worked with politically, but I had known one of them only by a pseudonym. Of the others, I knew half of them by name, for their political activities. The rest were complete strangers when I met them inside. We were not only strangers to each other, we were also very different sorts of people, often with strong ideological and psychological differences.

Our existence in prison naturally brought us into very close contact and immediately created infinite possibilities for tension. But the fact that we had all got there in the first place because of active opposition to one thing, apartheid, established bonds which might not otherwise have been there and these bonds were immediately strengthened by our day-to-day existence at Local which, particularly under du Preez, posed a challenge in the form of an ever-present enemy.

Coming into the yard on the first day and seeing it filled with similarly-khakied bandiete with some familiar faces among the khaki, I felt a sudden surge of relief: I was not alone. There were others in the yard too, cleaning their pots and laughing, looking relaxed and cheerful. I could not begin to think of the seven years ahead of me, but I could begin to think of the next day, or maybe the next week – when, du Preez announced, we would be allowed to talk to the others. But only after the 'psychos' had been to interview us and determine our grouping. Fortunately the psychos came within a day: two warders, one with pips on his shoulder, both with little pads and printed forms. How many rooms in the house where I lived? Did I live with my father and mother? Did my father often beat my mother? Did they/I ever smoke dagga (pot)? Did I have any qualifications?

It was predictable, and a farce – infuriating because they first delivered their set repent-ye-your-crime piece, then embroidered it with homilies about my political wickedness and therefore moral degeneracy. They displayed a tendency which we were to find quite common: of petty functionaries using their lowly but undoubted authority to lord it over us and pronounce grandly on matters of state, most particularly politics, and also rugby and motor-cars. These psychos, I had been told, were responsible for grouping – so, of course, I listened with polite indifference, and asked about grouping. D group, they said, that's where all prisoners begin. D group means one letter, one visit every six months. Smoking? You will never, said the psychos, smoke again while in prison. Work? You'll see, they said. They left, having – apparently – satisfied themselves.

One letter, one visit every six months. If you say it quickly enough you don't notice what it means. A letter in prison means a letter out and a reply, and no one letter can be more than 500 words long. (The Prison Regulations used to stipulate 'approximately 500 words or two foolscap sheets or four pages of writing-paper' but, for political prisoners, this has been interpreted with stunning obstinacy to mean 500 words exactly, no more.) A visit in prison, except for the condemneds, lasts half an hour and, for D and C groupers, can be taken by one person only.

I learnt, during my first twelve months, what these statistics mean in practice. I was sentenced at the beginning of December; four months later, on 29 March 1965, I handed in my first personal letter. I had thought about it for a month and had taken a week of evenings to write it. It was 504 words long, excluding the address. Six weeks later I received my first letter in: it was 500 words long, including date and address. Two months later, on 11 July 1965, I handed in my second 500-word offering. Three and a half months later, at the end of October, I received my second reply. That completed my first year's correspondence.

In November, I submitted a request to the commanding officer for permission to write a special letter to my mother for Christmas, pointing out that she was in England and that, as she was a priest's widow, Christmas was a time of particular significance for her. Du Preez read out the O.C.'s reply to me: 'No special letter. Tell him to use his ordinary six-monthly letter.'

Du Preez's initial silence rule lasted only two days but there was not much opportunity for talking in the early days of sentence. We were taken out of our cells for exercise each morning and afternoon, usually for half an hour a time. We could talk at these times in the yard – and did so, feverishly, busily stomping in two's or three's around and around the yard, in between emptying and cleaning toilet pots, or washing clothes, or (especially in the afternoons, when some sun shone directly into the yard) showering in the four cold showers. When we were not in the exercise yard, we were in our cells, locked up, alone, with no talking allowed between cells.

For the first two months, we had nothing to do. What we had, besides the Bible, were two library books a week. These came from the library at Central Prison which was stocked, it seemed, mainly from throw-aways from the State Libraries. This had an advantage for us in that the discards were often thick and long and with small print. What you hoped for were books that were thick and long, by Dickens or Galsworthy or George Eliot if you were lucky, or even Conrad and, once, Dostoyevsky; or, if unlucky, Lloyd Douglas, Cecil Roberts and the like. The luck of the draw was complicated by the fact that the Central Library ran a remarkable classification system (presumably prompted by rehabilitatory zeal) which divided books into 'Educational' and 'Fiction'. We had to take one Educational and one Fiction book a week. The distinctions were sometimes difficult to define: there was Educ/Lit and Educ/Hist, which happily catered for all of Dickens but only half of Jane Austen: *Northanger Abbey* made it as Educ/Lit, *Persuasion* could only make Fic/Romance; Tolstoy's *Tales* reached Educ/Lit, *Anna Karenina* only Fic/Rom; Graves got only to Fic/Hist with *Claudius the God*, while Sterne made it to Educ/Hist with *Tristram Shandy*.

These library books were our main solace in those first empty months. A lot depended on one's luck: I remember one long weekend, with short and early exercises (and therefore long and early lock-ups), having nothing to read other than a collection of ghost stories for children, and a dreadful (and short) Cecil Roberts. I remember too another such weekend when the hours seemed to mean nothing as I read my way, virtually without stopping, through the whole *Forsyte Saga* – and another when I read *All Quiet on the Western Front* through twice and was amazed to find it so fresh and timeless.

Du Preez complicated matters by refusing to allow us to exchange books. Each library book came with its own card, number and name, and du Preez would make a point of checking to ensure that each man had the correct two books in his cell. There we were alongside each other, each more than happy to see that no book was lost or damaged, yet he imposed his little ban – no swapping of books (with meals and no more books as punishment). It was petty, it was meaningless, it was du Preez.

This was the first of many such decrees from du Preez, remarkable for their being absolutely arbitrary and mindless, which – although we flouted them as often as possible – always imposed an extra unnecessary element of tension on an already tense existence. Du Preez was a petty tyrant, but he effectively controlled every aspect of our lives and so his tyranny was absolute and inescapable. He controlled everything from the issue of toilet paper to the censoring of letters and monitoring of visits. His power derived from the fact that he was in sole charge of our section, and, although only a head-warder (a rank equivalent to sergeant and achieved by long service, not by passing exams), he was given full backing by his superiors.

You could complain to the O.C. at the daily inspection but you complained always in the presence of your keeper, and the nature of the complaints was often such that, alone, they were ridiculous by being so trivial. Our lives were made up of trivialities. Du Preez's tyranny was based on the implementation of triviality.

Tony Trew needed a new roll of toilet paper. The first opportunity he got for asking for it was at morning exercise. 'Where's the finished centre-tube of the roll?' asked du Preez. Tony handed over the empty roll at afternoon exercise. Du Preez was busy then, preoccupied and joking with a visiting warder. Tony repeated his request; du Preez laughed and said 'Use your finger' and continued his discussion. Tony bristled and threatened to report du Preez, who burst into a flood of curses, his face suddenly purple with fury. The whole yard tensed; the search on the way back to the cells was severe and abrupt; and Tony eventually got a new roll with his supper.

I had spent one winter at Local. Before the next I wanted to prevent the chapped hands and lips I knew would come from washing in cold water outside in the cold. 'Could I buy a tube of lip-ice with my monthly toilet order?' I asked du Preez. 'No,' he said, 'you're only allowed to buy what's on the list.' 'Could I ask the O.C. then?' 'Put it in writing,' he said. So I wrote out a full letter, in duplicate, addressed respectfully to the commanding officer: 'Could I please have permission to buy some "lip-ice" from the canteen? – I have sufficient funds to cover the cost.' I handed the letter to du Preez, as instructed. Three days later he called me to the grille outside his new cell-office at the end of the corridor. 'No lip-ice,' he said.

I had kept, after sentence, my nailbrush – together with tooth-brush, razor, shaving-brush and some soap. The toilet list for purchases from the canteen listed no nailbrush, nor did the Prison Regulations. Three months after sentence, I returned from exercise to find my cell in the accustomed chaos which followed the regular skuds – the nailbrush was gone. 'Why?' I asked du Preez during his end-of-day wall-tap round the cell. 'You're not allowed a nailbrush,' he said. 'But what could I do with it? How could it be dangerous?' 'You're not allowed a nailbrush – good night.'

I asked to buy some nail-clippers to cut my nails. 'No,' said du Preez, 'use a razor-blade.' Without asking, I put the request in writing – a respectful letter to the commanding officer, asking, please sir, could I please buy a pair of nail-clippers to cut my nails – and if necessary the clippers could be kept in Mr du Preez's office. Three days later I was called to the grille: the O.C. says 'No, you can't buy clippers, use a razor-blade.'

The Regulations stipulate that, at Christmas, white prisoners should be allowed to buy up to R2 (about £1) worth of fruit, biscuits and sweets, maximum 3 lb. That means, said du Preez, 1 lb of sweets, 1 lb of dried fruit, 1 lb of biscuits. Could it not be taken to mean, asks Jack Tarshish (who's been at Central and seen it happen there with the ordinary criminals – and who didn't eat sweets), that someone who doesn't like sweets can buy up to R2 worth of fruit alone, as long as it doesn't exceed 3 lb? No, says du Preez – 1 lb/1 lb/1 lb. So Jack goes to the O.C. himself (you could do so, on request, once a week) and puts the case for 3 lb, not 1 lb/1 lb/1 lb. Of course, says the O.C., 3 lb if you prefer. So Jack returns to du Preez and says the O.C. says it's O K for 3 lb – and he hands in his order, his one little order for Christmas. The following morning he gets the order handed back by du Preez: the O.C., *he* says, says No – 1 lb/1 lb/1 lb. At inspection that day, the O.C. says yes, he's changed his mind: 1 lb/1 lb/1 lb.

In du Preez's cell-office were row on row of clothes. When we were sentenced, he issued us with a set, but the set he gave us did not include long-sleeved jerseys. These were there, in his cell-office, but he would not issue them – they were not, said du Preez, necessary until winter. Winter began officially in May. That was when the warders began wearing their winter tunics and that, said du Preez, was when we would get long-sleeved jerseys. It was cold, on occasion, before May and the O.C. was asked: could we please have the long-sleeved jerseys? Yes, of course, he would speak to Mr du Preez about them. There were plenty of them, weren't there, Mr du Preez? Yes, Sir, baie/ plenty. The jerseys stayed in his cell-office until 1 May, when we got them, one each – and not the newer ones: we must, he said, wear out the old ones first.

None of us, as C and D group prisoners, was allowed to smoke. The warders all smoked. Du Preez instructed them – on more than one occasion in the presence of a prisoner – that they were not to leave their butts lying around. The butts, and any broken matches, were to be thrown into the gutters around the yard – and not anywhere in the gutters, right into the water-sumps at the end of each gutter.

Du Preez's genius was not in inventing hardships, nor even in contravening the regulations. His strength lay in knowing – more by an instinctive cunning than any marked intelligence – just how far he could push the regulations without breaking them. He was, I suppose, the ideal prison warder in that he maintained, with deadly consistency, an active antagonism towards the prisoners. We came into contact, through the years, with a large number of warders, some of them capable of more immediate nastiness than du Preez ever tried with us. But none of them I met were ever able to match his ability to be so ruthlessly unbending. Given an opportunity where, without threat to his authority or even the possibility of appearing soft, he could show any goodwill towards one of us, he wouldn't. Even when he knew other warders were acting otherwise, he would never relent.

South African prisons maintain a tradition (surprising under the circumstances) whereby food-parcels are sent in to all the Jewish prisoners at Pesach and Rosh Hashonah. This means, in practice, that the Jews have two lots of ten days a year when their prison diet is supplemented by these extra parcels of plenty. By an equally happy tradition, these parcels are, as much as possible, usually shared out by the Jewish prisoners among their fellows. Except under du Preez. By the time of Pesach in 1965, there were twenty-one of us at Local, of whom seven were Jews and entitled to the parcels. And by that time, most of us had moved down from the single cells upstairs and were in the larger cells on the ground floor, sharing three to a cell. As soon as the parcels arrived, du Preez moved all the Jews into two cells, moved all their food boxes in with them and kept them locked up all the time, permanently out of the way of showing any charity.

This arrangement produced some bizarre incidents. The only access we had to them – and they to us – was through the judas-hole (which often had no glass in) or through the gap under each door. It thus became the task of those of us who were cleaners in the passage outside the Jews' cells to smuggle what we could, when we could. When du Preez or any of his cohorts were in the passage, there was no chance at all – when certain other warders were there, they became adept at turning their backs judiciously on us and strolling in the opposite direction. One young warder (he was not, unfortunately, a regular in our section) even went as far as unlocking one of the 'Forbidden Cells' so as to allow me hurriedly to rush in, collect an armful of cheese squares, sweets, taiglach and dates and rush out to disperse the goodies among the other cleaners and so, in time, among the whole Gentile community – who could be seen, if you knew what you were looking for, to be walking around the yard at exercise carefully chewing their contraband.

These merrier by-products of the regime – where it did not much matter to us if our banditry succeeded or not – hardly compensated for the effects of du Preez's bloody-mindedness on the more fundamental aspects of prison life. Having sharpened his spurs on us as 90-day detainees, he was ideally suited for continuing the Special Branch's policy of isolation which was applied to us as vigorously when we were prisoners as it had been while we were in solitary. No news for politicals – that, we were told by a series of officials, was the line, and it was the duty of the Prisons Department to implement it. Du Preez's interpretation of this was predictable: no news meant *absolutely* no news. Visits, he said, must be confined absolutely to family matters – or be stopped. Always that was the threat, with himself as sole arbiter.

Prison visits, under the best of circumstances, are difficult. With letters, they are the only means of contact you have with Outside, the only real life-line with normality. When rationed at our rate of one every six months, they assume almost grotesque importance: everything seems to depend on them, everything seems to move towards them, your whole being becomes involved in the fact of the impending visit as the only point of focus, the only imaginable substantial horizon. For days beforehand you scribble little reminders and begin drawing up a list of topics to discuss – so many priorities tumbling over each other for a place in that brief half-hour, so many seemingly vital points that cannot be omitted, must not be forgotten, and so many other things that would be good to discuss, so many silly little points of interest that would, normally, make chatty conversation pieces, make the matter of living seem relaxed and convivial. A shopping-list of your life. For hours before the visit you rehearse what you think you might say, what you would like to say, what you hope will be said. You spend hours discussing with others what they have said in their half-hours; hours discussing how, in the half-hour, to extract whole weeks of events (and not seem to do so), of ideas, of inspirations – enough to start the momentum again, enough to tank you up to last again till the next distant half-hour.

You wait, and wait. Then du Preez calls you – 'Trek aan/Get

your coat on. Nou is jy in die kak/Now you're in the shit. The O.C. wants you.' And you nod and smile, knowing he knows you know this is his kind of humour, but it's a visit – the visit at last – so you don't want to object, you don't want to be distracted or in any way risk losing any precious part of the half-hour. Through the corridors and up, waiting outside your side of the visiting-room, waiting for him to unlock your side of the box. 'Remember,' he says, 'remember – no news. No news, hey,' – and locks you into your side of the box with your attendant warder. Du Preez himself stands on the other side – and though the perspex through which you have to look is so narrow and though there is so little space there, he stands right next to your visitor, listening, watching always, ready to break in quickly with 'You can't discuss that' and 'Stop that'. And 'Time, thank you' before you feel you've begun – with the list hardly consulted, never completed, and the feeling always of immense dissatisfaction, frustration, unfulfilment, overshadowed by the oppressive presence that you can never escape.

Du Preez was there. So too was the thinly-disguised mechanism of tape-recording every visit. The visiting boxes were neatly panelled with sound-boarding; never more than one visit at a time was allowed; and there was always an elaborate ritual played out by the warders, signalling to each other that the visit could begin. This hidden presence was oppressive too, but we learnt in time to accommodate to it: it became part of the furniture, whether in the visiting-room or in our cells, another reminder of Special Branch attention which, because it seemed so petty and futile, seemed not to threaten.

What did threaten was the fact of du Preez's actual presence, looming over every visit. If it wasn't him, there was always the awareness of his presence: he tyrannized his subordinates as ruthlessly as he tyrannized us, and they, clearly fearful of allowing anything to appear on the tape which might later be brought to their account, were over-zealous in their attentions. I had a visit once from my former headmaster, monitored by a frightened-looking hospital orderly who rushed to intervene when my visitor began telling me, as a joke, that Jackie Kennedy had married . . . (I thought he said Onassis, but wasn't sure).

Another friend was stopped as he began a rambling story about 'Smithie's going off to meet Harold on a battleship'.

Such interruptions often gave us a fleeting indication of the sort of things that were happening outside. Whenever someone had had a visit we would collate any new snippets gained, any fresh nuances we could divine in the attitude of the attendant warders. The results were sometimes rather odd. For instance, towards the end of 1965, one intrepid visitor (the visitors too received the stern, no-news warning) began to tell his story but was abruptly cut short – so that the story, as we heard it, was that Smith had declared independence and that the British had imposed a complete oil boycott. What the visitor did not have time to mention was that this was all prognostication. We were thus able, through many long hours, to discuss and analyse and dispute and dissect events which had not yet happened. The next visitor must have been very puzzled when asked, obliquely, what were the results of independence when U.D.I. itself had still not become reality.

I found – and this was the case with most of us – that the desire to know what was happening outside in the world never diminished. I know that my own news-gathering instincts were definitely heightened by the fact that there were, effectively, no avenues open for any sort of news-gathering. I felt permanently challenged to discover or create ways of getting news – but I was, almost always, stymied. We were sealed off in our section, as if at the end of a long tunnel with only one small opening – and du Preez controlled that opening. Even if there had been warders who were sympathetic – or who were independent enough not to be terrified by the threat of Special Branch wrath – there was little chance of their passing on news to us. Two of them, I know, never read a newspaper anyway; two others read only the sports pages and the comics; and all of them were forbidden ever to bring a newspaper into the jail, let alone into the section. (It was not uncommon for the warders themselves, especially the younger ones, to be skud-searched on their arrival for duty.) And du Preez, with typical vigour, was particularly quick to notice whenever any of the warders in his section seemed to be talking to any of us too often or too long.

The only other outlets – inlets – for news were thus the very rare occasions when, because of some error somewhere, we were in a position to see a newspaper. This happened so rarely that it was indeed an event for us all (and must have happened about twice a year – two pieces of news every year). The seeing of a newspaper was, literally, that: a newspaper seen, for example, lying folded on a desk in an office you passed on the way to interview the commanding officer. You had time perhaps to see only the main headline, but that was sometimes enough for us to work out a complete train of events. Paul Trewhela saw the headline 'Mrs Nkrumah flies out of Ghana' – and from this we deduced that there had been a coup and that, in all probability, it had taken place while Nkrumah himself was out of the country and that he was, therefore, still alive. (It took six months to confirm our version.)

One other major news item which came our way was, over a number of months, divulged by the most unlikely source of all: du Preez and the Prisons Department. This was halfway through 1965 – for most of us, our first year in prison – but the final year for Harold Strachan, who had been sentenced for having explosives way back in 1962, in the days before the Sabotage Act and the minimum five-year sentence. Harold (we all called him Jock) got three years in April 1962, and was joined by Bennie Turok, also with a three-year sentence, in July that year – and together they had, for more than a year, been the only white politicals in Pretoria and had had a particularly rough time as a result. By the time we all joined them towards the end of 1964, conditions had improved a little, they told us, and there was definitely some psychological advantage in our being a large community together.

Jock was released in April 1965. His release, for the rest of us at the time, meant much in that here was someone actually leaving after serving a full three-year stint: it was good to see that people *could* leave. But, as is the way in jail, Jock soon joined the amorphous haze of Outside, fondly but infrequently remembered. Moreover, our thoughts in the next few months were more keenly drawn to a series of apparently unexplained and unconnected events.

First, we got hot water. It was early in June of my first year inside with the winter already beginning to give the walls a wet-feeling coldness. We had not, since being in prison, ever had access to hot water of any description. Now, suddenly one Saturday, we were called to the gates through which our food canisters usually arrived and there were half-a-dozen large drums of steaming water. Du Preez, smiling with largesse, pointed to the yard. We trundled the drums out and began, under Potemkin's cold showers, a dancing schoolboy splash of washing, prancing around naked in the yard's open-air chill and enjoying the sudden surprising feel of something warm.

For four weeks we had this Saturdays-only touch of warmth out in the yard. Our prancing diminished as the initial excitement wore off and the winter set in, leaving the yard a sunless expanse of cold walls and cold slate. During the fifth week we were told that we could, in future, use the inside bathroom for our Saturday washes: this bathroom, complete with cold showers, had always been at the end of our corridor but we had never been allowed by du Preez to use it for any purpose other than washing the food dixies (and, probably because of our conditioning under 90-days, we had never thought to claim it as a washing-place). The permission, we discovered, resulted from a complaint from Spike de Kellar's mother. What surprised us was the fact that, for the first time, there appeared to be some sort of official response to complaints made from outside: in the past, few complaints had received even the courtesy of an acknowledgement.

The next development affected not us but the African prisoners whom we spied through our windows – particularly through a small window under the stairway, next to the cleaners' table on which we dished out our food. The small window looked directly on to the Reception Yard where, day after day, we watched the two-by-two streams of Africans being led in, stripped, showered, handed their standard prison kit of shirt/shorts/jerkin, and led off again to the cells. This was the yard which I had watched for so many hours during 90-days and which, now completed, was no less cold during winter than it had been during the building operations the previous year. Nor were the prisoners any better dressed in their flimsy khaki and bare feet. Until suddenly one day – it was early in July – we noticed that there appeared to be something wrong. The two-by-two queue was there as usual, but it was acting very strangely, with several people shuffling, stumbling, awkwardly making their way in. Then we saw what it was: they were all wearing, or trying to wear, prison shoes. Most of the shoes had no laces; most of them were clearly not the correct size, but they were shoes. Shoes without socks, yes – but shoes.

We were busily constructing numerous hypotheses to explain the new sight in the yard when there was another development affecting us, which looked as though it could be related to the shoes. The cleaners were told to collect all the food and water dixies – and were shown a new stainless steel replacement. We objected: we were used to our old bowls which, though the enamel was often chipped, were deeper than the new offerings and, we said, easier to clean. And how, we asked, could we keep water in the new bowls? That point was taken: and we were told we could retain the enamel bowls for drinking-water, but the new steel dixies had to be used for food. The old bowls, said du Preez, were unhygienic. The same old bowls from which we had been eating, three times a day, for the past year at least – he said suddenly they were unhygienic. Something, clearly, was happening, somewhere.

Finally we discovered what it was. Denis Goldberg was called to the O.C.'s office and found there his father, introduced to him by a senior officer from Prison Headquarters. There had, said old Sam Goldberg, been some articles in the papers which made him fearful about his son's treatment; he had gone to Headquarters to ask about it and was now here to see how his son really was. Was he OK? Did he have any complaints? Yes, said Denis, he was OK – and complaints, yes, he had many complaints. He outlined a large number of them to his father and the attendant officer – then came back to us in the section where, by afternoon exercise, we were all busily suggesting theories to explain the startling news.

Only at the weekend did we learn the full details: one of us had a six-monthly visit at which, for once, there was no immediate intervention. The visitor was able to explain that there had been a series of three long articles in the *Rand Daily Mail* by Harold Strachan about conditions in prison. The articles, it appeared, made some 'shocking' disclosures and were causing considerable stink outside.

Inside, after the loss of our unhygienic, much-cherished food bowls, we watched with a mixture of eagerness and amusement to see what further changes would take place. We watched the warders too for signs of changes in attitude towards us: we had had enough experience by then of the ways of prison to know that there could well be some sort of backlash, but we were optimistic that we might see more changes. There was room for improvement. Our 'work' for instance.

By the end of December 1964, there were sixteen of us at Local, of whom a dozen had been sentenced since September that year, creating something of a political prisoner population explosion in white jails. The Prisons Department had clearly not done much pre-planning. Through December, through January, through February, we were locked in our cells for twenty-three hours a day, out only for the exercise periods. No work at all – except for three lucky ones who were cleaners of the section. It was very like detention – with the advantage that we could talk at exercises; with the disadvantage that we were now prisoners, allowed nothing from outside by way of food-parcels or private clothes. This was a time for embellishing all the time-chasing tricks learnt under detention, for devouring library books, and for devising new time-killers. (Raymond Eisenstein and myself, in adjacent cells, made ourselves tiny chessboards which could be hidden in our shaving-brushes. We played every evening, solidly from 5 p.m. to 8 p.m., gently tapping the moves on our walls. We had to stop eventually when the awaiting-trial [criminal] prisoners in a nearby cell reported us for continued tapping – for which we were punished with no meals for a day.)

At last – at the beginning of February 1965 after three idle months – our work arrived, the work we were going to be occupied with for the greater part of the next four years: mailbags. That is, repairing mailbags.

Four things can happen to mailbags: they can get torn; they

can burst their seams; the rope band at the top of the bag can become loose; or the rings at the top of the bag can work loose, even get lost. To repair a mailbag, you might have to do four different things: mend the tear-holes; mend the seams; mend the rope at the top; mend or fix on new rings. You must know two basic stitches: the mailbag stitch, for sewing the holes or tears together, which looks, when complete, rather like a scorpion with a stunted tail; and the seam stitch, which is a simple, self-locking stitch. You require a large darning-needle – large enough to take the tarred string used to mend the bags. (The string is fairly strong, sticky with pitch, and leaves a mess on your hands which is difficult to get off, especially in cold water.) You also need a 'palm' – a metal disc which you strap on to your hand and use like a thimble to push the needle through awkward or stiff places.

Mailbags, when sent to prisons for repair, are never new. The mailbags sent to our section were, for the most part, worse than old. They were often rotten. They were usually irreparable. When they first arrived, we welcomed them – with some reservations, but with a sense of relief to think that it was something to do, something almost active which might lead to something else. For the first six weeks, their arrival didn't much change the pattern of our lives: we had to do the bags, each locked alone in his cell with a quota of about half-a-dozen to complete every day. The cleaners would drag them in each morning, then deliver the needles and palms, string and spare rings – then the doors slammed locked again and there you were with the pile of musty bags and four-and-a-half hours of the morning (7 a.m. to 11.30 a.m.) and two hours of the afternoon (2 p.m. to 4 p.m.) ahead. The quota was introduced within days – along with rules: you had to sit facing the door, in front of your table, so as to be in clear view of the judas-hole; and no reading allowed during mailbag hours; and no sleeping – if you finish your quota, bang on the door and ask for more.

Six weeks of the cell-alone business – then we were taken out, each morning, fully-dressed in 'Sunday' dress (corduroy jacket and khaki longs) and marched clutching our stools, into our yard, out of the door in the wall, along the passage outside (which harboured two other doors, usually locked: 'Stoor/Store' and 'Morgue') and into the identical yard opposite. There, spread out around the walls of the yard, we sat and sewed mailbags – in silence. It was an improvement on the cell-alone arrangement: we could, at least, see each other and be together, but no talking, said du Preez, and the warders who guarded us were meticulous in carrying out his decree (understandably, because he was known to peep through unexpected doors or windows to keep a check on things). We had a warder with us, firmly locked in the yard, and another on the catwalk platform which was built on top of the end wall of the yard: *he* carried a loaded rifle.

Throughout that first year we sewed, in silence, perched on our stools around the walls of the yard. When there was sun, it was almost pleasant, shedding our jackets, then jerseys, then shirts, sitting sewing in the sun. When it got cold (and that year seemed to stay cold for much longer than usual) it was sheer hell. We were taken out to the yard at 7 in the morning when it was still freezing, were given a short walk around the yard and then made to sit through till 11.30, in the open cold, the only real movement being the needle in the one hand. You could get up from your perch and jump around in a stupid circle, clutching the bag over one hand with the needle in the other, but that was never enough to warm you – and the warder would disapprove before long. We used to return to the cells for lunch and I remember having difficulty raising my arms for the skud-search (two skuds every day, each time we came in from the yard), difficulty in getting any feeling back into arms and legs and feet. Sewing mailbags at the best of times is work fit for nobody – sewing in the cold doesn't bear thinking about.

I don't think that it would have helped much, then, had we complained. We did, on a number of occasions, complain about a lot of things to a number of people. But the only people we saw really in those early months were du Preez and Gericke (the O.C.) and possibly an occasional somebody higher up – and there was little point complaining, for example, to Colonel (as he then was) Aucamp, who was the man most directly responsible for the way we were being treated. *He* knew what our conditions were and he was the only man who could tell du Preez to change his treatment of us – and Aucamp, on the few occasions we saw him, was more overtly nasty and hostile than anybody we had to deal with in the daily run of prison life.

One of my cell-mates (whom I had known outside and who was doing five years), John Laredo, complained once to Gericke about the fact that so many of us had all to use the one tap in the yard for cleaning our toilet pots – could we please have another tap installed? Gericke at once fumed, raged at length to the effect that he had in the past had up to a hundred prisoners sharing that one tap at one time and *they* hadn't complained – and, by this time nicely worked up, he waved his swagger-stick in John's face and demanded why he hadn't shaved that morning. Laredo, in search of a tap, lost three meals.

We could, perhaps, have complained at visits about conditions. But we were still then at the stage when we had only two visits a year; we were warned that the ban on news covered, as it had done under 90-days, any discussion about prison itself; and, even had there been time or opportunity at these visits to say something about conditions, I don't think any of us wanted to let on to families or friends what it was like and so make them worried about conditions, when nothing they could then do could change anything. It was a related sense of pride too, which often – together with the feeling of futility – made us reluctant to raise issues, particularly the sort of petty, niggardly issues which du Preez delighted in and which seemed so silly alone, but as an accumulative whole made life so unpleasant.

There was a further consideration. We had all, without distinction, landed in prison because we felt that those in power were corrupt and evil, and maintained their position through fascist-type control. The treatment we received in their hands was therefore, in a sense, confirmation of our own beliefs. I think we would have been surprised if we had *not* been treated so. Added to this was the fact that we were all, even those who had been in jail for some years, abysmally ignorant of the ways of prison and the ways ordinary criminals were treated. Thus, before we spent our time with ordinary criminals at Central in 1966 (which was an eye-opener in so many ways), we were, as upstanding, respectable gents, too reticent to complain too much.

Bandiet

This reticence was, without doubt, mixed with a degree of fear – fear of a man like du Preez who had, literally, the power of life and death over us, and who was so fully responsible for every tiny aspect of our lives. The tendency not to rock the boat was often strong, if unrevolutionary.

It was this whole system which was rocked, from the outside, by Jock Strachan's articles. Before Strachan, it was ridiculous to complain to Gericke because du Preez had told you to wipe your arse with your thumb. Gericke would have laughed. After Strachan, du Preez might still have offered the same charming advice, but he would probably have thought about it first, and would certainly have ensured that he said it without witnesses present.

The Strachan articles – as we later confirmed when we went to Central – revolutionized the entire South African prison service, breaking open for the first time what had in fact become a secret society, subject to no sanctions beyond itself. The Prisons Act of 1950 had effectively banned the publication of anything to do with prisons, and nobody had dared to challenge this until the *Rand Daily Mail* with the Strachan articles. After the articles, the Prisons Department, with the backing of the entire civil service, made a fairly successful come-back, but the conditions within the prisons have never been the same. Everything related to prison reform in South Africa is post-Strachan.

We learnt the full extent of this revolution only later, when we were moved in with the criminals at Central the following year. The effects for us at Local were slow to filter through, and piecemeal. Some changes – like the replacement of the enamel bowls – were introduced without our pressing for them (though we discovered later that many derived directly from comments in Jock's articles – for instance, he had mentioned the bowls specifically). The obvious sequel to the bowl replacement came about ten days later when each cell was issued with a large metal canister – for drinking water. It seemed obscenely luxurious suddenly to have such a large, and covered, supply of water after so many months of a small uncovered bowl of water perched precariously on top of the toilet pot.

I was subject to another example of embarrassingly profligate luxury when, shortly after we heard of the Strachan articles, I got 'flu and was ordered to bed – bed at that stage consisting of my two felt mats on the floor of the cell. Just before supper of this first day-off in prison, I got the first shock: a mattress was brought in for me. A mattress! It was lovely on the floor, on a thick coir mattress. The second shock arrived the next morning: sheets. Two soft white clean sheets, making the mattress feel even softer and more comforting. If, the next day, they had added a pillow, I might have felt almost at home. Instead, I was better – and mattress and sheets disappeared abruptly.

Other changes fitted the more usual Local pattern: we had to fight du Preez for them. Like the Battle of the Window-panes. The pane-less casements in the cells were remarkably efficient wind-tunnels – however much you blocked the gap under the door, wind shot through the always-open window, quickly dispersing what little warmth had been left by the sun. We asked if the broken panes could be replaced. Du Preez, correctly, pointed out that the casements had been made in such a way that, once broken, the panes could never be replaced and that some of the gaps were never intended to have panes anyway – and no, we couldn't block the gaps. Denis Goldberg devised, from a piece of cardboard, a small pane that could be fitted into each gap and taken out, if/when required. Could we make enough of those and put them up, please? No, said du Preez. There followed the usual tense trek to the O.C., then an elaborate and prolonged inspection in loco, then muttered consultations between the major and du Preez (him looking belligerent, then angry, then pacified, then acquiescent, then obsequious) and yes, said du Preez, we can make cardboard panes and put them up, but he doesn't want any trouble, and don't dare hide anything behind them, and pull them down whenever he wants them down . . .

The next surprise – and possibly the most significant immediate result of the Strachan articles – was the visit to Local of Helen Suzman. An M.P., a vigorous parliamentary opponent of the Government – she came into our yard, brought there by Major-boss Gericke and an entourage of polite prison officials. A woman – in our yard. Incredible. Not at all unpleasant. The officials hung back as she came forward to greet us, and we –

ungainly hulks in coarse drab khaki – clucked around her, bubbling with surprise and curiosity. It was a very brief encounter, never again repeated in that way, yet the visit brought a breath of freshness to our lives which was, for us, a fitting celebration of Jock's articles.

In practical terms, Mrs Suzman's visit (and her subsequent ones, regularly every year) produced much. Within the same month (September 1965) we got permission to buy, and use, chess and draught sets (but no playing-cards); we were, for the first time, allowed to receive, and keep, one photograph from outside; and we were issued with 'P.T. shorts', blue sport-shorts which provided a welcome break from the ubiquitous khaki longs. The shorts were particularly useful the following month when, after a request for a tenniquoit or table tennis set, we were given a tennis ball and immediately initiated 'boop squash'.

Boop squash became our major weekend activity in the yard: basically it involved slamming the tennis ball up against the wall of the yard with your hand. We rapidly devised a set of rules, similar to squash, drew a service line on the wall and marked out a rudimentary court on the slate. Thereafter, furious battle was mixed, every Saturday and Sunday (except some Sundays when a zealously puritanical inspecting officer forbade such irreverent pastimes), providing the two contestants with remarkably strenuous exercise and the spectators with some entertainment and some irritation (the court encroached on the usual walking-track and the ball had frequently to be retrieved from the opposite end of the yard).

It is ridiculous, now, to think of us at Local at that time, initiating our new ball game, blissfully unaware of the storm raging about us. It was towards the end of 1965, in October, and we inside were concerned almost exclusively with the fact that the exams were upon us. That was for us the culmination of our first year's heavy study programme: we had been allowed at the beginning of the year to register with the University of South Africa, a Pretoria-based correspondence university. The study-courses had become the pivotal point of our existences: they provided both challenge and solace. But nothing can remove the forbidding nature of exams and it was the imminence of these which dominated inside life that October.

We were not entirely unaware of the real drama surrounding us: there had been a number of strange visitors to our section – we had all, one morning, been inexplicably locked up – and there were several occasions on which warders, muttering quietly to each other, shut up the instant any of us approached them. Clearly, something was again happening which affected us and which we were not supposed to know about. We eventually learnt about it all when lawyers arrived to interview Goldberg, Evans and Brooks – as witnesses for Jock Strachan in the case brought against him, arising from his articles. We learnt a fair amount about the case when the three returned from Durban, having given evidence – and we learnt even more about it when Costa Gazides returned from a brief sojourn in Johannesburg, where he was sent for further charges. He picked up an extra nine-month sentence but – which made the months well worth while, for us – had been treated at the Fort in Johannesburg, as any other criminal prisoner was treated – which meant he could bribe his way to access to newspapers.

From Costa and the three who went to Durban, we were able to piece together something of the way in which Prisons Department officials were helping to make the perjury charge against Jock stick – by telling a remarkable set of lies. In addition, they had (unhappily for them) procured the services of one of us, Raymond Thoms.

The Thoms affair was a sorry demonstration of what can happen to someone who does not achieve the necessary balance in prison between anger and acceptance, and of what can result from a system in which treachery is both expected and encouraged. Thoms was sentenced, in October 1964, to twelve years for sabotage (he and two others were trapped by an agent provocateur).

From the beginning of his sentence he showed signs of instability: an uncontrollable temper, in the face of both warders and fellow prisoners, and a marked reluctance to follow any group decisions. His behaviour resulted in some angry encounters, particularly with du Preez, which often heightened the tension among the rest of us, setting our antipathy towards du Preez against an inexcusable arrogance on Thoms's part. We were in no position there to draw any intellectual titillation from this classic conflict of individual and group – what concerned us was that Thoms frequently and without due cause made things a lot more difficult for us.

The crunch came when, in response to some threat from Breedt (one of the officers), Thoms made a counter-threat which disclosed one of our potential sources of information; he was challenged for this slip by Marius Schoon and replied by letting fly with his fists, first at Marius, then at Denis Goldberg and finally at Spike de Kellar, during which process he was un-peacefully pacified. As a result of this performance, Thoms was sent to Coventry by the rest of us. Thereafter, there were a number of equally unpleasant incidents involving him (he once ambushed Dave Evans in the passage and clobbered him nastily over the nose) and we were not really surprised when, at the end of the year, we learnt that he was going to give evidence against Jock. We were, however, surprised to learn that Thoms had been passing on information about us all to the authorities long before the Coventry business. His promised reward, we heard, was a speedy release.

The end of the affair was as sordid as could be expected. His evidence in the Strachan case was luridly fraudulent (the State tried to suggest through him that there had been an elaborate conspiracy inside to fabricate the stories Strachan told) and he was quickly demolished as a witness. This need not necessarily have discredited him completely with his captors, but he then slipped a note to Brooks, Goldberg and Evans (together in one cell after giving evidence for Strachan) in which he repudiated his evidence and outlined the lies he had been told to tell. This might have been useful, but the following day he told the authorities about his having slipped the note. The sad ineptitude of all this indicated something of the man's state of mind and the results of his actions left us with little time, let alone inclination, to reconsider our decision to have nothing to do with him: for the next two days we were subject to the most extensive skud ever seen at Local. We and all our belongings and cells were, literally, turned inside out.

They never found the note, and Thoms never got his release. The authorities, in fact, took a marked pleasure in keeping Thoms with us, thus further aggravating an already difficult situation. He continued to turn against us for some while – in June 1968 he planned an ambush for me and tried to assault me one morning in the bathroom – but then turned against himself: first a rope, from the top of a mailbag, was removed from his cell; then he made two 'bombs' of match-stick heads which he exploded in his eyes in an unsuccessful effort to blind himself.

The handling of this last sad incident by the authorities indicated their malicious indifference: they treated him in his cell for three weeks before removing him to hospital and during those weeks forced the rest of us (who, they knew, would have preferred to have had nothing to do with him) to look after him: clean his cell, bring his food and empty his toilet pot. I went to the commanding officer – Lieutenant Nel at that stage – and asked whether Thoms could not be moved from us: the situation for the rest of us was understandably difficult and for him, obviously, intolerable. Nel promised that something would be done about it when we moved, at the end of 1968, to a new section of the prison. When we moved, Thoms – back from hospital – moved with us, and the friction remained, and remains still. Without remission – and without due payment for services rendered to the State – he will be released in October 1976.

Du Preez did not forget the exposés and made up for it once Jock Strachan had, predictably, been found guilty on a number of technicalities arising from his articles. Jock got another two-year sentence for 'perjury', reduced to eighteen months on appeal. We got the backlash. Du Preez stormed into the yard one morning early in 1966 while we were sewing bags: he had already thought himself into a puffed-up rage and spluttered at us through purple cheeks. There was, he yelled, too much talking while we worked – in future, God help anybody caught talking, and we all had to sit on special spots, five yards apart. He produced a pot of paint with which Denis Goldberg had to mark, five paces apart, large spots on the slate. Some days later, du

Preez stormed out again, saw us sitting on our spots (each, as Laredo remarked, on our own group area) with our shirts off, sewing in the sun. He spluttered into purple again, turned furiously to his lackey-warder and demanded to know why weren't we wearing shirts and longs. The lackey, as ignorant of this decree as we were (understandably, because it had only just germinated in du Preez's head), looked dumb. We must, ordered du Preez, always wear shirts and long trousers when sewing, and God help anybody who didn't. He also found another use for his little pot of paint. He carefully painted over the window next to where we dished out food – the window through which we had seen into the Reception Yard and so witnessed the beginning of the Strachan revolution, the shoes-for-all episode. His blacked-out window was, we felt, a tacit admission of guilt.

There were indications of a backlash from other quarters too. Laredo, Eisenstein and myself had begun a special evening sing-song for Issy Heymann who, we understood, was being detained in a section somewhere above us. He got a year for refusing to give evidence against Bram Fischer – and then five years for membership of the banned Communist Party. Every evening we would whistle a stirring song and sing the International. To improve the effect, Laredo and I would clamber on to our tables and whistle and sing through the mesh grids by the door. One evening we were disturbed by a gruff curse below us: the night warder, watching us. Our protestations of innocence the following morning, when the Chief (Schnepel it was) challenged us with our crime, were futile. But anyway, we argued, everybody sings in the jail at night – why shouldn't we? Oh yes, says he, you can sing – but why were you on your tables? 'Wat was die doel/What was the purpose?' We shut up and, the next day, did our punishment of three meals: locked in an empty cell with no food for the day, learning to play klaberjas and reading the Maccabees in the only book allowed in punishment cells, the Bible.

It was particularly interesting at this time to watch the attitude of the warders towards us. Some clearly disliked du Preez's methods and either asked not to be in his section or, when there, acted with a decent correctness, never trying to harass us.

One mild-natured head-warder, for instance, clearly tried to be pleasant and polite to us. He came into our section only infrequently and, as a clerk in the front offices, was permanently removed from the influence of day-to-day key-warders like du Preez. This man Dunn handled our monthly toilet orders and we always watched with silent delight the prickly hostility between him and du Preez when he arrived each month with the large box containing our goodies from the prison canteen. Dunn – we nicknamed him, with some affection, 'Sad Sack' – would stand with the box at the entrance to the yard where we sewed our mailbags and call us out in turn: 'Mr Goldberg,' he would call, with unheard-of courtesy.

Du Preez would scowl and shout: 'Goldberg!'

'Here,' Dunn would say, 'is your order. Please check it and sign. Thank you, Mr Goldberg.'

'Hurry up, Goldberg,' from du Preez, becoming increasingly enraged as Dunn, unruffled, paid the same polite attention to each of us.

Besides his politeness, he had another distinguishing feature: he was one of the few English-speaking warders in the service. We were warned against seeing any correlation between his English and his manners by the presence of another English-speaker who treated us with unremitting nastiness, but Dunn was certainly a man apart in the South African prison department. He always tried, with us, to communicate a sense of understanding – and this was specifically because we *were* political prisoners, not ordinary criminals. Without actually saying as much, he indicated that he enjoyed talking to us and could respect our beliefs, even if he could not agree with them. He showed too that he disapproved strongly of the way we were treated, particularly by du Preez.

This, of course, made him very much an exception among the warders, and we were considerably shocked to hear (from a young warder who told me the news – then, after a reprimand, asked me to forget that he had said anything) that Dunn had one night shot himself. It was unlikely that his suicide had anything to do with us, but no other warders would ever discuss the matter – and no other warder ever again showed the same degree of sympathy towards us.

The pressures on the warders must have been great. It was obviously easier and more convenient for them to play du Preez's game. Not all of them liked to do so, but there were some who played it with relish. Like 'Keyhole Kate', who arrived when I had accumulated about two years' experience of prison life and had met quite a variety of warders. But never one like him. He arrived early in 1966, some time after the Strachan verdict, and quickly established his nickname (his actual name was Van Aswegan) by sneaking down the passage and peering in through the judases. He did this right in front of three of us, cleaners in the passage, without any sign of embarrassment. Without, it seemed, even seeing us there beside him, he stalked along and peered into each cell, often watching for minutes at a time. Perhaps he noticed how outraged I was at his crassness; perhaps he was bored and wanted somebody to torment and I was readily on hand. Whatever the reason, this Keyhole Kate latched on to me. He showed me no particular malice, he expended no particular energy, but he played with me and drove me nearer to violence than anybody else I met in prison. He would stop me suddenly in the passage, right there while I was busy sweeping or dusting, often wearing only a shirt and shorts, barefoot, and search me: make me raise my arms, open my hands, while he patted me and felt down my clothes with pudgy little fingers. Then he would smirk, shrug and send me back to work with a flick of his head as he went on down the corridor, peeping into more judases.

I was trying to devise ways of avoiding his passage performance (which he repeated three or four times) when he motioned me one morning into my cell. There he had my cupboard open and had pulled out a number of books, scattering them around on the floor. He had opened my packet of razor blades, removed the wrappings and scattered each of them on to the floor; and he had open in front of him my file of personal letters which, lazily, he was paging through as I stood waiting. He was, strictly speaking, entitled by the regulations to do everything he had done. For each little thing, I could gladly have kicked his teeth in. Then he said 'Staan reg/Stand up' and he searched me, standing amidst the debris of my cupboard, slowly going through my shirt and my shorts – I had nothing else on. In the pocket of my shirt I had my prison card, which he flicked away on to the floor, and a small roll of toilet paper – this he took, looked at it slowly and silently, then held it at one end and let it fall open, unrolling on to the floor. He watched it fall, smirked at me again, and left me in the cell to clear up the mess.

There were, fortunately, several other things happening at that time to keep me partially distracted from the attentions of Keyhole Kate. Our hypothesizing capacities, never slow to be activated, had been especially awakened by the visit of a senior prisons official in mid-January 1966. The visit stretched over two days and demonstrated security precautions gone mad: we were first all locked up in cells together, then taken out one by one to be interviewed by the man, Colonel Steyn, then taken back to the section to be locked up in separate cells, to prevent us discussing anything with those who had not yet been interviewed. The reason for this elaborate game of musical chairs was that Steyn asked each of us whether we would accept being moved to other prisons. The advantage, he stressed, would be that they could offer more constructive work – and he promised the company of 'prisoners of integrity'. He also wanted each of us to sign a declaration agreeing to the move; an attempted insurance by the Prisons Department against future complaints, which failed at inception because some of us signed, others refused to do so.

Steyn's visit naturally provoked endless speculation. The theories and counter-theories kept the yard buzzing right through February, but had almost died out by March – when another development generated yet another prognostic splurge: workmen arrived to tile the bathroom at the end of our corridor. One camp reckoned that this indicated we would be kept at Local; the other camp, with creditable bandiet logic, reckoned that the tiling would be completed just in time for us to be moved away from it.

In the event, both camps could be said to have been correct. It was not, I suppose, surprising that we should have begun to be able to read the prison auguries correctly: most of us, by then, had been bandiete for nearly eighteen months. Nevertheless, we were about to discover that in jail terms we were still absolute innocents.

4 Into the Jungle

As political prisoners inside Pretoria Local Prison, we knew very little of what was happening outside prison. We also knew remarkably little about what was happening inside the prison, even when it concerned us. When somebody was called out of the section, we never knew whether he would be back in two minutes or whether he would disappear from our lives for ever.

One afternoon in March 1966, three of the prisoners in our section were unexpectedly called and told to put on their jackets. They disappeared through the grille at the end of the section and were still not back by supper-time. We asked the duty-warder about them; he shrugged, said good night and slammed the door locked. I was in the three-man cell at the time and we spent the evening discussing the disappearance: why had they gone, and why those three? Denis Goldberg and Dave Kitson were an obvious pair: they had been involved in the same organization and were both long-termers, Denis doing life and Dave twenty years, and they had both been engineers outside. Marius Schoon, the third man gone, didn't fit any perceptible pattern: he was, in our terms, a medium-term prisoner, having twelve years, also for sabotage, but he had not been attached to any organization, had never shared cells with Denis or Dave, and had very few interests or acquaintances which could link him with the other two. There seemed no explanation for the three being taken off together like that. If their disappearance meant the beginning of a dispersal of us politicals to other jails (as suggested by the visit of the colonel the previous December), then it seemed that their choice of prisoners was going to be distinctly arbitrary. We went to sleep wondering whether it would be our turn in the morning – and who would be our partners if we were moved.

The next day was 14 March 1966. I remembered because that was the day I ate an entire sheet of writing-paper. Two days before I had been standing at the grille which separated our section from that leading to the kitchen: our lunch arrived, in two large canisters and an open tray. The tray was covered with a sheet of newspaper and, while the warder was busy opening and locking the grille, I was able to steal the sheet of newsprint and stuff it into my shirt. I managed to keep it safely hidden for the rest of the day: not a bad haul really, being the central news page from a local paper, and only about two months old. Right down to the ads, it brought in a bit of the outside which we tried to preserve by writing it out that night on a large piece of writing-paper (tougher and more easily hidden than the actual newsprint).

On the morning of 14 March – the day after Denis, Dave and Marius had disappeared – the makeshift newspaper had just been returned to me when there was a series of shouts from the warders and we were all lined up in the corridor, then marched into an empty cell to be searched.

There's nobody so guilty as somebody who knows he's not innocent. I was convinced that the sudden search had to do solely with the large, bulkily-folded piece of paper, filled with snippets of illegal information, which nestled uneasily in my trouser pocket. I stood, as if nonchalantly waiting, with my hands in my pockets but frantically working the paper into a tight ball which I managed to slip unseen into my mouth. It tasted foul and became more and more unpalatable with each chew. I smiled soggily at the warder searching me and was so intent on willing him not to speak to me that I hardly noticed that he had finished pawing me all over and was directing me down the corridor and out – out with the others to the truck drawn up in the inner courtyard of the prison, ready with an armed escort to take us away.

I was still chewing when we left Local, more than a dozen of us crammed chattering in the back of the truck with silent warders. The sides of the truck were closed but there were two small airvents through which it was possible, fleetingly, to catch a glimpse of green, of flashing colours, a tree, and a child walking, and of the road stretching far away, uncluttered, into the distance. We drove hardly a quarter of a mile, round the corner and up the hill, and stopped at Central Prison, the hanging jail.

Three of South Africa's jails are particularly famous. First, there's the Fort in Johannesburg which squats like a flattened frog among the skyscrapers of Hillbrow and which was preserved in 1964 from much-needed improvement by being declared a national monument. The Fort is largely a remand jail, housing (in strictly segregated sections) both black and white awaiting-trial prisoners. The second famous jail is South Africa's own Devil's Island: Robben Island, off Cape Town, a former leper colony where the Xhosa chief Makana drowned when attempting to escape from his British captors in 1894 and where now Nelson Mandela and all black political prisoners are kept.

And then there is Central Prison, Pretoria, the maximum security jail for white criminals, which also houses one of the few places in South Africa where black and white live legally along-side each other: Section B2, the death cells. Central Prison, Pretoria, is the only prison in South Africa with gallows. Up-wards of seventy people, mainly black, are hanged there every year.

Cold Stone Jug is what Herman Bosman called it. Forty years before we arrived there, Bosman had been sent to Central for murdering his step-brother: condemned to be hanged, he was later reprieved and spent eight years in Cold Stone Jug. He wrote an absorbingly funny book of his experiences at Central – *Cold Stone Jug*, which I read for the first time inside Cold Stone Jug. In forty years, very little had changed.

The entrance to Central looks like a medieval castle: you enter the prison through two huge wooden doors set into a crenellated façade of stone and pass immediately through a portcullis of heavy bars into a small forecourt. This forecourt forms a no-man's land between Outside and Inside: if you're a visitor to the prison from Outside, you never get beyond the forecourt but are led off into one of the visiting rooms in the office-block on the left as you come in, and, once you're inside Central as a prisoner, you never get back out beyond the fore-court. You go from the forecourt through a heavy steel barred door: from open-air lightness you are led into a dark narrow passage and, like a lion at the circus, through another steel grille-door out into a huge inner hall, a hollow and echoing cathedral dome of heavy grilles and bars and cold stone walls.

This is the Saal/Hall, the nerve-centre of the prison, a vast spider's head with gloomy passages leading off it into the distance, dominated by a large notice opposite the entrance saying Stilte/Silence, and smelling of floor polish.

The fifteen of us from Local were dumped in the Hall, three rows of puzzled, somewhat intimidated politicals, pushed into line against the wall and told to shut up. Stilte/Silence. But there was no silence in the Hall's hugeness: from directly behind the notice opposite us – Stilte/Silence – came a chant, a rising and falling chant of hymns, slow, mournful, filling the Hall's emptiness, eerily drumming through the bars, amplified by the bare walls. The chant of the Condemneds. You can never, at Central, forget the Condemneds, up in their cells behind the notice in the Hall saying Silence.

Nobody else in the Hall seemed to notice the singing. The Condemneds' chanting formed a background to several other sounds which rang across the polished black floor of the Hall. There was a young warder with a set of keys, busily rushing from one side of the Hall to the other, opening a grille-gate to let in, sometimes an officer, sometimes bandiete, slamming the grille closed and accompanying them across the Hall to open another grille and slam it closed behind them. There was a cleaner, on his knees, endlessly making his way backwards across the floor, polishing, polishing, never looking up, never stopping, always polishing. And another cleaner, ferreting around with a duster, ever-attendant on the young warder, bowing and jumping to his commands, running errands back and forth across the Hall, from one grille to another.

None of them seemed to hear the singing and the chanting. They seemed oblivious, busily threading an invisible web of indifference within the head of the spider. We watched in silence, fascinated. There was so much activity, so many people passing in and out, so many different faces. For the past sixteen months, we hadn't moved from the closeness of our cell-corridor-yard existence at Local, where we saw only ourselves and the same familiar few warders, where we never saw further than the wall at the end of the corridor, or the wall at the end of the yard, or the wall of the cell. Now suddenly we had gone beyond the walls and stood in this Hall where there was so much activity and so many people – and the warders, seemingly so busy as they passed through the Hall, seemingly intent on something purposeful, so different from the warders we knew; they seemed somehow less threatening, seemed to lack the bored malevolence of du Preez and Local. Central Prison, with its persistent chant of death, seemed to us to be so much more alive than Local.

The Hall warder and the cleaners ignored us, at first. Then another warder from the Reception Office brought through some suitcases belonging to the short-term prisoners amongst us. (Those of us with sentences of more than five years had no such 'property bags' – our belongings were sent home at the beginning of our sentences.) The suitcases had been brought across with us from Local Prison and their owners were told to mind them until we were officially signed into Central Prison. The cases provided some unexpected bounty several boxes of cigarettes, some packets of tobacco and, it seemed, some sweets. We were all ridiculously excited at this sudden reversal of the lean smokeless months at Local. Costa Gazides (doing a year for membership of the Communist Party, and a delightfully resourceful bandiet) signalled to the Hall cleaner as he passed on one of his errands and got from him, behind the back of the Hall warder, a match and 'slatch'. The Hall warder ignored our whispered antics and seemed not to be bothered as we sneaked a lighted cigarette from hand to hand. Certainly he could not have failed to see our inept attempts at concealment. We had still much to learn.

The cleaner – who, said Costa, claiming to have met him while awaiting-trial at the Fort, was called Pieletjies – became markedly attentive as more and more packets of cigarettes and tobacco appeared from the suitcases. He moved with his duster to a brass hydrant near us and, busily polishing, indicated that he would store all our tobacco for us and save it from definite confiscation. Gratefully we passed the packets down the row towards Pieletjies and watched as he slipped them under his duster and then out through a doorway to our left which, it appeared, led into some sort of store where someone else sympathetic was working. Thank you, Pieletjies, we nodded, and he smiled back OK, a pleasure.

Meanwhile, Norman Levy (he was doing three years for membership of the Communist Party) had investigated his suitcase and found, with a whispered chuckle, 'peppermints'. We had seen no sweets for months – Norman eagerly popped a little white sweet into his mouth and, as quickly, out again. His sweet was a mothball.

We should have taken the mothball as a sour omen of what to expect at Central – of what, for example, to expect of the tobacco and cigarettes hidden for us by Pieletjies. Pieletjies told Costa in a hurried exchange the following day that there had been 'trouble' with our goodies; and the day after he reported, with deep sadness, that he had been 'ramped' by the boere (i.e. heavily searched) and that everything had been confiscated. He was, said Pieletjies, very very sorry.

We were also sorry to have lost so much, so easily, to so obvious an operator as Pieletjies. But it was a useful lesson: at the price of about a month's worth of smoking material, we had been quickly introduced to one of the essentials of Central society. It is dangerous at Central to trust anybody, particularly those who seem to be sympathetic and helpful.

But on that first afternoon, we were still new boys. We stood for about an hour in the Hall and were then led off into 'C' section, the two-pronged arm leading off the Hall to the right: three storeys, with a double row of cells in each prong, about 250 cells altogether, smaller cells and narrower corridors than at Local. This was the underprivileged section, for all C and D groupers, who were not allowed to smoke. (The more privileged B and A groupers lived in the 'A' section, stretching off on the other side of the Hall. In the 'B' section were the punishment cells, and the Condemneds.) We were all, at that stage, either C or D groups and were assigned to cells scattered out in the six corridors of the three floors. We were shown where our cells would be and were then immediately taken out to the workshops:

scattered again, some to the Sheet Metal 'shop', some to Carpenters, some to Blacksmiths, and four of us to Fitters and Turners. (Only three of us had been posted to Fitters: Raymond Eisenstein was actually posted to Blacksmiths but, not liking that idea, ignored instructions and joined me at Fitters.)

The first surprise at the shop (reached by a seemingly endless march through doors in walls, endless walls) was to find Denis Goldberg whom we had last seen the previous evening disappearing down the corridor at Local with Dave Kitson and Marius Schoon. Denis was equally surprised and delighted to see us: they had been brought from Local and dumped, without explanation, at Central. They had visions of themselves being the only politicals among 600 or so criminals and imagined that the rest of us had been similarly dispersed in other prisons. (We never discovered the reason for sending the three others on ahead of the rest of us to Central – perhaps just another little administrative game, teasing the mice.)

My next surprise was to discover what a Fitting and Turning workshop actually is. Unlike Denis, an engineer, I had never before been inside an industrial workshop and in fact had little idea of what a Fitter and Turner was. I saw rows and rows of lathes and stamping machines down one side of the large hall, and metal tables and a huge bending-brake down the other; everywhere was activity, with ear-tearing screeches and clatter, brightly lit up by flashing welding arcs. And everywhere workers, bandiete in khaki uniforms, busy, shouting, working, and now staring with interest at the four new shuffling figures. It was, so soon after the sedate silence of sewing mailbags, shatteringly alive.

We were presented to the chief-warder who looked at us without comment, then assigned us to different jobs around the shop. Some seventy-five bandiete worked in the Fitters' shop which was concerned, mainly, with the manufacture of metal doors and window frames – all for new prisons. The shop was in the shape of an L: I was posted to the shorter leg where most of the activity seemed to consist of bandiete smashing at bits of metal with hammers. The din inside was matched by more din outside where, with metal grinders and bigger hammers, other

bandiete hammered, working in lean-to sheds. I was sent to one
of these sheds and introduced to two of the biggest men I have
ever met: huge, with muscled arms, playfully wielding huge
hammers – straightening metal window-frames, they said,
pointing to their anvil-table and a pile of frames. The larger of
the two large men, nonchalantly crushing a frame into align-
ment, nodded to me to stand next to him, then shouted into my
ear as his large mate continued with the crushing process. 'My
name,' he said, 'is Rapers (that's what it sounded like) and I'm
your friend.' I nodded, a little surprised. 'And watch out: don't
talk to nobody here, don't trust nobody.' (I nodded.) 'You must
trust me.' (Nod.) 'Don't tell nobody nothing. Only tell me.'
(Nod.) 'You see that boer there' – pointing with hammer at the
chief who introduced me – 'he's all right. He's my friend too.
Actually – now don't tell nobody, hey' (nod-nod) 'we're related,
outside. Outside we're cousins. So he's my friend and you just
tell me everything and I'll look after you, see.' I nodded thanks,
then tried to indicate: can I help here? Big-boy Rapers shook
his head and tapped me lightly on the chest with his hammer:
'Just don't tell nothing to nobody. Only tell me, see.' I nodded,
standing aside to watch the two of them smashing the frames
into submission.

Later in the afternoon my solicitous big friend Rapers and his
big mate left the shed for a while, having explained to me what to
do with the hammer and the frames. I had hardly begun to take
a preliminary bash at my first frame when a young bandiet
rushed up, glanced anxiously over his shoulder and said hurriedly: 'For God's sake, don't say anything to that guy. Don't tell
him a thing. He's one of the biggest narks in the place.' He
rushed off as quickly as he'd come. I had not seen him before: I
did not see him again. I had no opportunity that afternoon to
consider either the advice of the stranger nor the attentions of
Rapers – but when I got back to the section after work, I found,
to my relief, that my new cell was diagonally opposite Marius
Schoon's. Marius, having already been at Central for a day, was
able to guide me through the bewildering rituals of the place and
to slip me a small packet with tobacco and paper for two
cigarettes, plus match and slatch.

Each cell doorway had both barred grille and solid door: they lock the first grille and you must stand behind this while they count, then recount, and only then lock the outside door. During the count there is a chance to talk to the person behind the grille opposite.

I mentioned to Marius my encounters, first with Rapers, then with the unsolicited stranger. Marius too had experienced much the same thing the previous day: someone who had latched on to him at once with the same confide-in-me patter and another who had approached him with a warning against narks, informers. The warning for Marius had differed from mine only in the fact that he had been warned against *everybody* at Central, not just one person; and Marius's friend had given a healthy supply of tobacco and smoking wherewithal together with the warning.

We agreed that these first signs of reaction from the criminal bandiete at Central were encouraging. We had been worried, when we originally heard that we might be moved in with other bandiete, that they would react towards us in a predictably white South African way and, having absorbed the propaganda of the Government, would consider our anti-Government activities as un-South African and treasonable. We expected considerable attention from informers (and I assumed that Rapers, somewhat ponderously, fitted this role for me) but we also expected hostility. It was a relief, after the first day, to have found not hostility but what appeared to be quite genuine friendliness.

I encountered a related reaction the next day at the shops. I was dutifully hammering in Raper's lean-to when I was tapped on the arm by a well-built bandiet who introduced himself as Andy. 'Don't work here,' he said, 'these are narks. Come work with me, inside.' I explained that I had been specially assigned to Rapers by the Chief, so Andy, unabashed, went straight to the Chief and returned to say that I should work for him, not Rapers and Co. I moved off to join Andy, at which stage Rapers returned from the toilet and started complaining vigorously that he couldn't cope without my assistance. Andy intervened abruptly: I was going to work with *him*, he said, and he would gladly break Raper's head open for him if he pressed the matter any further, or did anything to me. Andy's protectiveness was not entirely altruistic. He worked at an electric grindstone inside and had beside him two large drums, both full of small triangular pieces of metal: parts for window catches, which had been stamped out on a press and which now had to have their sharp edges ground off. Several thousand little bits of metal with sharp edges. And Andy had been alone at an electric grindstone with two wheels. Together, in four days, we completely smoothed the edges off all the little triangles in the one drum – and I had also smoothed off a considerable amount of skin from my fingers. I arrived at the shop the second week to find that Andy was being transferred: 'promoted' to the more open prison at Kroonstad. (From Central, the maximum security hanging jail, you could as a non-political criminal only go up.)

Andy left me with the second drum of metal triangles all for myself. But he had, during four days at the grindstone with me, given me a remarkable run-down of life at Central. Andy had already been at Central for more than two years: he was a thief; had served time before and was now pushing a twelve-year sentence for armed robbery. He reckoned that, with remission and amnesty, he would make it out after about five years in all. We laughed together at that: he had a much longer sentence than me but would be free a long time before me; and already he was in B group and would, once he got to Kroonstad, be promoted to A group. (By the time I got to A group, Andy would have been released.)

The bandiete at Central had heard, said Andy, that we politicals had been having a rough time. No remission – yes, that was bad, he agreed. And no news. And bad grouping too: look at us, with all of us still in C group, and some still in D after two years. No criminal, said Andy, ever started his time in D group – that was for punishment. But he'd heard, he said, that -he boere at Local were giving us a rough time (heard, it seemed, from the usual prison grapevine, possibly from talk among warders, passed on to bandiete) and, of course, we were Strachan's people, weren't we? We were the guys with Strachan who had written those newspaper articles and 'they' hated Strachan for exposing them like that. They hated us too, yes. Never tell them the truth, said Andy – tell them the truth, like you guys told them the truth, and they'll hate you.

I thought perhaps that this was an overtly political statement by Andy and that his sympathy was motivated by radical white views of the state of the outside society. But not at all: he was, in outside terms, a good white South African, content in an un-questioning acceptance of apartheid and white dominance. He had never, in fact, thought about 'politics' – it was something apart, beyond his interest, a game played by 'them'. 'They' were Authority, Government, anybody in control, especially the cops. He knew that I was a political prisoner and was therefore, by his definition, one of them that play politics – but this didn't matter: I was now pushing time, like him, and that put me apart from 'them'. And because they were, for no reason, trying to make my time more difficult, he sympathized with me and helped me. But not before he had sorted out for himself his one puzzle: they had said, said Andy, that we politicals were dangerous people. '*You* don't look very dangerous,' he laughed. 'You're quite an ordinary sort of guy.' Yes.

So he helped me. The help he gave was simple for an old hand like him, but it was fundamental in teaching me about Central society. Andy taught me to smuggle, particularly smuggle tobacco. Tobacco. For those of us who smoked, tobacco was one of the first things we thought about when we arrived from the wilderness of Local Prison. Tobacco was the first thing that most people thought about at Central, whether they smoked or not. Tobacco was the basis of the Central economy. Officially, only A and B groupers were allowed to smoke. Unofficially, everybody who wanted to smoke, smoked – at a price. The whole economy of the prison revolved around the process whereby tobacco was smuggled from those who had it to those who hadn't.

There were two sorts of tobacco available: 'private', which was brand tobacco, bought by the privileged A's and B's as part of their monthly toilet order; and 'issue', a fortnightly free issue to A's and B's. 'Private' seldom cost more than 20c (10p) a packet: it was, in outside terms, cheap and of poor quality. Inside, it was high quality and re-sold for R1 (about 50p) a packet. 'Issue' tobacco – usually black, dirty, of very low quality – was issued free but could seldom be obtained on the Central market for less than 40c (20p). The prices fluctuated according to the time away from each monthly order and the availability of dwindling supplies. The number of non-smoking A's and B's seemed always sufficient to keep a fair amount of tobacco available for all, but the market was never flooded enough to let us clandestine smokers feel content. I never had too much tobacco, often had too little, and had always to be prepared for a search and the possibility of losing all my secret stocks.

To smoke involved two prime manoeuvres: buying the tobacco, and then keeping it. Both processes could be hazardous. Prisoners have no cash. What money you may have on arrival – or any sent in to you – is put in an account, through which all financial matters are handled. Before any purchase is made – e.g. by a warder buying the monthly toilet order – the account is checked to ensure there is sufficient credit. To be found with actual money is a serious offence: it is assumed (correctly) that the money is required for bribing warders, or for use outside the prison – i.e. that the bandiet is about to escape.

Having no ready cash inside, you pay for contraband either in substitute currency or in kind. At Central, the monthly toilet order provided the basic currency: you buy as much toothpaste, soap or shaving cream as you are permitted by the regulations and use these items as currency. (This has side-effects: you learn to conserve precious items of toiletry like shaving cream by shaving with soap; or by not washing too often; or by using only the poor quality issue soap and toothpaste. You can learn a lot about a person at Central by knowing what sort of razor blade he uses.)

Having bought some currency, you have to find a trader. This was more difficult than might be imagined. All the unprivileged C's and D's were in 'C' section; all the privileged A's and B's were in the opposite, 'A' section. Nobody was allowed out of a section without a jacket on and all jackets had your tell-tale group badge on the pocket: red C's and D's, green A's and B's – both groups easily identifiable by the section warders watching at the gates. Direct contact was therefore difficult, if not impossible.

There were two possible channels of supply: through a go-between, a 'steamer', or directly through someone you worked closely with in the shops, where all groups mingled freely. The best sort of steamers were the cleaners in the sections: they spent all day in the sections, were usually well in with the section warders and had time and opportunity to look after contraband. When Marius Schoon and I first arrived in C3 (section C, top floor) we were lucky to have a sympathetic cleaner – or so it seemed, initially. The cleaner, 'Wam', offered us a week's supply of 'snout' (tobacco) on tick, at the usual rates, without interest – and also said he could keep it for us during the day. Every evening, as we rushed in from the shops, we'd grab the small packet (snout, matches, slatch, paper) and keep it hidden till after lock-up. That worked fine for a few days, until Wam, crestfallen, told us he had been searched and all our little packets lost. No tobacco left, but could we please pay anyway? We paid, had to borrow for the night from another bandiet, and the next morning find another way of getting and keeping the snout.

This was where Andy, my workmate in the 'shop', advised and helped. The shops offered the best solution, both for available steamers from whom to buy, and places of safe keeping. It was a relatively simple matter to collect the snout there – but then, how to pay for it, and how to get it back to the sections? Both difficulties arose from the fact that you were subject to a very thorough search, once going out to the shops, and once again coming in from the shops. Every morning, after breakfast eaten in the sections, you lined up downstairs and then marched, two-by-two, out through the Hall, through the C-group yard and into the B-group yard: a large gravel yard where, at weekends, the B's and A's played soccer.

On weekdays, the yard was cut off by a line of warders at the one end: you arrived in your two-two line and joined one of the queues in front of a warder. Everything in your pockets had to be held in your hands as you presented yourself – arms out, legs apart, jacket open – as he glanced at your hands (sometimes shaking out the hanky), then felt along your sleeves, down your armpits, torso, hips, down your legs and up again, inside to your crutch, with a final couple of pats up your back. The evening procedure, on the way back from the shops, was similar but even more thorough: you had then to take off both shoes and socks and hold them dangling from your fingers, together with hanky and anything else from pockets. The evening searchers were always more probing, more observant to match jacket badge with illicit tobacco pouch. The exercise, obviously, was to prevent tools and equipment from leaving the workshops, but the effect was to make the passage of all contraband difficult, and that meant trouble for us C and D smokers.

Andy helped arrange a regular supply of tobacco for me which I paid for once a month, in toilet goods, and which I kept safely locked in the tool-cupboard of a friend in the workshop. He was a B-grouper and therefore allowed tobacco. Each evening, I would fill my little plastic tobacco pouch with sufficient snout for the evening and, just before marching off from the shop, tuck the pouch into my underpants. My arrangement worked well, except one Friday evening when my packet had to be larger than usual – to cope with a long weekend ahead – and I had the misfortune to be searched by an earnest young warder with the reputation of all but undressing one at the skud. He was known to take great delight in feeling high into one's crutch.

On this Friday evening, I approached for the daily crucifixion bit, my shoes dangling in my right hand, my socks and hanky in my left, my jacket open, and my eyes frantically searching out how I might avoid the dreaded boer and get in front of the pleasanter boer next to him. As I edged nearer the line of boere, I could see evasion was going to be impossible and I decided to brave it out. I stepped up to him (his name, I think, was Snooi-man) and put feet apart, arms out, looking straight ahead, the packet between my legs feeling obscenely large. Snooiman tipped both shoes up and peered into them; ran his hand down the socks and hanky, milking them empty; then heavy pats along the sleeves, jerking up into the armpits, then carefully rubbing around the back, down to the waist, around to the front, sliding down over the hips. Then he knelt down – with one knee in the dirt so as to be better able to feel all the way down my outer legs, and round the ankles, and up, inside along my calves, then knees, inner thighs (I've had it, I thought, had it) then firmly into my groin, two hands pushing in on both sides, easing upwards (he's missed it) then one hand easing down again, firmly feeling me, cupped. I looked straight ahead, over his head, feeling the queue build up behind me, feeling all the eyes to the left and right and behind me looking inwards at me – there in the middle of the soccer pitch, with Snooiman, now on both knees, feverishly tearing my fly open and wrenching my under-pants down and holding up, triumphant before the world, my little yellow packet of snout. 'Staan daar/Stand there!' he shouted, pocketing my packet as I slunk off to stand by the wall, doing up my flies before the assembled eyes.

My punishment on that occasion was to get three meals – which meant, at Central, a grimmer form of punishment than at Local. Central had a special row of punishment cells in the 'B' section, below the Condemneds. When you were given meals, you had to report to the 'B' section warder at open-up in the morning, before breakfast, and were locked away in one of the cells for the entire day and night, being opened up only briefly in the afternoon for a wash and to empty your toilet pot. The cells were inside-cells, without an outside wall which might catch some sun and warmth: ill-lit and viciously cold. I was there in mid-winter and sat for the entire twenty-four hours, huddled into a ball on the mats in the centre of the floor, wrapped in the four available blankets. I had managed to smuggle a library book with me: Gogol's *Dead Souls*, which I read only partially. Immediately above me, on an inner steel catwalk, one of the white Condemneds paced up and down at exercise, sharing with me the ceaseless chants from further down the section of the black Condemneds. The punishment cells are commonly referred to as the 'Bom' – a contraction of 'Bombay', because the major punishment for criminals, besides 'doing meals' as I did, is to be sentenced to so many days on rice water. When bandiete return from the Bom having done time on rice water, they come out looking very pale, like roots of grass drawn out from under a rock, like people who have been living with the dead.

On the morning after my twenty-four hours under the Condemneds, the chief-warder passed on his inspection and said jovially: 'Ag, man, just don't carry so much tobacco around with you next time, hey!' His remark reflected the generally relaxed attitude of the authorities towards smoking. They knew perfectly well that everybody who wanted to, smoked; they knew too how the market worked and they let it work, intervening only when they wanted to, or when they couldn't avoid doing so (like when Snooiman triumphantly presented me to the chief, complete with inescapable corpus delicti). It was, like much else in prison, an elaborate game they played: a game of cat-and-mouse, with the bandiet-mouse permanently at the receiving end. It was the arbitrariness of the way they played the game which made their actions questionable, particularly when the issue – smoking – was such a petty one. (The pettiness was confirmed three years later when smoking was made permissible for all groups of bandiete.) Where it concerned something as petty as smoking, this arbitrariness was relatively harmless. But it was indicative of a more serious tendency which was dangerous – and which was markedly evident in another aspect of the prison economy, the 'boom' trade.

'Boom' is an Afrikaans term for 'dagga', the South African pot or marijuana. It was impossible to gauge how many boom-rokers/boom-smokers there were at Central, but boom was clearly a most highly sought-after contraband and my impression was that a fairly large percentage of the bandiete were 'rokers' – possibly as many as half the inmates. The boom-trade was one of the most closely watched of all smuggling operations and was therefore also one of the most expensive. The boom-trade, more than most things, mirrored and laid bare the essential corruption of the Central society.

Boom could be obtained only from outside. A single internal source was discovered in our time: a nifty patch of boom – it looks like 'khaki-weed' – found planted on top of the roof of the officers' office in one of the workshops. The only possible way for boom to be smuggled into the prison was by bandiete who worked outside the prison during the day, or by warders them-selves. The outside workers – for instance, members of the building group – were always subject to the most stringent searches, twice a day, and were always subject to close official supervision. But the boom came in, regularly.

One of the men I worked with once, Johnnie, was part of a three-man combine which bought boom at least once a week, always enough for at least one weekend 'trip'. Sometimes during the week too Johnnie would get a nod from a passing friend and would laughingly invite me to join them outside the shop for a quick borsie/chesty, chestful of smoke. Twice I accepted and got a headache, no kicks.

The boom stakes were high. A boom 'pinch' was one of the most serious offences which could be marked on your record and the price of boom was correspondingly exorbitant. A 'bale' of boom could be bought on the black market outside for about 50p – inside, the bale would be broken up into about a dozen 'arms', each of which sold for as much as the original bale. Sometimes too the 'arms' themselves were sub-divided into 'fingers' which would sell for as much as 25p. The inducements to join such a profitable market were therefore great and it was clear from what I saw of Johnnie's operation that the dealers involved were certainly not only bandiete. The boom-trade could never have flourished as it did without the direct interven-tion of warders – and, Central society being what it was, the authorities were as aware of this as they were of the workings of the tobacco trade. But in the eight months that we were at Central, there were only two known occasions when there were boom 'pinches' and both of these were significant for the way in which they originated.

The first took place on a building site outside: an African bandiet (black and white came together, outside their respective prisons, to work) turned to someone who looked like a white bandiet and said: 'You're a spy.' The spy turned out indeed to be a warder, dressed as a bandiet, who had been 'working' there for some days and who, as soon as he was unmasked, searched the bandiete and uncovered several bales of boom. The bandiete were charged and sentenced – which did not, said the grapevine, please the authorities. What they had been hoping to achieve by sending in the boer-spy was to nail one of the other warders in that group who was kingpin of a large smuggling ring. One of the bandiete in the ring had informed on the warder and the authorities, with the help of the informer, had devised their abortive plot to trap the warder.

The second pinch was less complicated. One of the bandiete who worked in the kitchen wanted to improve his position in the kitchen hierarchy. The kitchen was a central point in most smuggling deals, with a strict hierarchy of positions maintained among the bandiete. The aspirant bandiet was cramped by the fact that the man he wanted to replace was an old hand in the kitchen, on good terms with the kitchen warder. Aspirant bandiet had also, alongside his aspirations, developed quite a strong friendship with Old Hand – so much so that Old Hand, as a special token of friendship, one day offered Aspirant a borsie of a boom-cigarette. Aspirant took the borsie, waited for another invitation from his friend, then asked and got – again for friendship's sake – a small amount of boom for himself, to smoke in his own cell. He took the gift, not to his cell, not even to the kitchen warder, but to the chief at the front. Old Hand's cell was thoroughly ramped that night, his boom was confiscated, he was charged, sentenced and lost his place in the kitchen. The kitchen warder too was cautioned – why had *he* not spotted Old Hand's tricks? – and was ordered to replace Old Hand with a more reliable bandiet, Aspirant.

Crucial to both of these incidents were informers – 'narks' as they were called, in Afrikaans or English. (The official languages at Central were English and Afrikaans, although the latter, as in the outside white society, tended to dominate.) Narks, in fact, were an essential part of the whole system of control as practised at Central. The authorities maintained control very largely through narks and narking; and the trading of information was used as a prime inducement for social advancement.

'Don't trust a soul in this place,' was the first piece of advice Andy gave me – a warning which was often repeated by new acquaintances (some of whom subsequently themselves proved the validity of their own advice) and which was usually accompanied with the rider: 'Especially, don't trust cleaners, storemen or clerks – they'll sell their grandmothers for half-a-packet of snout.'

Clerks, storemen and cleaners: these were the top positions at Central. These were the prison administrators. They, rather than the warders, in fact ran the prison; apart from actually opening and locking the doors, they did virtually everything, organized everything, administered everything. They were the complete functionaries, leaving the warders to sit back comfortably and watch. Each section, for instance, had a warder in charge, and several cleaners. The section was effectively controlled by the head cleaner: he organized the cleaning, he collected, kept and distributed the cleaning materials; he supervised the laundry and issued clothes to new prisoners; he gave out the issue tobacco and issue toilets; he collected the letters in the mornings; he assigned new prisoners to their cells; and he accompanied the warder to help with the count in the evenings, he closed the doors so that the warder could lock them, and he helped with the count again the next morning. With a good head cleaner, a section warder needed to do nothing all day. With a well-organized section warder, a head cleaner could wield tremendous power in the section, often more power than the warder himself because the cleaner, being a bandiet, was always in a better position to know about the bandiete in the section than the boer.

The best way a bandiet could get to such a position of power was to let the section warder know *all* about all the bandiete in the section. The authorities encouraged informing and rewarded it. For instance, the position of C section storeman was particularly influential and lucrative: in charge of the clothes' store for the entire prison, the C section storeman was in direct touch with storemen in the kitchen – between them they controlled a vast wealth of eminently smuggleable commodities. The C section store was always a key point in any large smuggling deal.

The man who got the job while we were there was one Trembath (he succeeded an old-timer who finally left prison after a stretch of more than ten unbroken years). Trembath's history was not much different from that of any number of bandiete at Central: sent to reformatory as a teenager, convicted for theft or fraud in his early twenties and sent to prison, first for eighteen months, then for two-to-four years, then four-to-eight, then for the nine-to-never indeterminate sentence (known as a 'coat' after the blue coat originally worn by habituals). He was about thirty-five years old and had spent nearly half his life as a bandiet. He had also served a couple of extra years for attempted escapes. Here Trembath's history varied slightly from that of his companions: he had taken part in an escape planned by five of his friends from a small jail near Johannesburg; he had participated fully in the preparations for the escape, so much so that he kept a detailed diary of the whole episode. He had then escaped with his friends and, as soon as they split up and went off to their various hiding-holes, Trembath presented himself at the nearest police station, complete with diary and information about where everybody else was hiding. Nobody at Central was surprised when, finally, Trembath made it to the C section store.

He was storeman at the time of stock-taking. Stock-taking in prison was an annual joke, an elaborate game of deception played out in open cooperation between boer and bandiet, yet with the boere earnestly adopting an honest façade. Du Preez had introduced us to the farce at Local: we carried pile after pile of clothing out of his store, laid some of it out in the yard to be counted, and then spent more than a day hiding his vast surplus: sacks of extra clothes under the manholes covering the drains in the yard; stacks of extra mats and stools put by the grille for hiding in other sections; extra blankets, dixies, brushes – all sorts of equipment, accumulated each year and hidden. Why? Du Preez said he was worried he might be found short of something and would have to pay. He hoarded and hoarded throughout the year, giving out as few items as possible. When he got something which he could, legitimately, claim was irreparable and therefore swappable, he would tear it in half and then claim two items from the store instead of one.

Du Preez need not have worried about shortages. Trembath in the C section store at Central in 1966 had to account for a shortage of nearly 2,000 pairs of underpants. Somehow – through miscalculation, theft or mismanagement (probably a combination of all three) – 2,000 pairs of underpants had been lost within twelve months. Trembath sent out messages to cleaners in all sections, and their warders, asking for help. They searched everywhere and found loads of illicit tobacco, some banned comics, and one bandiet with a cupboard full of stolen vests and towels, all neatly stacked and unused. But no underpants. They searched the 'shops'. No underpants. So Trembath, obviously with connivance from above, sat down with a pair of scissors and carefully cut up 200 brand-new, untouched pairs of underpants, making more than 2,000 bits of underpants – which were duly counted, and accepted as correct, by the inspecting officers.

This type of collaboration between boer and bandiet was common, especially amongst the storemen and cleaners, and the narks. Where it did not involve the immediate welfare of prisoners – as in the case of the underpants – it was fairly harmless. But it was an indication of a sick system, and it could be pernicious. The C2 section-boer, Kleynhans, wanted a transfer to A section, where the bandiete were less rough and the work even less onerous than in C section. He therefore hatched a plot with the cleaner in his section whereby the cleaner would negotiate a smuggling deal with the A2 section-boer in such a way that Kleynhans could trap his fellow-boer, get him sacked, and so get his place. The C2 cleaner was offered a handsome reward of R10 – in cash, the most sought-after commodity in prison. The plot was a great success: the A2 warder disappeared within days, Kleynhans was praised for his initiative and duly rewarded with the A2 job – but the cleaner, having been used, was never paid. Kleynhans, now A2 boer, denied having offered any reward.

There were some instances where authority *was* exercised without recourse to narks: here crude force took over, like when Thys Jakobs was assaulted by the mad boer du Plessis. Head-warder du Plessis was boss of Moulders, the workshop with a forge which ran alongside one end of Fitters. He was short, walked with a sailor's roll, had trouble breathing and was an avowed Bible-puncher. He also had an uncontrollably violent temper. His fellow boere treated him with hardly-disguised derision. It was inevitable that, when Thys Jakobs was moved in to work near Moulders, there would be a clash, sometime. Thys, as far as was possible in jail, was a playboy, a flamboyant and rather nasty rogue. One day he annoyed du Plessis too much and did so within reach of a compression grinder. Du Plessis grabbed the grinder (it was, as I knew from having had to work with it, solid and heavy) and clobbered Thys over the ear with it, screaming pentateuchal abuse and all but frothing at the mouth. Thys was not badly injured by the blow but it was unpleasant and unprovoked. There were also plenty of witnesses around and there was therefore some point in reporting the matter. 'But don't forget,' the wiser witnesses advised Thys, 'to ask for a doctor's examination immediately.' Thys left for the office and was seen, later, being led off towards the front. Shortly afterwards, du Plessis stomped off in the same direction.

Thys was taken to the hospital, where an orderly examined his wounds. He was then taken to the front. He wanted, he told the chief, to lay a charge against head-warder du Plessis for assault. No, replied the chief, *he* was being charged for assaulting head-warder du Plessis – and already there were three other warders who had reported that, not only had he assaulted Mr du Plessis, but he had also disobeyed a lawful command. Thys, eventually, settled for three days on rice water on the second count. It seemed, he said, the easiest way out – and he dropped his assault charge.

Thys Jakobs's battle with the mad boer happened a couple of months after we arrived at Central. By then I had graduated from the grindstone and the little bits of metal with sharp edges to the compression grinder (a sort of portable grindstone, akin in nature and noise to a road-builders' compression drill) – and from that to a welding bay, where I was apprentice to Jackie, a man sentenced to life for murdering his wife. Jackie was not much older than me but he was, in jail terms, an old-timer: he had done time as a teenager and again in his early twenties. He was also an old-timer in terms of jail philosophy. He hated narks, and he hated the system whereby the authorities now maintained their control through narks. It wasn't clear at what stage the change had taken place but even Jackie, with a history of only about ten years' jail experience behind him, could still talk of the 'old days' and the type of rough justice that functioned when narks were universally loathed inside, when to be a nark was to invite a blanket over your head in the section and a silent thrashing from the rest of the bandiete.

'Those were the days,' said Jackie, 'when you knew where you were in boop, when you didn't have to betray all your friends to get to B group and arse-lick your way to A group.' Jackie's answer to the 'new' system was to be a loner, associating only with a small group of close friends whom he knew well and who had a common interest in remaining 'staunch' to each other. They were all long-timers who, disliking the system and refusing to participate in it, could make their time comfortable only by sticking together and helping each other.

This 'staunchness' among the old-timers produced a strange alliance when we arrived at Central. The Minister of Justice liked to say that there were no political prisoners in South Africa, tortuously arguing that there were merely some people sentenced for offences against the security of the State. But we were, very obviously, a group: we had all been sentenced for actions arising out of our opposition to apartheid and none of us considered that we had done wrong. This was immediately recognized by the other bandiete when we were put in with them – and it was well recognized, though not acknowledged, by the authorities in their treatment of us as a group. The bandiete at Central called us simply 'the kommies' – they had, for so long, been subject to Government propaganda which labelled any real opposition as communist and there was little point anyway in trying to explain, say, to Jackie that I was not actually a member of the Communist Party and never likely to be one. It was sufficient, within the South African context, to talk of us all as a group of 'kommies'.

'Hey, man,' said one of the old-timers, 'you kommies all wear glasses, man' – an observation which was largely true and which did identify the fact that most of us were middle-class intellectual types, 'egg-heads' to the Central bandiete. We were softies, lost in a society such as Central. We were, identifiably, a group, with strong group loyalties, who were there because of our opposition to the corrupt society outside. And this group loyalty immediately established a bond between us, the softies, and those of the old-timers who continued to rebel against the corrupt society inside. These men were generally the roughest of the bandiete at Central and we joined them at the lowest, least privileged levels of the society.

Together, we were the blacks of the Central society. At Local Prison, however grim our conditions, we had been daily reminded of the fact that we were white and therefore, inevitably, privileged. In our special section of what was basically a black jail, we had always been aware of the difference in treatment between us and the blacks.

There was one particular early-morning scene at Local which regularly came as a sobering reminder of the difference. Immediately opposite the alcove under the staircase where we used to dish up the food was a concertina gate leading through to one of the black sections. The cells in that section were identical with those in our own section. (We were once taken into them in search of mailbags.) They were 'double-cells', like those which three of us whites shared – with room for our three mats and lockers and small tables, but no more. While dishing up the porridge in the mornings, we could see through the concertina gate into the section and watch the black double-cells being emptied. A large retired warder – whom we knew as 'Snowball' and who occasionally came to our section, watching over us with surly geniality – stood in front of each cell-door and shouted for the black prisoners to come out 'Kom-kom! Kom-kom!' – and the bandiete would run out, five, ten, fifteen of them, never less than fifteen, often as many as twenty from the three-man cells. Snowball would stand counting them, using his heavy wooden truncheon as a tally-stick and clobbering each one firmly over the head as they rushed out and, ducking, passed him. 'Kom-kom, kom-kom,' he would shout, and the young warders guarding us would watch and laugh.

Whenever our warders wanted anything carried from the section they would open the concertina gates and shout down the black corridor: 'Kom, kaffir! Kom, houtkop! (woodenhead)', and a black bandiet would come scurrying with a quick 'Ja, baas, ja, baas', ducking to avoid the inevitable clout.

Now, in the all-white society of Central, it was our turn to be the blacks, sharing with the rebels and recalcitrants all the worst jobs in the place. Now we were the scurriers and the carriers. We didn't have to duck and ja-baas our way to safety, but we were clearly among the least-privileged of that society, with the least chance of social advancement and, together with the long-timers with their often blackened records, at the receiving end of all the hierarchies of buck-passing.

As the blacks of that society, we were also caught in an official Catch 22: if we misbehaved and actively bucked the system, we were kept down; if we behaved and accepted the system, we were still kept down because we were politicals – and the catch worked equally for the roughies who, having bucked the system in the past, inevitably had bad prison records which were against them whenever they asked for improvement.

Being white, it was a useful lesson to find out what it is like – in a South African context – to be black. It showed how the endless and inescapable drudgery of menial and mindless tasks could produce resentment and tension, and how, at the same time, common suffering could also produce strong solidarity between different people. It showed too how the system could generate frustration and anger.

This was, for me, most clearly demonstrated in 'Gums'. I first met Gums when I was sitting at the electric grindstone, rubbing my fingers raw as I grazed off the sharp edges of those thousands and thousands of little metal triangles which would one day become catches on thousands and thousands of windows. Gums worked the windows: he had to check each newly welded window-frame and hammer it square on an anvil. He always had beside him piles and piles of frames still to be hammered – and as he finished one pile, so another new pile would be delivered to his corner. 'Windows,' said Gums one day, 'is eternity.'

Gums was in his early twenties, serving an eighteen-year sentence for armed robbery. He had been sentenced when he was eighteen, an orphan, with neither friends nor family. He had grown up in institutions, mainly reformatories. They had taught him to trust nobody and to expect, in any institutions, that everybody was a nark and that the only form of advancement was through being a nark, or through having money. Gums arrived at Central with no money and no prospects of getting any money: he had nobody outside who could provide for him and he immediately got into trouble at Central which meant that he would have difficulty getting gratuity for his work there. He got into trouble because, on arrival at Central, 'I either had to sell my body or become a nark.' Gums didn't want to do either; had a fight with a bandiet who wanted his body and who, not getting it, 'shelfed' him by planting boom in his cell. That put the first indelible blot on Gums's record.

So Gums decided to survive by the only other way possible: make money. How to make money in a moneyless society, and when you've no means whereby you can make money? Gums's solution was simple: he'd make money by selling things. But Gums had nothing to sell, so he became a jail thief. There were many jail thieves at Central – which is why the grilles of the cells were locked during the day. But Gums became a special jail thief: he made a key which could open cell-grilles. Gums was a good jail thief, which made other jail thieves jealous. One of them again shelfed Gums by reporting him just after a good haul, and the boere found Gums with the haul, and with his key. There is only one jail crime inside worse than having boom – that is making a key. With a key you can escape, maybe – and that's the worst crime of all. Gums's record now looked very bad: boom and a key. Gums had little chance of gaining privileges for a long time, least of all getting gratuity for his work in the shops. So Gums had little chance of getting any money at all, legitimately.

So Gums made another key. He had it when we arrived to work in the Fitters' shop. Three of us 'kommies' worked near or with Gums, and got friendly with him – and Gums liked us. One day Gums heard Costa Gazides explaining how he was being cut up by one of the cleaners in his section. Costa had an arrangement with a compatriot who had one of the top jobs in the prison: cook in the officers' mess. The compatriot, Achilles, had access to the most delectable goodies in the whole prison.

Achilles was Costa's friend and Achilles wanted to help his friend: he wanted to give Costa cheese, and milk, and meat, and snout. But Achilles left for the officers' mess very early in the morning, long before anybody else was opened up – and he came back late at night, long after we'd been locked up. So Achilles made an arrangement with the section cleaner, Sakkie, to leave the goodies for Costa in the section store, where Sakkie would pick them up and later hand to Costa – taking a small commission, of course. Costa, once or twice, found some lovely goodies in his cell at night: some cheese, even the odd half-packet of snout. One day he had a chance actually to meet Achilles and thank him for the oddments. 'Oddments?' asked Achilles. 'I've been sending you a regular supply, never oddments.' They compared notes and discovered that the small commission which Sakkie had taken amounted to something like seventy-five per cent of the deliveries. Costa told us about it at the shops, while drinking our clandestine morning coffee with Gums.

Gums was angry, but silent. He said nothing about it until the weekend when, during exercise on Sunday morning, he told Costa to drop by his cell on the way back to the sections. There Gums handed over a week's supply of goodies for Costa, from Achilles – the full supply. Gums had stayed behind in the sections during Saturday exercise and had visited Sakkie's cell, using his new key. He removed Costa's goodies and then took his own commission from Sakkie in the shape of everything else in the fully packed over-commissioned locker.

It was a crude sort of justice but it was the only sort of justice possible at Central. It also characterized a protectiveness towards us which we often found from the rough lags. What we had to offer in return was very little, but it was unique at Central: the chance of friendship which was neither demanding nor threatening. 'I can talk with you guys,' Gums said to me once.

He could talk perhaps, but our discussions were always superficial or hurried: we met while working in the 'shops', or at the mess at lunchtime, or occasionally in the sections. There was never an opportunity to get to know each other at all well, and certainly no chance of offering any assistance to Gums at a level beyond the superficial. I once complained to Gums about the fact that I was still in C group (kommies progressed very slowly) and therefore still had to face the endless grind of smuggling tobacco, of having to be in a permanent state of watchfulness and tension. I wanted to relax. 'Oh no,' said Gums, 'that would be terrible. I must make moves all the time. The only way to get on in jail is to be in a permanent state of crime. Crime keeps you going, keeps you thinking. I must keep moving – that keeps me alive and kicking.'

The prime move that Gums wanted to make was to get out. He wasn't dumb so he knew that his prospects of staying out if he managed to 'break' were slim. Few breakers ever lasted more than a couple of days outside: the police network was too extensive and, for a criminal, there are few really safe places for you to go.

While we were at Central, two breaks that we heard of were successful: that is, the men managed actually to escape the walls. The first was where two bandiete dug a hole in the wall of the Carpenters' shop and escaped through it one night while taking part in an experiment to introduce overtime at the workshops. The experiment came to an abrupt halt and the two men were away for a week: they were picked up trying to break into a jeweller's shop on the way to Cape Town. The grapevine reported that there had been no need for them to break into the jeweller's – just that they happened to pass the window and couldn't resist the temptation.

For the rest of us the second break was far more dramatic and entertaining. It happened one Saturday afternoon while we were watching the fortnightly movie in the Hall. It was a dreadful movie – '*Son of Spartacus*' – and some sort of cataclysmic interruption was required to make it memorable. The Son of Spartacus – alias Mr Universe – was flexing his muscles against the Roman Empire when the sound-track was joined by a rising air-raid-warning wail. For a moment we couldn't tell whether the siren was part of the screen-action or not, but then the sudden scurrying of boere in the shadows confirmed the wail wasn't from Spartacus. The wail became overwhelmingly loud while the boere ran around and around each other in circles, shouting at each other and at us, getting nowhere and achieving nothing, and not even pausing in their circles to watch as Mr Universe brought the Empire to its knees. We sat huddled on our benches, happily watching this unexpected double feature which continued until a senior officer directed the boeres' attention towards the kitchen.

There, it seemed, one Pat Russell and two friends had managed to hide in a cupboard, then hack their way through a window and so over the kitchen roof on to the outside wall – in full sight of a young guard in a wall-post a couple of hundred yards away who had become hysterical trying to phone through to the main gate, completely forgetting that he had a loaded rifle next to him. Pat and his mates made off in one of the warders' cars, but were picked up the same day, at a garage north of Pretoria, when they offered to pay for petrol with the spare wheel of the car.

'They were stupid,' said Gums, 'they could've thought of a better lark than the spare-wheel.' And Gums still wanted out. 'I must move,' he said – and it was some time before we discovered how desperately earnest he was. His plan for getting out involved using the courts, quite literally. He maintained that it was simpler breaking from the cells below the Magistrates' Courts in town than it was from Central. He would use his key to break from the cells there.

He had support for his theory from other bandiete with experience in escapes: the court cells, they said, were easy. There were two problems: getting to the courts, and getting a key to the courts with you. This second problem explained why it was that most groups of bandiete planning a break from the courts liked to take with them one 'hasie/bum-boy' (homosexual): it was easier for him to 'bottle' the key for them and get it, undiscovered, to the court. (To 'bottle' something is to hide it up your arse.) The first problem – of getting to court – was usually solved for the old-time bandiete by the authorities themselves: they were taken to court to face further charges and they took with them as many of their mates as possible – witnesses for the defence.

But Gums had no mates facing further charges who could call him as a witness. Therefore his only chance was to engineer an incident which would get him taken to the Magistrates' Court. This was a dicey sort of thing to try because the incident had to be pretty serious to merit being heard outside the prison, since the Prison Regulations gave the authorities wide powers for hearing internal disciplinary cases and imposing punishments. The Regulations also provided for magistrates to hear cases inside the prison, for instance in attempted escape cases. Which was why, said Gums, he'd make his case so serious that they would have to take him out. It wouldn't be anything small like assaulting a warder or smuggling boom. 'Just watch,' he said, 'you'll see.' No advice from any of us who knew him would help. All we could do was wait and watch.

Gums made his move one lunch-time, in the workshop mess. Most people had just finished eating when shouts from one side of the mess and a clatter of benches falling and tables being pushed back announced a fight. Immediately a circle of bandiete fell back to form a large ring around two men, one of whom was Gums. He had a knife in his hand and had already slashed his opponent across the face. The other man was a Hungarian called 'Shabby', doing time for robbery: he was defending himself by flinging the metal food-dixies at Gums, and ducking, edging away as Gums tried to move in, ducking too, knife in one hand, a dixie in the other. It was sudden, menacing, very nasty. A strange quiet everywhere, broken only by the murmurs of the bandiete in the inner ring trying to force the encircling watchers back, fearful of the flying metal plates. Nobody tried to intervene. No bandiet ever intervened at Central in the jungle fights between other bandiete – that only brought trouble and unnecessary involvement with the boere.

At first, no boere appeared at all. Normally at lunch-time, a couple of them were left behind in the mess, locked in with the bandiete. That day, as soon as the fight started, both boere vanished. They returned within minutes, heavily reinforced, and tore into the watching circle. Gums saw them coming and flicked his knife backwards, over the wall behind him, then stood waiting to be collected. They took him away at once, with Shabby following, off to the hospital to have his bloodied face treated. Gums was soon brought back to the shops, to the blacksmiths, to have chains fixed on him: two shackles around the ankles, the chains leading up through a waistband and on to more shackles at the wrists. The shackles stayed on, permanently, for the month that the wearer was kept in solitary, in the Bom under the Condemneds. Shabby returned to the shops the same afternoon, looking surprisingly cheerful with plaster covering what would always be a long battle-scar down the side of his face.

'It didn't ought to have been Shabby at all,' Gums explained when he emerged, pale and spiny, from his month's cool-off in the Bom. 'I'd thought to fight Giovanni [doing fifteen years for bank robbery] because he'd cut me up over a cigarette lighter. But Giovanni wasn't around at the time I went looking for someone to fight, and Shabby was there. I've nothing against Shabby personally,' said Gums. He had needed an opponent to fight, not a pretext for fighting. Any opponent would have been OK.

The knife was from the Fitters' store: one of a number of classified tools (like hacksaws) which were issued only on request and which had to be booked back into the store at the end of each day, but not necessarily before lunch. 'The time in the Bom,' added Gums, 'wasn't very nice, with the chains and all. But you'll see – I'll get to court in a month or so. Just watch.'

We left Central before the case was called. Two years later one of the shop boere came through to our new section to fix a door and I asked him about Gums. Gums, it seemed, never got his chance. He got an extra year on his eighteen years and was stripped of all privileges – in a specially-convened court, inside Central.

'He's finished,' said the boer, who quite liked Gums. 'You'll never change him now. He's rotten, finished.' So they've written him off, finished. I doubt whether Gums will ever get out of there, and I don't think either that he will survive in there. He could have: he was young and energetic and he had it in him to do better things, even after he had come to Central. But he became desperate and brutal because there seemed, in the system at Central, nothing else that he could do to break his frustration.

What was so terrifying about Gums's actions was that they were the logical outcome of the system itself. And thinking of Gums – like us, a black in the Central society – I thought too of the thousands of young, energetic men in South Africa's cities who, being black, are confined to a life of drudgery and frustration – and desperation. I could see why so many of them ended up, like Gums, in prison, and why so many end up at Central – the place where you live to the sound of men being killed, officially. Central Prison is South Africa's hanging jail.

5 Hangings

The only gallows in South Africa are at Central Prison, Pretoria. On average, while we were there, about two people were hanged to death every week at Pretoria Central. In the second half of 1966 alone, according to figures given in the South African Parliament, sixty-six people were hanged. Of these sixty-six people, forty-six were African, nineteen were Coloured, and one was white.

I remember the white one. It was characteristic of Central society, like the society outside, that sixty-five blacks could die unknown and that one white should be known and talked about. He was called Steve Grobbelaar. He was hanged to death on the morning of 7 July 1966, having been in the Condemned section for fifteen months. Quite a few of the bandiete at Central had known him and two had known him well. He had come to Central originally with a seven-year sentence, for robbery. He had escaped from Central once, had been caught and sentenced again, to an indeterminate nine-to-fifteen-year sentence. He escaped again and contacted two of his mates in Johannesburg, one called Tom, one called Whitey. Steve Grobbelaar told his two mates to meet him, with a car, and a gun. 'When Steve Grobbelaar said bring a gun,' said Tom, 'you brought a gun.' On the way out of Johannesburg, they stopped at a small cafe in Braamfontein and tried to rob the till. The cafe proprietor objected and they shot him dead. Steve Grobbelaar got the rope for that; Whitey got life; Tom got fifteen years.

Tom and Whitey were with us in C section. When Steve Grobbelaar was hanged after fifteen months in Condemneds, Tom asked the boere in the workshops how Steve was. Steve was all right, said one of the boere who had been there, early that morning: he went all right. He took it well, said the boer.

Tom, I noticed, took it well too. He nodded and went back to his work. Then, the same afternoon, he walked back from work past the place where his mate Steve had been hanged that morning – just as, in the morning, he had walked past it on the way to work.

We all passed it, every day, in the morning on the way to the workshops, in the afternoon on the way back from the workshops. Every morning, every afternoon. And, on an average of twice every week, we waited, outside the gallows, while they cleared up after they had hanged people.

A friend of mine, John Harris, had been hanged there in 1965 (for the bomb he had put on the Johannesburg Station). I wondered, when we arrived at Central, what it would be like to live in the place where John was hanged. I wondered whether, as an ordinary bandiet, one would be aware of the Condemneds and the hangings.

Hangings usually took place on Tuesdays and Thursdays. We lined up as we did every day in the sections after breakfast, four-by-four, waiting for the instruction to march off. On Tuesdays or Thursdays – sometimes both days – there would be a delay, some minutes extra for you to chew on a final piece of breakfast katkop, to try to catch an extra puff or two in cupped hands, hiding behind the back of the man in front and waving your hand to disperse the smoke so that no wandering boer would see. Then off, two-by-two, through the Hall in silence, out through the C group yard and along to the B group yard, the long sandy yard with the line of boere across the near end, waiting to search you. And after the search you line up at the far end of the yard, four-by-four again, in teams, a team for every workshop.

On your left, as you stand facing the end of the soccer yard, is a high wall. On your right is the tall length of A section, three storeys of sheer wall with its three rows of window after barred window. In front of you, as you stand waiting in the soccer yard, is a tall two-and-a-half-storey building: roof and fanlight atop two-and-a-half solid storeys of windowless wall. No windows looking out of the gallows. You stand in the soccer yard, each morning, facing the wall of the gallows, waiting to lead off through to the workshops.

You go from the soccer yard up some steps and through a gate in the wall at the side of the tall gallows building. Two boere stand counting as you go through the gate into the short passage, then left up some more steps and out through large double doors, out into the inner road which runs the length of the workshops. On your right as you go through the first gate is a flight of steps, steps leading down to a single door, one door at the bottom of the tall building but no windows at all in that building, where the gallows are. Opposite the steps, immediately on your left as you go through the first gate, is a small room with a door and windows. The door on the right, at the bottom of the steps, and the door and windows on the left, are usually shut as you go through to the workshops.

On Tuesdays and Thursdays, after the unusual delay in the section after breakfast, you come through into the soccer yard and stand waiting in teams. The gate ahead – the gate next to the wall of the gallows building – is shut. You stand, silently waiting. The workshop boere, in their overalls, stand waiting too, silently watching to see that you stay silent. You can hear knocking. From behind the wall ahead, the wall beside the gallows, you can hear a distant knocking. You stand in the soccer yard in the early morning and hear knocking. Sometimes a prolonged knocking, sometimes not much knocking – as they put on the coffin lids.

The small room on the left as you go through the gate is the laying-out room. The bodies are brought through the door on the right, up the steps and across the passage-way into the small room on the left, and into the coffins.

You don't see any of that, waiting in the soccer yard. All you see is the locked door in the wall. And you hear the knocking of the coffin lids being put on. Then there's a long silence, broken sometimes by the distant sound of a truck pulling off, or by a boer ahead opening a gate and peering through, and coming back to wait until it's all right for us to walk through to the shops. Until everything's been cleared up and finished.

Then you're marched off, two-by-two, up through the door in the wall and along the short passage on the other side, past the steps going down on the right and the small room on the left, and through the large double gates leading to the workshops.

Once – it was early in May, I remember – we were kept waiting a particularly long time, and there had been considerable knocking. I glanced into the small room on the left as we went past. The windows that were usually shut were open. Inside was a table, like an operating table, flat and hard. On it lay a pair of khaki shorts, the short khaki shorts worn by African bandiete. That day, said one of the young boere in the shop, they hanged six of them at the same time. That was why we had waited so long in the yard. Six at once, he said. The man who does it, he said, is very good with them: he puts the blindfolds on quickly and easily and talks to them all the time and pulls the lever without the guy even really knowing it's going to happen when it does happen. They go all right like that, he said. Sometimes – not every week – there's sawdust scattered on the pathway between the door on the right and the room on the left. Sometimes there was not enough sawdust to cover the dark marks on the ground. Why sawdust, I asked. For the blood, explained one of the young workshop boere. There's often lots of blood at a hanging, he said. It comes from all over the place. When they hang women, he said, they have to strap them up between the legs beforehand. They scatter sawdust on the ground so that on your way to the shops you don't step in the blood from the bodies on their way to the coffins.

One day at the shops – on a morning in the week when we had waited in the soccer yard – another of the young shop boere came in looking grim. He was normally a sunny sort of person and spent quite a while every day chatting to Jackie and me in our welding bay. This day he looked bad, green about the gills. We laughed at him, joked, and made some remark about people who came to work with hang-overs. He had been to his first hanging. Every warder is required, at least once, to attend a hanging. This was Henning's first. He said he didn't want to see another. There was this guy, this kaffir, who was hanged and the rope sort of came up and pulled his face off. His whole face sort of came off. All the skin from his chin upwards was up over his nose. All the blood around and everything. They leave them hanging for twenty minutes to see that they're dead. It's all a hell of a mess, said Henning. He didn't want to see another one like that.

The first thing you notice as you come into Central is the singing, the sound of the Condemneds. Up behind the huge sign in the Hall saying Stilte/Silence, the Condemneds sing, chant, sing through the day and, before an execution, through the night. At times, the chant is quiet, a distant murmur of quiet humming, softly. Then it swells: you can hear a more strident, urgent note in the swell, sounding through the prison, singing the hymns that will take them through the double doors into the gallows. Fifty, sixty, sometimes seventy at a time up in the Condemneds, waiting their turn, singing their fellows through their last nights.

My cell in C section was right at the end of the far corridor, on the outside, away from the inner wall. Once in my cell, the singing receded – only occasionally, especially late at night before a hanging, the swell of chanting would surge through, eerily filling the night. But those in A section – the privileged A's and B's of the prison – were directly opposite the Condemneds in B2. For them, the singing was ever-present, close at hand, right through the long nights before hangings. 'Abide With Me, Abide With Me' – all night, 'Abide With Me' – swelling with intensity towards morning and then, as the lights came on in the cells around the prison, a final intense burst and sudden silence, silence as the double doors open and close.

In June 1966, three of the political prisoners with short sentences were upgraded: Paul Trewhela, Lewis Baker and Norman Levy. The rest of us under-privileged politicals envied them, jealous of their new status with the right to smoke and the prospect of more visits and letters and better facilities – and we helped them pack their oddments and watched them leave C section, across the Hall into A section. We saw Lewis at lunch the next day, looking pale, haggard from his first sleepless night of privilege. The Condemneds had sung that night, sung through till dawn, right across the way from Lewis and the others, until the lights came on and sudden silence.

The hangings took place at about 5.30 in the morning, about the time they switched our lights on. For those of us in C section, the singing and the sounds surrounding the hangings were indistinct. Our early mornings when the lights came on were cold, silent times: it was always difficult waking up, returning to the reality of the mats and blankets on the floor and the cold cell. It was always difficult to wake up – except the day when they brought through a young woman to be hanged.

Women's Jail – the section for women – was alongside Central. The wall of Women's formed one of the walls for the kitchen/hospital yard at Central. Our cells, up at the end of C section, overlooked the kitchen yard. We were close enough to Women's to hear, sometimes at night, babies crying; and the shouts of the wardresses next door, switching the lights off at 8 in the evening with cries of 'Stilte/Silence' – and one who always screamed 'Bliksem/Bitch!'

They brought the woman through as the lights came on. Into the silence and darkness outside our windows there was a sudden whimpering and crying, deep sobs of crying moving across the yard. A woman, a young woman it sounded like, gulping deep whoops of weeping. I thought at first I was asleep, dreaming the nightmare cries, then I turned in my tight-drawn blankets and saw the black polished floor and the light bright in the ceiling and I lay puzzled, listening, then cold with horror as I realized where I was and what it was, and I followed the cries past my window in the yard down below and round the corner, disappearing inside. And I lay, cold still, imagining how she walked up the iron stairs and along the passage, and then through the two heavy doors leading into the gallows.

They had to bring her through, said the boer later, strapped up in a strait-jacket. She was an African who had smothered her child. She had hysterics when they hanged her, he said. She didn't go well.

We learnt no more about who she was. We seldom knew anything about individual Condemneds, except the whites. We just knew they were there. On the board in the Hall, inside the Hall boer's office, was the daily tally of prisoners in each section – and each day, if you peered in quickly as you went past, you could see the tally for B2, the Condemneds, always at about seventy or more, awaiting execution. Predominantly blacks, always. Blacks in the otherwise all-white jail. If there were whites like Grobbelaar, they were kept separately in the same section, but at the end they all went through the same double doors to the gallows.

There was always considerable interest among Central bandiete in any whites who were in Condemneds. It was so with Steve Grobbelaar, the only white hanged in the second half of 1966, and so too with Deisel, hanged in the first half of the year, in May. I met him, the day before his execution, crossing the Hall. I was coming in from the shops and he was crossing towards the Condemneds' visiting room, looking up into the sun streaming through the top of the Hall dome. I wasn't watching where I was going either and we collided. He looked down from the sun, smiled an apology and walked on, accompanied always by his boer. He looked calm. It was the first time I had been so close to anyone from B2 and I couldn't help noticing that his jacket had tabs on, instead of buttons. No buttons, I was told, so that they couldn't kill themselves before being executed.

Deisel, like Grobbelaar, was well known at Central. He had been an ordinary bandiet there for a long time, had then escaped and killed a cop in the process. He wasn't very long in Condemneds. The night before he hanged there was a special record request programme for him. Every evening, from 5.30 to 8 p.m., records were played over the loudspeaker system in every section with interruptions at 6 p.m. and 7 p.m. for the evening news from the South African Broadcasting Corporation, one in English, one Afrikaans; and, sometimes, announcements from the secretary of the Entertainments Committee, who played the records from his cell at the entrance to B2. Before he began playing the records that night, the secretary announced that this was a special request programme for Deisel in B2. For two and a half hours, with brief interruptions for the news broadcasts, Deisel's last programme blasted through every section. The loudspeakers were loud. The programme consisted of a number of cowboy songs – 'Home on the Range', 'Don't fence me in' . . . with some hymns – 'Abide With Me', 'O God our help in ages past' . . . with lots of 'opskud' and 'tiekiedraai'; and ending with 'Nearer my God to Thee'. The secretary played the last record, then read out a final message to everybody from Deisel, saying good-bye, and then, over the loudspeakers: 'Well, OK, and good-bye to you too, Deisel. It's been nice knowing you. Good luck, hey' – and he signed off the evening's entertainment with 'I'll See you in My Dreams'.

The next morning we waited in the section, and waited again in the soccer yard. In the workshop, one of the boere said 'Ja, it was OK, Deisel went OK.'

Another Condemned whom we once saw close-up was a young African. We saw him in the Hall, going through to a last visit, but in circumstances very different from my encounter with Deisel. It was one Saturday, during a movie, the whole Hall darkened with drapes and closed doors. For once the Silence rule within the Hall's huge dome was relaxed as we squashed onto the benches, eagerly chattering. But the no-smoking rule was not relaxed. Nobody was allowed to smoke in the Hall and the temporary darkness made it all the more difficult to light an illicit smoke. A sudden flare was immediately visible to the watching boere.

No boer was more attentive than Faan Jonker, the Hall boer. Faan Jonker was a swine, a mean man. He had small eyes, little red pins glaring out from above a sharp nose and a bristling moustache. Below the bristle was a tight loud mouth, bursting with obscenities – and below that a large bursting belly. Faan Jonker was the man who administered lashes. The only time I saw Faan Jonker smile was once as he strode across the Hall, rolling up his sleeves in anticipation of giving six lashes to a young dagga-smoker, strapped on to the triangle in the yard outside. The story at Central was that Faan Jonker had once been Chief in the kitchen, but was caught at the head of a vast smuggling racket, and was demoted to head-warder, head-warder in charge of the Hall.

He had an office at the entrance to the Hall. It was really a box, built up against the wall, with a glass front – from which Faan Jonker could survey his silent polished empire. Or he would stand at the door of his box watching as the lines of bandiete passed to and from the workshops. You would see him sniff through his bristle, then a large paw would reach down beneath his belly and scratch tenderly at his crotch, then nudge the belly into place. Suddenly Jonker's whole form would pounce forward and a bandiet would be dragged from the line and led off into the box, to be searched. Jonker liked patting people and finding illicit things hidden in their underpants.

Saturdays, movie days, were frustrating days for him. His Hall was defiled, filled with benches and chattering bandiete. Benches filled the Hall, except for an open passage left down the middle, from the entrance-gate on the one side (next to Jonker's box) through to the B section grille on the other (leading up into the Condemneds). Jonker sat with the boere in his box, watching the darkness for a flare of matches.

Halfway through our movie programme one Saturday, the grille of the Condemneds opened and a young African was brought through into the central aisle by his black warder. I was sitting just back from the aisle, which was partially lit by the projected light of the movie, enough to distinguish clearly the two standing forms against the rest of the hunched shapes. But still dark enough to highlight the flare of the match as the Condemned stopped at the grille and lit himself a smoke. Down from the Condemneds for a visit, which meant passing through the white man's afternoon entertainment, passing through Jonker's No-Smoking Hall. He stood at the grille, pausing while his warder locked the grille behind him, and lit a smoke with an open flare. Drawing in a deep lungful of smoke, he flicked the match off into the darkness and began a slow easy stroll along the aisle, drawing deeply on the glowing smoke.

There was a scuffle and confused muttering from Jonker's box, then the box light went on and Jonker burst from it with a roar – 'Wie rook daar/Who's smoking?' – as he pushed his way into the aisle. The black Condemned with his warder stopped and waited in the centre of the aisle. Jonker advanced towards him, shouting: 'Jy rook, kaffir, jy rook/ You're smoking, kaffir, smoking!' – and pointed a quivering finger at the infidel. All the weight of Jonker's authority went into that gesture: he could charge the culprit; he could take his meals, his privileges; put him in solitary, get a black mark on his record. He could point a finger at him and shout 'kaffir!' The young black man smiled at Jonker and blew a puff of smoke into his furious face. Then he brushed him aside and walked off with his guard to his visit. Jonker returned to his box and switched off the light. We could laugh quietly.

There wasn't much else about the Condemneds that you could laugh at. They were there, the inescapable chanting centre of the prison, usually unseen, always present. It was like living with a murdered man permanently in the front room of your home: you have to pass the corpse every day, you have to work around it, you have to sweep under it and dust over it, you have to live with it. You cannot get away from it. You have to learn to live with it. This was the most terrifying thing about Central, the hanging jail. Not that it was difficult to live there, but that it was so easy to learn to live there.

I had wondered how I would feel. How would I feel, knowing that every day, twice a day at least, I was walking past the place where they killed a friend of mine, past the place where John Harris had been hanged? That, there, that in front there, that was where he had died; that was where they brought him through, that was where they packed him up, nailed him down, and they took him away that way. I could repeat that each day as I walked through Gate No. 5 on the way to the shops, and back through Gate No. 5 on the way back from the shops. I couldn't escape it. It was there. I was there. There was nothing I could do about it. It was not that I could not live with it; it was only that I *had* to live with it. And I did live with it, through no particular act of positive will, no definite effort, no long sleepless nights wrestling with remorse or fear or agony, torment, misery. Only a feeling of immense sadness, watching the lines of life tread past the door behind which people die an official death. They talked about John at Central. He had been hanged less than a year before we arrived. They remembered him and they had their stories about him, like the stories they have about most whites who hang. Oh yes, they said, he went well – singing too, they could hear it in the section before the doors shut: 'We shall overcome.' He went OK. The boere, so the story went, didn't give him a chance: gave him an extra long drop, just in case. He was all right, he went singing.

It must take a great deal of strength, a great deal of courage, to be able to go out all right, to go out singing, when you are so alone, facing the rope, walking out alone to die. All those people around you – warders and a priest and a doctor – most of them involved in seeing that you are killed, getting you dead as soon and as officially as possible.

You learn to live with it at Central because – for all the blood on the ground and for all the singing, the stories, all the awareness and the closeness – still there is a final remoteness which keeps you separate. The routine keeps you unthinking about it, lets you walk past the gallows every day and not notice it, lets you care and yet be remote. As long as you can walk past every day, there's always Them-in-there and Us-here: them is for dead, us is us, alive. So you stay remote. You are always remote as long as it doesn't happen to you. Until it does happen to you, it's not you. Particularly when you're so near something so diabolically unthinkable as a crowd of officials gathering round to kill somebody in the cold light of early morning – particularly then, you can't really imagine what it would be like if it was actually you. The more you talk about what happens to others, the more you hear at close quarters what it's like for others – the more it remains *them* and not you.

That is why hanging, as a criminal deterrent, doesn't work. Until it *has* happened to you, you can't imagine it. I worked for four months at Central with a man who, on his own admission, qualified for the rope. He thought he was going to get the rope – but he thought that only *after* he had committed his crime.

Jackie was a knife man who was doing life for stabbing his wife to death. He was the one who taught me to weld; the one who hated the narks so much. He was about two years older than me: born in Port Elizabeth, he had been brought up by his widowed mother in South End, a tough part of town, one of South Africa's twilight areas where the races had mixed, settled and intermingled long before the Government began introducing its laws for racial purity.

Jackie, with an Afrikaans surname, spoke English at home, and a mixture of both at the factory where he started work, aged fourteen. 'We had this gang,' he said, 'and there was this other gang, Italians, and they had knives and fought us, so we got knives and learnt to use them too.' Then he got 'busted' (I forget what for) and went to Tokai Reformatory for a year; then back to the factory, and knives, and fights, till he got a year for car theft, served mainly at an 'open' prison near Pretoria. Then he got married and later, in his own way, divorced.

'You see,' he said, 'she'd gone off [his wife] with another guy, sudden like, and took the kids too. I was the hell in, man, and chased them all over town, till she came back and moved in with her old man. Then she came across to chat about it, with a let's-talk-it-over line like, hell, we haven't even kissed before. And I think: I'm going to get you, girlie, get you. But we chat and talk, sitting on the bed there and chatting, till she says OK, Jackie, she's off now and she gets up off the bed and starts going and I think you can't go now, please don't go now, but she says yes she's off now going with her back to me as she gets off the bed. So I reach down to the drawer by the bed and take out one of my long knives and I think you can't go now, girlie, not now and reach up and pull her back with the tongue deep in her back and she sort of screams and there's blood and I think God, Jackie, you've done it now, better do it properly now – so I hit her again hard in front too, hard and real deep. Six inches, I'm telling you, six inches each – each fatal, they said in court – I got her thirteen times altogether. First in the bedroom there where she was lying against the wall pushing me off with her legs and then running down the passage towards the kitchen, like a chicken, you know, with blood jumping out all over. So then I got her again in the kitchen, a couple more times as she sank down by the sink sort of, and my Ma came in and was pulling me, screaming.

'I just left them there and went and had a couple of drinks. They all saw the blood and laughed and said, 'Had another fight, hey, Jackie?' – and then I went to another goose's place. She nearly fainted when I told her but I waited there and they picked me up. You should have seen – it was all in the papers – and they had hundreds of photos in court. I knew I was for the chop, yes, and I thought well yes maybe I'd get the rope even, though they'd told the court about the other guy and her running off, or I thought maybe fifteen years or twenty years or something. Then he said life, life, and it seemed funny somehow

– I couldn't think about it proper, not something fixed like the rope, or fifteen years; just life. It seemed like for ever.'

I asked Jackie if he had thought about the rope before. 'Before I did her? No. It wouldn't have made any difference anyway, y'see, I just lost my angry.'

I asked Eddie Meyer about the rope. Eddie was serving a fifteen-year sentence for armed robbery (a capital offence in South Africa) and would certainly have faced hanging if the policeman he had shot had died. What about the rope, I asked.

'What about it?' he asked. 'It's there, isn't it? But maybe the cops'll get me first, after I've got some more of them. Or maybe' – and he looked almost pleased at the thought – 'maybe I'll end up going out of here feet first, through Gate No. 5 – and they'll talk about me and say I went singing too.'

That was part, perhaps, of Eddie's bravado, but it showed how even he, who – more than most – had been in a position to fear the rope, remained remote from it, unable to consider it as affecting him directly. And beneath the bravado was a fascination – a fascination felt by the boere as much as by the bandiete.

We encountered this even before going to Central – for instance with 'Duckpond', a young warder at Local. Duckpond was the son of a warder and a wardress, and he wanted to see a hanging. He wanted to see a hanged man. He had his chance once when we were sewing bags in the yard at Local and the boer on the catwalk told Duckpond that a corpse had just been brought into the mortuary outside in the passage. Duckpond wanted to get out of our yard and into the mortuary to see his first corpse. But he had no key for the yard (du Preez kept that and let us, and Duckpond, out only at lunchtime) and he ran round and round the yard like a puppy, squealing up to the man on the catwalk to get somebody to come and open the door quickly for him; round and round, like a little boy outside a locked toilet, wanting to see his first corpse. Eventually somebody came to let him out – and let him back in again. Duckpond looked quietly content, his curiosity satisfied. He thought about it a bit, then started chatting to the man on the catwalk: what he wanted now, he said, was to see how corpses were *made*. He could go to Central for that.

I asked Henning, the young boer in the workshop, what he thought of hanging.

'I don't want to go again,' he said. But did he think it a good thing?

'What do you mean good thing?' Did he think it worked?

'Oh yes, it worked fine: they all were dead straight off.'

Yes, but did he think it a good thing that some people should hang other people?

Well, it was their job, wasn't it? They're only doing what the courts tell them to do. Yes, but did he think the courts *should* tell anybody to do that sort of thing?

'How come,' he asked, 'all you kommies are so damn clever?' – and he walked off and wouldn't again discuss the rope.

That was a predictable white South African remark: I could have encountered it even before I went to prison. Before I went to prison I had not really seriously considered capital punishment: I was against it and was horrified at the thought that South Africa was responsible for about half the world's executions. But I had not considered this as a close-up fact: it was merely one among many horrifying facts about life under an apartheid government. Even when I joined an organization involved in activities which were offences under the Sabotage Act – an act carrying a possible death penalty – I did not think about capital punishment itself. The possible penalty was an active and serious one, but so too was the possibility of imprisonment – and that in itself was sufficiently serious to absorb all musings.

Only after I had lived at Central did I come to realize, fully, the utter horror of capital punishment, what it involves and the responsibility it imposes on man. I do not think that any man can be asked to exercise that devastating responsibility. I do not think that any man can carry out the demands of the system or live with the system without himself at once becoming degraded, corrupt and brutal. This question is not peculiar to South Africa but it assumes particular significance in the South African context. I used to watch those figures on the board in the Hall at Central: seventy-plus in B2, awaiting hanging, sentenced mainly for murder or rape or armed robbery – and most of them black. And I realized that Central is a mirror of the outside apartheid society: the violence inherent in the laws of apartheid – in the laws which break up families, which deny freedom of movement or expression, which deny to men their basic humanity – this violence has its natural counterpart at Central in the gallows, the essential symbols of official violence.

But even more hideous than the gallows themselves was watching at Central how it was possible to accommodate to the horror – how you could become accustomed to it, how you learn to live with it and accept it. So too have people become insensitive in the outside society.

Shortly before we left Central in November 1966, they began building a new 'Maximum Security' section on the rise immediately behind Central. It was soon known among bandiete as 'Beverly Hills' and was reported to contain new up-to-date gallows and more room for more Condemneds, all out of sight. The new section, we heard, was eventually opened some time in 1968 – a fitting monument to a Government which had just passed a Terrorism Act and which was claiming greater efficiency and an 'outward-looking' policy.

6 Sex

As a schoolboy, I spent ten years boarding at a leading church school in Johannesburg. This was a useful preparation for prison. It prepared me to accept an endless and often meaningless routine. It taught me to cherish and to be deprived of privacy. It taught me to expect arbitrary pettiness from the authorities. It also prevented me from being surprised by the fact that men, put together in close proximity for many months, might find sexual satisfaction with other men, whether they were homosexual or not.

The prison authorities, as in most of their actions, professed one thing about the sex trade and practised another. Most cells are single cells in Central, about ten foot square, with room for your felt mat on the floor as bed, plus a small table and stool, a toilet pot and sometimes a small locker. The regulations do not allow two men to be locked up in a cell together – this, they say, might encourage sodomy – but Central is overcrowded so there are numbers of single cells with three men in them, with just enough room for three mats to be squeezed alongside each other, and three toilet pots, but little else. These three-men cells are known, both among the bandiete and the warders, as 'married quarters'. It is common knowledge at Central that you can, without much difficulty, make arrangements with the section warder to be moved into 'married quarters'.

Hennie asked me to move into married quarters with him, one weekend. Hennie became cleaner in our section in about July. He was young – about twenty-five – good-looking, and tough. He had just come, he told me, from the Madhouse ('observation' section) at the beginning of a fifteen-year sentence. They had made him a cleaner while they decided whether to send him for further observation at a mental hospital – because of his crime, said Hennie, looking down at me. I looked up, showing polite interest. The beak, said Hennie, gave him only fifteen years; he had asked for the rope, he said. It was the second time he'd done it and he had asked the beak for the rope, but the beak only gave him fifteen years. Hennie had sharp eyes, watching me. I had, by then, been at Central long enough not to rise to any baits about people's crimes – everybody told you their crime: this was their key into the society. I looked at Hennie with mild interest. Fifteen years, said Hennie, for rape. He had raped a six-year-old girl. They made him cleaner in the section, pending further observation at Weskoppies, the state mental institution.

As cleaner, Hennie had considerable freedom of movement, with a cleaner's access to several sources of extra goodies. I once asked him (foolishly) whether he could get an extra katkop at the weekend. Hennie obliged, and, without being asked, continued to oblige: sometimes katkop; sometimes extra butter; sometimes sugar; once, half an orange. I would return from the shops in the afternoon and find, after lock-up, the goodies hidden neatly inside my cupboard – which was clever of Hennie because it indicated that he could unlock my carefully locked cupboard at will, while I was away, and he ruled the section. He would pass my doorway in the morning, helping the boer with the count (you had to stand behind your locked grille after they had opened the outside door, each cell with door and grille, both locked). As he passed, I would nod thanks, and he'd smile back.

Then one Saturday, Hennie came into my cell during the pre-supper pause between the fortnightly movies and lock-up, when cleaners were free to wander through the section. It had, I remembered, been a good week for me: at least one extra katkop and, special treat, an extra pie on Wednesday. Hennie came into the cell and started chatting, leaning on the table – about the movie, about cars, about rugby, about his crime. Then, looking into my open cupboard with its stacked shelves of books, he said:

'Hell, man, but you *read*, hey!'

'Yes.'

'You play chess?'

'Yes.'

Hennie smiled. 'We must play sometime' – idly fiddling with

my *Complete Shakespeare*. 'You know,' he said, 'I like you.'

I felt trapped. Hennie was leaning on the table between me and the grille, and he was big. The cell began to feel more than usually cramped, small, without corners. I moved towards the open grille, awkwardly: 'Yes, very nice, Hennie. So let's just stay friends, shall we?'

He followed me into the passage, smiling. 'Yes, of course, beautiful. And sometime we'll play chess together, hey?' He disappeared down the corridor. When I went back to put the Shakespeare away, I found a chunk of white bread tucked into the cupboard, large and very fresh.

Next Saturday, after I'd been locked behind my grille, there was Hennie. 'I've fixed it,' he said. What? 'The chess, of course.' He'd arranged, he said, with the boer who would be on the following weekend, that we could go three-up over the lunch-time lock-up. Three? 'Yes, three,' said Hennie, 'Wally's got a board.'

'Hennie, you play chess with two people, not three.'

'Sure. But Wally's a great player too. We can play lots. Wally and me's been together often. You'll see.'

'No, Hennie, I don't . . .' But he was gone, and my grille was locked.

Hennie was not with the boer at the count that night, only Wally – assistant cleaner to Hennie, who slammed the door closed for the boer to lock before I had a chance to say anything. Next morning, I couldn't find Hennie. In between emptying my pot and cleaning it, between grabbing my breakfast and eating it, I couldn't find Hennie in the section – his cell was open, empty. Then we marched out to the workshops, for the day. In the evening, there was hardly time enough to grab a dixie of soup and a mug of coffee, bump with them down the narrow corridor and leave them in the cell, then tear off clothes and dive for the cold shower, rub down and tear back to the cell for immediate lock-up (and cold food) – little enough time for that, let alone for searching out Hennie.

I had to wait until Saturday of that week, when there was slightly more time over breakfast. I was just finishing my mielie-pap when Hennie came in again, into the small cell. I immediately said: 'No, Hennie, no chess, no chess for me.'

'What you mean?' – very bland, sitting down on the edge of the table, between me and the grille.

'No chess, Hennie. I don't play three-man chess.'

'So we'll teach you, man, we'll teach you, don't worry, man.'

'No, Hennie. Leave me alone.'

'But it's all fixed, man. No trouble. The boer says it's fine. All fixed, beautiful.' He smiled. 'Look, the three of us will play chess. I promise – chess. Really, man, chess. You trust me, don't you?'

'No!'

'Then come along and I'll show you you can trust me.'

'Forget it, Hennie.'

And I made to leave the cell. Hennie's leg was there, stretched across the doorway, leaning on the grille. Sweetly: 'Don't go, man, don't go. Come and play chess rather.' So it went on. Stupidly. Hellishly. No chess – yes, chess – no chess – chess. My very small cell, with Hennie's large leg stretched across, leaning on the grille.

It couldn't last. It ended when the call came for us to go down into the yard for morning exercise. One of the other politicals passed my cell and called for me to join him. Hennie left, still smiling. He didn't press his point that weekend and the following week there were no extras for me in the cell. And then Hennie, instead of being sent for further observation at Weskoppies, was upgraded and transferred into A section. His upgrading to B group came after he had served only four months of his fifteen-year sentence for rape. That was the usual promotion schedule for criminal prisoners. It took John Matthews – a political prisoner doing fifteen years – eighteen months to be upgraded, from D to C group. I hardly saw Hennie again, but he had given me a chilling idea of how difficult it could be at Central to avoid unwanted advances.

Of course, it was easy for me. Had Hennie really pressed his case with me – had I, in fact, not had an initial inclination to be polite and, instead, had told him to push off at once – I would have been all right. I had nothing to fear from Hennie. I could, as a recognized member of a recognized group (the politicals), withstand any nasty moves he might have made against me personally. I was, in a real sense, protected. Others weren't.

One night in April, there was a scream from downstairs, a scream similar to those we used to hear at night at Local: lingering, hideous in the lonely silence. It was, at Central, a sound which provoked discussion next morning. One of the hospital orderlies explained (the screamer had been taken to the hospital during the night): 'Oh, it was nothing much really: the boy was raped in the married quarters at Sonderwater [prison, outside Pretoria] and is still crying about it.'

Some others had other methods of defence. Like 'Dopey'. Dopey was a young bandiet in our workshop who had once been a keen and very proficient boxer, but he got hammered silly in a series of boxing matches in jail and he was also a prolific smoker of boom, and anything else he could lay his hands on. He once laid hands on some mal-pitte/mad-berries, a rare type of wild berry with L.S.D. effect. Punch-drunkenness and mal-pitte had left Dopey dopey. He was at Central on a four-to-eight stretch for robbery. He should have been in hospital. He wandered around the workshop all day, harmlessly chatting and singing to himself, incapable of any work. The boere tolerated him, sometimes giving him a broom to play with, sometimes trying to make him do something constructive like using a file to round off window-catches. They once tried him at a small punch-machine which stamped out small holes in sheet-iron bars – Dopey sang and chatted and joked with the machine for a couple of days, then tried, successfully, to stamp a hole through his thumb. You couldn't talk to Dopey: if he ever joined a group, it was to bum some tobacco, roll a quick 'zoll' then head off, swinging away gaily in long discussion with himself or Eileen, the girl in his head.

One night Dopey was put in a cell with two others, one of them a 'lifer' from our shop, named Don. At some stage during the evening people in cells near by heard a series of shouts, a scuffle, then silence. The next morning at the shop Dopey went past singing and chatting to himself, apparently oblivious of Don at one of the lathes, sporting two black eyes. The grapevine soon reported that Don had made a pass at Dopey in the cell and

Dopey, momentarily pausing in his monologue with Eileen, had dealt Don a neat left-right with his sugar container, and then continued his chat with Eileen.

Don's reaction to the incident typified the attitude of most long-timers: he had been locked up in a cell with two others for the night (not from asking, but because of overcrowding in the prison) and, wanting sexual relief, had gone for it where it was, right there on the mat next to him. The fact that Dopey had objected was – with a shrug – 'stiff'. There'd be others.

The third man in the cell laughed: I've been locked up like that before,' he said, 'and I just turn over and let them get on with it.'

But not everybody had Dopey's instinctive powers of defence. Central society was clearly divided into two categories: 'hawks' and hasies/rabbits. The hawks were the sexual predators: hasies were their partners, either willing victims of the hawks or bandiete who could not, like Dopey, withstand the advances of the hawks. For someone without friends or resources, Central did not offer much protection from the hawks.

Alf was a hawk. About forty, Alf had been in and out of prison for more than half his lifetime. With a long drawn-out face, long nose and thin lips, and scraggy eyebrows, he even looked like a hawk. Being an old hand at Central, he had organized himself into one of the better jobs at the workshops: storeman for the sheet-metal shop, which had the distinct advantage in that the store itself was apart from the shop, on its own, opposite the paint shop, with no resident boer and subject only to occasional checks. Sheet-metal shop storeman was a respectable and envied post at Central, corresponding in power to the C-section store-man.

The ordinary bandiete who had dealings with Alf cursed him for his respectability: you could not, they complained, do business with Alf except at the highest rates. He could, it was reported, get you anything you wanted, at a price. (Except liquor. Liquor, at Central, was unobtainable. Even the most susceptible of the smuggling boere baulked at dealing in liquor.) Alf's power derived from his links with the boere, involving not just small-time smuggling with things like tobacco and boom, but the big time too. Like when Alf arranged to issue new scaffolding to the building group and then, after it had been used only once, having it written off as scrap: a warder then saved the Prisons Department the cost of having to dispose of the scrap by kindly removing it to his home, and reimbursing storeman Alf.

So there was a mixture of surprise and delight among the bandiete when Alf got busted. One afternoon, soon after lunch, four boere burst into Alf's store and caught him with his pants down, on top of a juvenile. The news was around the shops in minutes. 'Must have been a pinch,' said Gums, 'otherwise he would've been warned.' And several others, who had suffered the strain of trading with Alf, hoped he would be 'busted' hard.

But Alf was not even charged. He spent some days locked up in the awaiting-trial section then returned to the shops, looking pale and thinner. He was demoted: taken away from the prosperity of his sheet-metal store and relegated to the ranks of us lower workers, where he was quickly lost and forgotten.

The incident gave an interesting indication of official attitude. (The fact that a juvenile was let loose with someone like Alf was, admitted one warder, a mistake. Juveniles – convicted teenagers –were normally kept separate from long-timers and transferred immediately to other prisons.) Official pronouncements, ringing with boarding-school propriety, condemned 'unnatural' sex and made great play of avoiding the evils of sodomy and homosexuality. The prison authorities could offer no solution to this 'problem', so hid behind a veil of pontifical hypocrisy. Everybody at Central – bandiete and boere alike – discussed the sex trade openly: it was, after all, the most immediately available source of social interest and was one of the few free areas of gossip between warders and bandiete. Everybody knew the hawks and everybody watched with interest to see who would be the latest hasies or laities/young boys. The official practice, as opposed to pronouncement, was to encourage rather than discourage the sex trade.

'It keeps the peace,' Mr Lappies explained to me one day. Mr Lappies was a head-warder, in charge of welding in our shop. I got to know him quite well: he was a good worker himself (he actually did work), helpful and without malice. He had a boilermaker's ticket and had worked in a private firm – but he also had a large family and was enticed into the prison service by the handsome side benefits offered: cheap housing, free medical services, reasonable pay for little work. While we worked, Mr Lappies would discuss most things with us – but never, with me, politics. Mustn't disturb the peace.

One day, Mr Lappies described why he liked doing night shifts. When you're on night shift, explained Mr Lappies, you can creep around the sections while the music's playing and peep through the judas-holes and nobody inside the cells knows you're there. It's amazing, said Mr Lappies, what some guys will get up to when they're alone, or locked up together in a cell. You should see the things some guys make. They use their radios as lizas. ('Radios' – cell blankets, according to prison practice, have to be specially folded into a tight bundle which, when complete, resembles the front of an old wireless or radio. 'Lizas' – things to lie with.) One bandiet made himself a liza out of a plastic bag: each morning he collected and stored away some pap (mielie-pap/crushed maize – the daily porridge) until he had a full bag of the stuff. It seemed, said Mr Lappies with a giggle, rather a messy sort of liza. Another bandiet made a hole in the side of his cupboard which he lined with cloth. Another had a special tin-can with a hole in it: he had fixed the tin up in the shops, then smuggled it back into the section and his cell. You'd be amazed, said Mr Lappies, what you can see when you peep through the judases on night shift.

It was spooky listening to him. As boere go, he was one of the best but he would have felt hurt if I had questioned his relish for peeping secretly through judases. Peeping into privacy, he thought, was his duty and a laugh. And the sex trade, he said, kept the peace.

There was a degree of truth in what Mr Lappies said about peace-keeping but his statement, like his voyeurism, was superficial and reflected official hypocrisy. The prison authorities wholly ducked the problems involved in locking men away, sometimes for years and years. They took no steps whatever to relieve or to compensate for the tremendous tensions which are inevitable in this state of enforced celibacy. Their attitude seemed to fluctuate between a sneer and a giggle – a dereliction which, taken with the rest of their corruption, could be either harmlessly amusing (if one was strong enough to survive) or perniciously nasty (if one wasn't).

I had already experienced something of the nastiness with Hennie in the section. In the workshops I saw how the nastiness could be really dangerous – and I saw too some of the amusement, through 'Blackie'.

Soon after I met him, Blackie said to me: 'Come and be my laitie.' After Hennie's deviousness, Blackie's directness was almost endearing. I said: 'No thanks, Blackie,' and he nodded, then went back to his mice.

Blackie, with his mice, was one of the better things about life at Central. Blackie (so-called because of his complexion) was an inveterate member of Central society. About fifty, he had spent more than twenty of those years in prison. When I met him, he had served six years of his second coat: on the previous coat, he had got out after the minimum nine years and been picked up within a week for swiping a bottle of milk from somebody's front door and a packet of sweets from a station kiosk. For these misdemeanours he got a second, mandatory nine-to-fifteen-year sentence. (These sentences are automatic. If a person is found guilty of an offence within ten years of serving, say, a two-to-four sentence, he automatically gets a five-to-eight; and thereafter a nine-to-fifteen, the 'coat', or 'nine-to-never'; and thereafter another coat; and another . . .)

Blackie was fairly relaxed about it. He was painter in the Fitters' shop. This meant he painted the protective undercoat on the metal window-frames, door-frames, doors and grilles which the shop produced. (Window-frames, door-frames, doors and grilles were made at Central Prison for new prisons elsewhere in the country.) Blackie stacked the door-frames in long rows outside the shop in such a way that he had a completely enclosed encampment within a palisade of door-frames. It was a fascinating place where you could go for a quick smoke out of sight of the boere, where you could bum spare coffee or sugar, where the boom-boys often went for a quick chestie – and where Blackie kept his mice. Blackie had once arranged a smuggle with a boer and got in a pair of white mice. The pair had 'increased quick' explained Blackie, 'like in the Bible where they begatted and begatted.' The mice were carefully housed in the series of cages Blackie spent his days making, in among his door-frames. Blackie was in business. There were very few houses on the Prison Reserve, he said, which didn't have mice from him. It was good business, bringing him a prestige he had never had outside.

'Come be my laitie,' muttered Blackie to me, within a week of his last request. (It was often difficult to make out what Blackie said: he spoke a remarkable mixture of English, Afrikaans and prison slang, and he had no teeth. He had once had a set of false teeth made for him, free, by the Prisons Department, but he had soon 'flown them off' to another bandiet for tobacco.) 'Come be laitie,' said Blackie. 'No thanks, Blackie, not today.' 'Then, OK, come look' – and he led me off, not in the least offended, to see the latest experiments on the mice.

Blackie was embarking on genetic experiments on his mice. First, tails: he chopped the tails off a pair and mated them, to see whether they would produce a breed of tail-less mice. They didn't. Next, colour. Business would be even better, he said, if he could produce different-coloured mice, maybe rainbow mice. 'Watch' – as he took first one mouse by the tail, then another, and dipped them carefully into the pot of red paint. And brought them out, wriggling and spluttering. 'It won't work like that, Blackie,' I said. 'Wait see.'

He came across the following week. 'Didn't work. They dead.' Then – 'Come and be my laitie, man.' 'No thanks, Blackie.' So he went off back to the mice – this time, he said, he'd try painting them, not dipping them. (That didn't work either.) Blackie's designs on me – which he pressed with inoffensive regularity for a couple of months – lacked Hennie's menace because, for Blackie, asking me to be his laitie was rather like asking me for a cigarette. If I said yes, well and good. If no, he could ask somebody else. If he couldn't get from anybody, he could wait until somebody said yes. There'd always be somebody, always somebody like Blackie himself who had spent so many years inside, waiting, asking around, and waiting. Blackie was no hawk like Hennie, or Alf. Or Krappies.

Krappies worked next to our welding bay on the huge bending-brake which bent and shaped sheets of metal ready for welding. Krappies, like the brake, was square and solid: he had a high, flat forehead and huge flat ears, with square mouth and jutting square jaw. Krappies looked as though he had been a convict all his life. He had. He kept complaining that the shop boere refused to transfer him to better prisons because he was so good on the bending-brake that they didn't want to lose him. This was probably true, but Krappies made it no easier for himself by working excessively hard, guarding his job jealously and, in effect, making himself indispensable.

Then Krappies got Bobo. Bobo was half Krappies's age, a handsome tough rogue, doing a two-to-four for robbery with G.B.H. (grievous bodily harm). Bobo was also bright. By Krappies's standards, Bobo was almost sophisticated. But somehow, within days of Bobo arriving in the shop, Krappies had got him: as assistant on the brake and got him, we heard, into married quarters with him in A section. Krappies now worked just as hard with Bobo straining beside him but he never complained. 'The love birds,' remarked Mr Lappies quietly, 'them's love birds.' And everybody, keeping a safe distance from Krappies's massive forearms, laughed.

Nobody discovered what actually went wrong. Everything appeared unchanged, but suddenly one afternoon, without warning, three boere dashed out of their office door in the corner of the shop and ran in behind the bending-brake. There, alone, they found Bobo putting the final touches to a key: making a key, one of the most serious crimes in jail. Bobo couldn't argue. He was led off by the boere, to the Bom and a charge of attempted escape. No Krappies. Where was Krappies? One of the bandiet-clerks who worked in the boere's office reported that Krappies had been seen, shortly before the pounce on Bobo, hastily talking to the Chief, round the side of the building. By the time Krappies reappeared at the brake, Bobo had gone. Krappies made out that he was surprised and came round to our bay, asking what had happened to Bobo. Jackie chased him away, angrily cursing him for his treachery: 'Pimp your own laitie, hey!' Krappies retreated sullenly back to work behind his bending-brake.

'Just a little lovers' tiff,' quipped Mr Lappies gaily, the next day. A little tiff, perhaps, to a boer's eyes, and well in line with normal Central practice – but it was a tiff which got Bobo an extra six months on his sentence for attempted escape, which put off his possible remission by several months, and which meant that Bobo had a permanent black mark on his record. Mr Lappies could laugh, but he knew as well as everybody what lay behind the incident: Krappies had pimped his 'lover' for his own sake. His due reward from the boere came through within a week: a transfer from Central to one of the better, more open prisons.

7 Narks

The Krappies–Bobo affair showed how the intrinsic corruption of Central society could poison everything. Nothing had value unless it could be traded: tobacco, boom, bodies, friendships – they were all commodities – and none with a greater value from the official point of view than information. We spent eight months at Central and it was inevitable – particularly as we were politicals – that we could become a focus for the attention of the narks. I had met my first nark on my first afternoon at Central but his attentions, like many we met during the time there, were too obvious and crude to be anything more than amusingly harmless. Far more serious were the attentions we received from the bigger-time narks who centred round the 'School'.

The School is a remarkable establishment presided over by an equally remarkable gent called the Schoolmaster. The School is not a school, and he is not a schoolmaster, but all one's studies are handled by him from the School. The School houses the prison library and is used on Sundays for church services.

The School is a large room on the first floor at Central, immediately opposite the Condemneds, above the Hall. You can stand at the door of the School and look across the Hall through the bars closing off the Condemneds above the huge Silence notice and through to the two huge doors leading to the gallows. This view is not altogether unrelated to the Schoolmaster himself who had, before his elevation to the intellectual heights of schoolmastering, served for many years as warder in charge of the Condemneds. Bandiet history had it that the reason for his subsequent long reign as Schoolmaster was that he, unlike his predecessors, did not smuggle the exam papers which were placed in his care for the various exams run by the School on behalf of outside educational institutions.

All prisoners, say the Prison Regulations, should be encouraged to study, but it was our impression that the encouragement had been confined largely to bandiete doing technical trade tests, some occasionally taking pre-matriculation school courses and some, very occasionally, doing undergraduate university courses. Then suddenly in the early sixties came the mass of political prisoners, most of them already with at least one university degree and all of them more than anxious to respond to the officially pronounced 'encouragement' to study.

This, it soon appeared, was not going to be quite so simple for politicals: we were granted permission to study only through one university, the correspondence University of South Africa in Pretoria, and there were several problems about the type of courses we would be allowed to follow. I was initially given permission to study for an Honours course in English and I took French as a second subject. I wrote exams in Introductory French and French I and was continuing with French II when I was told that French was banned – just as Dave Kitson's Russian course had been banned earlier and as were all language courses except German. Then I was told that no post-graduate courses were allowed – i.e. that my Honours course was to be stopped. I objected, pleaded and got nowhere, so asked to see my lawyer so that I could sue the Prisons Department for the money they had already allowed me to spend on the Honours course and which would be wasted if I could not continue. I was told I could continue the course, but had to write the exams immediately (which I did, a year before I'd wanted). This meant that I still had three years to go in prison and couldn't, for instance, do a masters. I shopped around and did a diploma in librarianship instead.

That was fine for me – I was leaving – but the ban has meant unnecessary hardship for the longer-term prisoners, like Denis Goldberg doing life. Denis came to jail with an engineering degree and registered to do a B. Administration, which he completed in three years, with three firsts. On the strength of his outstanding results, the university automatically granted him a scholarship to proceed to post-graduate studies in any of his majors. The Prisons Department refused to give him the scholarship and still persist in their ban on post-graduate studies. So Denis is now doing a B.A. in a different set of subjects and faces the prospect of proliferating undergraduate courses.

The long-term frustrations produced by this official policy of deliberate meanness were matched by the day-to-day exasperation of having to have all study matters passed through the School. The process, even when we were at Central in the same building as the School, was a tortuous one. No prisoners had direct access to the School, whether to discuss study problems or to exchange library books: library books were delivered to the sections once a week by School monitors and to get to the School you had to hand in a note in the mornings before going to the workshops and you were then, if lucky, specially called through from the mess at lunch-time. This was a hurried and aggravating procedure: you had to be accompanied by a warder, who objected to the unnecessary strain of walking from the mess to the School and back again, and there was no opportunity of getting to your cell to collect your study files or letters.

I was called through to see the Schoolmaster one lunch-time, some weeks after I had ordered several books, including the poems of Stephen Spender.

'Here,' said the Schoolmaster, dubiously handling the packet on the desk in front of him, 'is a book. You ordered a book.'

'Yes, sir, many books.'

'This,' extracting the book slowly from its wrapper, a book indeed, not a bomb, 'is one book.'

'Yes, sir.'

'This book is Poems of Edwin Spender.'

'Oh, sir, I ordered *Stephen* Spender.'

'Stephen Spender?'

'Yes, sir.'

'This is Edwin Spender.'

'That's the wrong book, sir. I ordered Stephen Spender.'

'Does it matter?'

'Sir?'

'Won't this do just as well? It *is* Spender,' he said. 'Won't it do instead?'

'Sorry, sir, no, sir.' And you feel almost cruel for causing so much anguish and unnecessary effort.

The Schoolmaster looked up hopefully but saw that I would not understand, so shrugged resignedly. Spender, Edwin, would have to be returned to the booksellers to be replaced by a similar-looking book with similar-looking words in it by a man with a similar name.

But at least this Schoolmaster did order the books and deliver them, sometimes. Then, probably because of the increased pressure of work from the exam-writing politicals, he got an assistant, a man called Rabie who had intellectual pretensions. Rabie was bone idle, so the School suited him admirably. He also thought of himself as something of a political expert, which was bad news for us politicals because this Mr Rabie was put in charge of our studies, including book orders.

I have a record of one attempted book order executed by Assistant Schoolmaster Rabie. My initial order was dated 23 October 1966, for twenty books for my Honours course, all of them taken – as required by the prison regulations – from the book-lists provided by the university lecturers. It took three months for ten of the books to arrive so, on 2 February 1967, I wrote a note to the School asking about the other ten. Silence. A month later I wrote another note. Still silence, and still no more books. After another month, on 2 May (three months after my initial query) I wrote yet again – and, a month later, got a reply from the booksellers referring to some of the outstanding books but failing to mention anything about several others. These I queried, again by way of the regulation note to the School. 'We can't,' replied Rabie, 'find the order for the books you're asking about.' This was in May, for books I had ordered seven months before. So I repeated the order, and halfway through June came another note from Rabie: 'Please repeat the order, original's lost.'

Inclinations to fury – being helplessly subject to such inefficiency – were increased by the fact that Rabie mixed his inefficiency with a considerable amount of politicking. Among the books I ordered, from the tutors' lists, were some Sartre plays and Dostoyevsky's *Brothers Karamazov*. These, I was told by

Rabie, one day in April, I could not buy. I wrote back a brief note the same night asking him why not – and, as was the p actice, handed the note in the following morning for transmission to the School. I received the note back that evening – across it was scrawled: 'Requests of this nature can only be answered on Wednesdays.' That happened on Thursday, so I had to wait till the next Tuesday night before writing the note again and handing it in on Wednesday morning: 'Why no Sartre or Dostoyevsky?' Reply that night, from Rabie: 'No reasons need be given for such decisions.' So I wrote a letter to the commanding officer, explaining that both books were recommended in my lectures, that Sartre was a leading Western European philosopher and that Dostoyevsky was a leading nineteenth-century novelist. Could he please reverse the ban on the books? The commanding officer – displaying the trait which seems common to most officials, that they *never* read *any* letter – sent the letter on to the School. Rabie sent this comment to me: 'No book – NO BOOK – by Jean-Paul Sartre will ever be allowed in by me! And Dostoyevsky also!' After that, I gave up the exercise in futility of writing to Rabie and waited for an opportunity to tell Rabie about the lovely long book which I had read in the early days of my time at Local, Dostoyevsky's *Possessed*, which I had got from his own Central Prison library. 'Makes no difference,' said Rabie, 'Sartre's a communist and Dostoyevsky's also a Russian and you can't have any of their books.'

Controlling studies was only one of a series of operations handled by the School but, involving as it did the invigilation of exams, it was the one which most required the personal attentions of the Schoolmaster. For the rest, he and Rabie relied on a number of bandiete: bandiete who controlled the issue of library books, controlled the circulation of newspapers (to A-groupers only) and magazines (to A and B-groupers only), controlled the delivery of stationery and study assignments and post, and who organized the calling of students to the School. They controlled, in bandiet terms, a great deal and to be top bandiet in the School meant being in a position to wield more power in the prison than most other bandiete and, often, more power than a large number of warders too. These bandiete were the white-collar workers of the society. Outside they were probably fraud artists, con-men, gentlemen rogues or petty cheque-snatchers and housewife cheats. Inside they quickly got jobs as jail clerks and administration men, and became, effectively, the controllers of the prison with a degree of responsibility shared only by the storemen and head cleaners.

Top bandiet in the School was Bill. It was impossible, as an ordinary bandiet at Central, fully to gauge the extent of his empire, but it was considerable and virtually bridged the gap between boer and bandiet. Bill was large and smooth, with a charm and articulateness uncommon among bandiete. He could have been a bank manager (probably had been – bandiet rumour spoke of embezzlement and extortion). Certainly, he managed the School: newspapers, books, magazines, stationery, exam timetables – if you had queries, Bill knew the answers. Rumour had it too that you could, at a price, get most things from Bill (excluding exam papers – even Bill couldn't break the Schoolmaster on that). In the best traditions of jail managers, Bill could seldom be approached directly: always through intermediaries, so you never knew whether to thank him personally for the newspaper slipped into your cupboard one weekend or to thank one of his minions, of whom there were a number. To be on the safe side, you thanked everybody.

Bill's position and obvious influence inside and outside the School meant, in terms of day-to-day peace of mind, that he was a man to be avoided. This was not as easy as it might seem because the School was also the Church hall on Sundays and Bill was supervisor of Church activities too. There were several official chaplains who visited Central: the three regulars (Catholic, Anglican and Dutch Reformed) shared the School each Sunday, holding services at different times throughout the day. There were also less frequent visits from the rabbi and ministers from denominations like the Methodists and Christian Scientists. The Sunday services were supplemented, in the case of the three regulars, by a weekday visit for private consultation.

The Sunday service was a regular draw-card, providing not only the possibility of spiritual uplift but also a necessary break from the excessively long weekend hours of lock-up. Anglicans gained an extra half-hour out after morning exercise; Catholics were opened up a full hour before the end of lunch-time lock-up. In addition, the services in the School provided an ideal and unhurried opportunity for smuggling. At the price of sitting through two hymns and a sermon, you could arrange to collect most things. The Anglican chaplain, Reverend Don Martyn, was under no illusions as to the sincerity of the majority of his congregation. I suspect he worked on the mud-slinging principle that something might stick, somewhere. At the same time, he was an affirmatively genial man, full of good sense and pleasantly lacking in aggressive piety. His services provided a short interlude of welcome entertainment, and he spiced his sermons with wit and worldly fun.

In attendance always, beside the drooping boer, was Bill – or his substitute, one 'Fire'. If you wanted to see the chaplain privately the next week, you handed your name to Bill or Fire and it was their responsibility to see that the list was handed in the following Wednesday so that your name could be called out before you left for the workshops. Rev. Martyn would arrive during the week for these private sessions and hold court in the School, at a small table on the dais across the room from the Schoolmaster. Always there to greet him was Bill, sometimes with a cup of tea, and always, I noticed, with a first-name greeting. The greeting was perhaps unimportant in itself but it did indicate the extent of Bill's familiarity – a familiarity which his deputy, Fire, a far less presentable sort of person, tried to ape. Martyn, expansive and smiling, always replied in similar manner, and warmly greeted too his old friend the Schoolmaster. Then, one by one, he would call us to his table and spend a few minutes with each of us, offering advice or comfort, and occasionally passing on greetings from friends or family outside. For many of the criminal bandiete he was far more than a friendly father-confessor: he would arrange finances for things ranging from study books to false teeth and glasses, and he was primarily concerned with finding jobs for prisoners who were about to be released. In all of this he was scrupulously fair and – while some of his ministrations could not strictly speaking be said to be in accordance with a rigid interpretation of the regulations – they were patently innocent and harmless, particularly so when viewed within the general scheme of things at Central.

But when we, the politicals, arrived, we became the unwitting wreckers of the good that Martyn had been able to do at Central. It was impossible to establish what actually happened and who did the major damage, but it is doubtful whether Bill was un-involved and certainly Fire was deeply involved in the Martyn affair. Martyn got into a great deal of trouble and so, very nearly, did we. The basic problem – and cause of all the trouble – was the inducements held out by the prison authorities to those who would trade in information. As politicals, we were fair game for the narks. Whatever we did was watched and reported. People seen associating with us were noted and, on one occasion at least, warned away. This provided the authorities with a very full account of all our movements – plus a large measure of pure fantasy. One such fantasy began circulating within weeks of our arrival at Central: the head cleaner in C2, known as Sholly, drew aside another cleaner and with ostentatious furtiveness showed him a roll of banknotes, real banknotes – which, said Sholly through the side of his mouth, had just been slipped to Lewin by Rev. Don Martyn at a spiritual consultation. I have no idea how Sholly got such a hefty roll for himself but I know that I had not, as Sholly suggested, seen Martyn that week, nor, unfortunately, did I ever have the pleasure of receiving any clandestine cash, let alone a roll as large as Sholly's.

Nothing further was heard of the bank-roll, but Sholly's story did indicate that the narks – of whom he was one of the most notorious – were busy covering all areas of our life. A month or so later, when being called on Wednesday morning to see Martyn, we were told to go to A section instead of the School, and there was Martyn, forced to hold his 'private' consultations in the company of an ever-attendant boer in a cell in the mad-house. Martyn, understandably, was most upset.

Then, shortly before we left Central, came the news that another Anglican priest, Fr Dill, had been caught in a boer–bandiet trap at Sonderwater Prison outside Pretoria, accepting a letter to post from a prisoner who had been primed by the authorities. He was immediately deported. His case seemed un-related to Martyn, until we arrived back at Local and I asked when Martyn would again visit. 'You'll never see *him* again,' said a boer, 'he's been sacked.' For several months we saw nobody, then Martyn's successor was appointed – Fr Hills – and we divined (he could never tell us anything directly, being closely attended always) that things had not been well between Martyn and the authorities at Central. The implications were that Martyn had been 'caught' at some subterfuge and had been asked to leave his work in the prisons.

We assumed that Martyn's alleged subterfuge had to do with the sort of thing Dill had been trapped into. Our assumptions seemed partially verified when, shortly after we left Central and returned to Local, seven of us were charged with smuggling letters while at Central. The charge alleged that, during 'the months October and November 1966 [we] conspired or attempt-ed, with a fellow prisoner Michael Gerhardus Hertzog Jansen van Vuuren, to smuggle an uncensored letter out of the prison'.

Michael Gerhardus Hertzog Jansen van Vuuren was Fire, Bill's deputy in the School. Fire was another white-collar criminal, a middle-aged bandiet, doing a coat for fraud. His case was complicated by the fact that his lawyer had advised him against testifying in the box when both Fire and his subse-quent advisers felt that he would have gained an acquittal had he in fact testified. One of his subsequent advisers at Central was one of us, Lewis Baker, who helped Fire draw up (and lose) an appeal – and who then continued to help him, trying to bring a private prosecution against some of the witnesses on the assump-tion that they could be discredited and so give Fire good grounds for appealing to the Prisons Department for an early release. Throughout all the time that the appeal, and then the private prosecution, were being discussed, Fire was – through Lewis – our man in the School. Fire was always willing to help any friends of Lewis's and was more reliable than other sources in supplying newspapers, and he was never reluctant to help out with other necessaries – sugar, or tobacco, or matches. Always he would smile, 'Yes, my friend,' and produce the goods without fuss.

If ever we wanted, said Fire more than once, to send out any extra letters, just let him know: he knew the boer who censored the letters and entered them in the book, and he could always work a point. My immediate reaction on hearing Fire's offer was to shy away: letters were too precious to jeopardize in any way, and letters could be evidence. Fire's offer seemed like so many other offers we got daily, bait from the narks. But I considered it, especially in the light of common practice at Central, common practice for people like Leon, down the passage from us in C section. Leon was in C group and therefore, like us, entitled to only one letter every three months – and, after the announcement in April 1966 of improved concessions, one letter every six weeks. But Leon had a wife and half a dozen girlfriends outside and all of them wrote to him regularly. He used to receive at least six letters every week – nearly a full year's quota in one week. And Leon used to reply to them all, every week. 'How?' I asked, enviously. 'Easy,' he said, 'the boere don't mind. As long as there's no filth in the letter and it's not *too* long, why should they worry? Only a few bandiete write letters anyway, they're not going to be swamped with work.'

Fire confirmed this, and repeated his offer: not to smuggle the letters out without their being censored, but merely to speed their delivery to the right boer and to ensure that he didn't keep a tally of how many were sent. There didn't seem much to be lost: if he was trying to trap us, there could be no come-back on us if we acted quite openly, handed the letters to him on the strict agreement that he would take the letters downstairs to the boer – just as, every morning, he collected from us any material for the School, and delivered it to the Schoolmaster. In the event, I don't think I gained more than one extra letter through Fire. All the letters I handed to him were duly received outside, with the Prison stamp – and I received replies, through official channels. The risks involved in any larger enterprises seemed too great to be tempting, and there was always the feeling that what went for others, like Leon, didn't go for us politicals.

Still Fire persisted in pressing to help. And all the while he was consulting with Lewis, hoping with increasing desperation to earn an early release through his private prosecution. But it was taking a long time, and Lewis noticed a change in Fire's discussion. Fire began asking different questions: questions about Lewis's past, about political groups and church groups, opposition groups. And wouldn't it be possible, asked Fire, for him to join the Communist Party? Fire, it appeared, had despaired of getting his release through his own actions. Now he was going to get it through the Special Branch, using us. And, I suspect, Rev. Martyn. Martyn was asked to leave. We were presented with a charge sheet alleging misconduct during the final two months only of our stay at Central, whereas, in fact, most of the dealings with Fire had been before those two months, before the time he suddenly started asking Lewis about joining the C.P., before the time, presumably, when he first began hatching his plot with the boere.

The end of the affair was sad because it affected the only person who should *not* have been affected: Don Martyn. Martyn was sacked, I'm sure, largely because of false evidence insinuated against him by Fire and others. The charges against us were almost welcome: they gave us an opportunity to see our lawyers and, more important, raised the possibility of exposing, in open court, some of the malpractices of Central. We gave our lawyers a pretty full picture of what happened at Central and they, we heard, discussed the matter with the authorities – who decided, not to our surprise, that they would not press the charges.

The case was actually even more bizarre than seemed apparent at the time. When our lawyers went to discuss the case with the commanding officer at Central, they found that he was totally unaware of the case. He had heard nothing about it, had not instigated it, nor sanctioned it. He began calling in various of his staff whom we knew to be involved in the case. Gradually the pattern emerged of an elaborate intrigue, of which we politicals were only a part: an intrigue hatched at the Prisons Department headquarters by the O.C.'s antagonists who had set out not only to shelf us but also to discredit the commanding officer for having allowed such things to take place in his prison. I was not surprised, after those months at Central, to learn about chicanery in high places. It confirmed my view of Central as a mirror of the outside South African society: a rotten regime, devoid of moral justification, maintaining control through deceit and double-dealing, and, in the process, befouling everyone.

One lunchtime in November – 14 November 1966 – our names were called out 'for the School'. As we were being led off from the mess we realized that the list of names called included only politicals. We got to the Hall to find the entrances closed off and there, spread across the Hall's vastness, fifteen pairs of boere (some familiar, very familiar), two boere for each of us.

'Kom,' they said, 'back to Local.'

8 Back to Local

Issy Heymann – who, during five years in prison (for member-ship of the Communist Party), never failed to have a joke to suit every occasion – once told of the man who goes to hell and, being well-connected, is offered three choices of residence, on condition that any choice he makes is irrevocably final. He is shown first into a chamber of fire where writhing figures scream in sweaty agony – No thanks, he says. He is taken into a second chamber, icy, full of shivering forms in freezing anguish – Not for me, he says. The third chamber consists of a slow-flowing, stinking sewer: several occupants stand up to their knees in the sludge, daintily sipping tea from bone-china cups. Ah yes, says the man, this I prefer – and he steps forward boldly, just as one of the satanic guards yells out: 'OK, mob, tea-break's over. Back on your heads!'

Going back to Local Prison from Central Prison seemed, in many ways, to be going back on our heads. The tea-break at Central was over: no more daily news broadcasts, no more smuggleable tobacco or newspapers or extra goodies, no more work in the workshops, no more movies or music, no more of any of the advantages of being in a community of several hundred other bandiete. We were back on our heads, in the same isolated section at Local, with the same small yard and the same smashed face of du Preez there to greet us.

But for all its advantages in terms of daily comfort, I don't think any of us really minded leaving Central. It had been a place of death and corruption and to be back at Local was like being back home, among the familiar things of old. Du Preez was familiar, and clearly no different personally. But he was no longer in sole charge of our section: a chief-warder had been brought in, immediately above him, a challenge to du Preez's authority which was confounded for him by the fact that the new man, Van Staden, was at least ten years his junior, and already a rank ahead of him.

Van Staden had occasionally deputized for du Preez during our 90-day detention at Local and had once brightened my weekend by telling me that, if anybody tried to liberate me from my cell, he would take great pleasure in preventing that by throwing bombs into the cells and locking us in. Nevertheless, Van Staden was an improvement on du Preez and some sort of conflict between them was inevitable. We watched anxiously during the next few months to see who would win the confrontation. Occasionally we could help: Van Staden and du Preez began playing chess together at lunch-time and I taught Van Staden Fool's Mate, which he proceeded to use against du Preez, regularly, every couple of days, never failing to mate in four, using the same moves day after day. We needed some mild diversion of that sort to take our minds off the fact of being back with du Preez and being subject, it appeared, to an attempted re-imposition of the old hard-time regime.

Soon after our return, the man responsible for the treatment of all political prisoners, Colonel Aucamp, visited the prison and ranted at us. We had, he thundered, been 'superior and unco-operative' at Central. We still had to learn, he said, who was in charge. He was wrong. We knew who was in charge: he, Aucamp, was in charge, and du Preez was his favourite running dog. Back with our mailbags and isolation, we were clearly in for another battle with du Preez, where life would again be reduced to simplicity and squabble, toothpaste and toilet paper. Du Preez was known well by old-hand bandiete at Central: they called him simply 'Kaffir'.

In those first few months back at Local, I decided to keep a tally of our battle with du Preez because I thought I would never properly be able to remember how ridiculous and petty were the things that caused the crises in our lives. I am glad now that I did keep the notes because I would never have remembered. I drew them up in the form of a sort of profit and loss account of the battle (another borrowing from school-days) – from the middle of November 1966 till the middle of August

1967, by the end of which I had completed my first thousand days in prison.

The account went something like this:

18.11.66   Aucamp says we cannot swap each other's books. Borrowing is verboten.

21.11.66   Du Preez finds Bram Fischer washing his hands in the newly built basins in our bathroom and combing his hair in the newly installed mirrors. I thought, says Bram, they were for us. Moenie dink nie, says du Preez – don't think; a prisoner must never think.

22.11.66   Yes, says the commanding officer, those *are* your basins and mirrors. You may use them.

23.11.66   Du Preez bans any books being taken into the yard at exercise time.

24.11.66   Du Preez bans all talking while mailbags are being sewn. The O.C. confirms the ban on books in the yard.

25.11.66   We get a tennis ball, so can again play 'squash' against the wall with hands.

28.11.66   Eisenstein, Arenstein and Trewhela are charged for disobeying an order. The three had been exercising round the yard with Laredo who stopped with a sore foot. They stopped too. Walk, said Van Staden. Why? asked Eisenstein. Because you must. Why? Because I say so. I prefer to stand still, says Eisenstein, to talk to Laredo. Laredo can stop, says Van Staden, the rest of you walk – or else. No, say the three, we'll stand, not walk. So they get charged. Jack Tarshish is charged for being in possession of illicit goods, found during a cell search: i.e. a newspaper cutting, found tucked into a book.

29.11.66   Jack reveals that the contraband cutting was in fact hidden *before* we went to Central and had travelled there and come back again, without detection.

29.11.66   Headquarters say: No, I may not send a letter to a lawyer, Miss Pat Davidson, asking her to handle my affairs. Let my wife handle everything for me.

I have no wife. (I wrote to Pat after Aucamp told

me I could no longer see my former attorney, Ruth Hayman, because she had been banned. I appeal to the O.C.)

30.11.66 All our 'late light' cards removed from our doors on the grounds that we're finished exams and therefore no longer studying. (The cards gave us, as students, lights till 11 p.m. instead of the usual 8 p.m. for non-studying prisoners.)

1.12.66 We appeal to commanding officer who says OK, keep your cards.

8.12.66 Charges against Eisenstein and Co. all dropped after intervention by lawyers.

14.12.66 There will, says du Preez, be no extra visits for Christmas.

17.12.66 Van Staden, on du Preez's off-weekend, allows us at lunch-time to be locked up with more than three in the large cells, thus allowing us to 'entertain' friends during the lunch-time lock-up.

19.12.66 Yes, says the O.C., you have no wife – so you can send letter to lawyer.

22.12.66 Yes, says O.C., you will be allowed one extra half-hour visit for Christmas.

2.1.67 No, says du Preez (starting off the New Year), you may *not* entertain friends at lunch-time.

10.1.67 No, says H.Q., you may not order 'foreign literature' (in reply to my request to order *The Times Literary Supplement*).

13.1.67 Friday the 13th – good day for bandiet's luck: I get upgraded to B group, so there are now four of us officially allowed to buy tobacco (and supply another eight secret smokers).

14.1.67 Van Staden again allows communal lunches.

21.1.67 Du Preez again bans communal lunches.

22.1.67 I may not order *Newscheck* (a fortnightly news magazine from Johannesburg. My B group status allows me two magazines a week).

I may order *Die Huisgenoot* (an Afrikaans family weekly magazine).

24.1.67   I'm stopped from continuing my English Honours studies: H.Q. says no more post-graduate studies. (H.Q. had allowed me to register for this three-year-minimum course the previous year and I had already spent considerable time and money working at it.)

29.1.67   I see my lawyer, Pat Davidson, about my Honours and ask her to investigate an action against the Prisons Dept for stopping my studies. (She contacts Helen Suzman, who contacts the Minister of Justice – and, on 8 February 1967, I get permission to continue – until the ban's imposed again at the end of 1968 and I have to write the exams immediately.)

2.2.67   Great excitement: no du Preez in the section and rumour that he's been transferred.

3.2.67   Crunch: du Preez's not transferred – merely looking after Lewis Baker in hospital.

3.2.67   We can, says O.C., borrow books from each other (thus legalizing common clandestine practice).

7.2.67   Du Preez screams at Schermbrucker for pointing out that the mailbags we have to repair are rotten, filthy, irreparable. Du Preez screams at Ernst for daring to go into someone else's cell.

11.2.67   Du Preez (having a ball) refuses to give Lewis Baker his tobacco order: Lewis is out of snout and knows the orders have come. Wait till Monday, says du Preez.

    Du Preez interrupts Laredo's visit to prevent 'news' being transmitted.

12.2.67   Du Preez stops Heymann at a visit telling his wife about Baker's trip to hospital.

18.2.67   Van Staden again allows communal lunches.

25.2.67   Du Preez again bans communal lunches.

26.2.67   Du Preez says the O.C. also bans communal lunches.

28.2.67   Van Staden, in civvies, visits section and says good-bye: he's leaving, to go farming.

    (Du Preez, we had to admit, was having a good run. Round One of the battle very definitely to him. And there wasn't, immediately, much sign of improvement for us.)

2.3.67 Du Preez decrees that Jock Strachan, back with us for a year and not allowed to study, may not borrow our books.

3.3.67 Du Preez refuses to accept letter from Dave Evans asking to see a specialist. (Dave had been suffering, for over a month, from a severe type of diarrhoea, unsuccessfully treated by the prison doctor.)

4.3.67 John Laredo initiates the first Saturday morning lecture. The O.C. had sanctioned this self-education-entertainment idea of ours. Laredo's offering: first steps in sociology.

9.3.67 No, says H.Q., I may not order *Le Monde Hebdomadaire* as recommended in my French notes.

Seven of us charged with trying to smuggle letters through Fire van Vuuren while at Central.

21.3.67 No, says du Preez, no books allowed in the yard during the day. (This was after the mailbag supply had run out and we were left in the yard with nothing to do.) Du Preez ordered the warders to hand out brushes and soap – with which to scrub the concrete gutters. We scrubbed the clean gutters and scrubbed the slate paving and scrubbed the brick walls and scrubbed the urinal.

28.3.67 Helen Suzman visits. She was not allowed the previous facility to see everybody, so had to choose one prisoner. I was the one. The visit was held upstairs, in the lawyer's room adjoining the usual visiting boxes, with a sort of post-office grille between us.

A fearsome assignment for me because I had to present the grievances of the whole community: lack of upgrading, lousy work, study problems, no news and no remission, and a clear policy, via du Preez, of giving us a bad time – e.g. with absolutely *no* possibility of smuggling *anything*, still we are searched twice every day, in and out of the yard. The visit lasts about two hours, with du Preez standing outside the window of the room, but no interruptions.

A bad cell-skud the same morning, which

uncovered sugar kept in several cupboards, and a chunk of bread rolled in a vest, under Arenstein's cupboard.

30.3.67 Yes, we may, says the chief, keep sugar in our cells, but we may not keep bread, especially if rolled in prison clothing.

(The same day saw the first of the reforms arising from Helen Suzman's visit, the nature of which made it difficult for some to decide whether it was profit or loss: the lunch-time lock-up was reduced by an hour, thus getting us out into the yard earlier, to sew mailbags, and thus also reducing what had by then become a common and welcome aspect of life at Local, a long lunch-time schloff/siesta. In principle anyway, it was a plus for us, and promised more to come.)

31.3.67 Yes, of course – says the O.C., with unusual and ill-fitting charm – of course you can take books into the yard, any time.

15.4.67 John Matthews is brought back from hospital (piles operation) in great discomfort – but a bed is moved into our cell for him. A real bed, with a mattress.

20.4.67 Du Preez storms at Jock Strachan for shaving after breakfast, not before.

23.4.67 Fischer and Laredo are called to the front, as representatives of the rest, to be read a letter from the Commissioner of Prisons replying to a number of requests. None of the requests granted – but unprecedented that he, boss-man, should reply in this way. Also, he specifically states that parole applications *will* be considered.

(His parole bit turned out to be a meaningless platitude, which served at the time only to raise some useless flutters of hope.)

1.5.67 May Day message, via Eli Weinberg's visit, that Bram Fischer had been awarded the Lenin Peace Prize. Bram admits he's known for some time.

4.5.67 Hurried visitation from the O.C. in the morning to announce that Evans and Goldberg would shortly be seeing a specialist about their diarrhoea. General puzzlement about the major's sudden show of concern: it's two months since Evans first asked for a specialist, and was refused.

Puzzlement solved the same afternoon: arrival in the yard, with free access to all of us, of Mr Senn, special representative of the International Red Cross, and an accompanying Red Cross doctor. They personally interviewed everybody, with no interference at all from the boere. (It was obscene, watching du Preez being charming.)

5.5.67 Evans and Goldberg see specialist about their continuing stomach ailment.

8.5.67 We all get new blankets.

16.5.67 Our case (letter-smuggling) has apparently been postponed, probably forever. (We heard no more about it.)

17.5.67 New regulations announced: C groupers now get one letter a month, not every six weeks.

25.5.67 Yes, we may buy a small cricket bat.

26.5.67 Du Preez refuses to pass my once-a-month personal letter out: 500 words, yes, but it's 'too telegraphic'. He can't understand some of the things I say – and he must, he says, be able to know about everything I write. He won't return the letter – says I must write another – first one's for the file.

31.5.67 Second letter, he says, still too telegraphic. Write another – and another for the file.

1.6.67 Yes, we may cover the pane-less windows and mesh openings with sheets of plastic – for the winter.

2.6.67 (My way of testing the political climate:) I apply again for permission to buy a pair of nail clippers. Permission refused – use a razor blade.

3.6.67 The daily yard searches stop. The O.C. says he told du Preez to stop them a month ago.

4.6.67 Du Preez intervenes at a visit to stop the visitor telling her husband that war had broken out in the Middle East. Husband and wife protest, pointing out they have relatives in Israel. Du Preez maintains the ban –

and is later backed up by the O.C.: nothing's happening, he says, about which we need know anything.

6.6.67 The doctor prescribes a daily pint of milk for Baruch Hirson's ulcer. Du Preez has the order cancelled on the grounds that a milk bottle is a dangerous weapon.

7.6.67 A smooth concrete square is laid in the yard to replace the rickety, bumpy slabs of slate on which we play 'boop squash'.

10.6.67 A visitor mentions having just come from a service at which prayers of thanksgiving were offered for the ending of the Middle East hostilities. (That must, we reckoned, have been a damn short war.)

13.6.67 Raymond Eisenstein, sentenced with me to the same seven years, disappears suddenly. Du Preez and the boere refuse to comment. We hear later that Ray's been released and deported, following representations by his family, as had also happened earlier to Spike de Kellar and Tony Trewk. Nice to know it can happen.

26.6.67 (A neutral observation on the state of things by John Matthews: 'Freedom Day is here – and so are we'.)

30.6.67 The O.C. comes specially to tell us that Mrs Suzman has been granted permission to give us a record-player, with loudspeakers.

1.7.67 Du Preez attends the sixteenth of our Saturday morning lectures: Norman Levy on historiography. After the lecture, he confiscates Norman's notes – which outlined various approaches to history, including the marxist – and announced shortly afterwards that there would be no more Saturday morning lectures.

(Previous lectures included Hirson on physics and maths; Goldberg on dam- and bridge-building; Weinberg on photography; and Lewin on Falstaff.)

7.7.67 Another visit, to me, by Helen Suzman; still in lawyer's room, but shorter. The music, she says, should be here by next week. Have there been improvements in our sports facilities?

(26.7.67 Du Preez takes Jack Tarshish to the dentist at Central. Jack overhears a conversation with a Central boer. Central Boer: Kan jy hulle mooi ry?/Can you ride them nicely? Du Preez: Nee, dis jammer/No, unfortunately, we can't any more.)

27.7.67 Poles are installed in the yard, so that on . . .

29.7.67 . . . we can fumble through our first game of volleyball (which was, for the next four years or so – while there were enough bandiete left to play it – to become our greatest source of entertainment, every weekend).

1.8.67 Another neutral event, possibly good in the sense that it happened at all, but futile for what it meant productively: a visit from no less than the (acting) State President, Tom Naude, with a flutter of Special Branchmen in close attendance: the only man with the ultimate power of reprieve over all prisoners. What chance was there, Bram Fischer asked him (two white heads nodding together), of political prisoners getting remission and amnesty? Oh, said the State President, oh yes, he hoped there would be a chance. He sincerely hoped so. And passed on.

2.8.67 Loudspeakers installed in each cell, but . . .

3.8.67 . . . still no music. The O.C. ordains: we will never, *never*, be allowed to control the record-player ourselves. Only full sides of records will be played. And remember: the music is a privilege, not to be abused.

4.8.67 More new regulations announced – incredible: henceforth, everybody in all groups is allowed tobacco. Everybody allowed three photographs (maximum 6 ins × 8 ins – previously, only one photo, for A's and B's). Everybody can buy playing cards (previously verboten). Visits: C's, one half-hour a month from one person; B's, one a month from two at a time; A's, two a month from two.

 Letters: 500 words – C's, one a month; B's, three a month; A's, five a month.

(5.8.67 Unprecedented sight at Local, Saturday morning in the yard: four bandiete perched on their stools around an upturned water canister, playing bridge, cigarettes or pipes in their mouths – and watched, almost benignly, by du Preez.)

7.8.67 Our first night of our own music – from a remarkably long-wearing collection of two dozen records sent in by Mrs Suzman: Brahms' four symphonies, Beethoven's Triple and Brahms' Double, Beethoven's 9th, Mozart horn concertos, a Richter recital, an Oistrach recital, Chopin's 1st piano, and a Bach harpsichord recital.

(The collection had to be long-wearing from all points of view: we played from it, every night for a couple of hours, for the next three months, until we eventually got permission to supplement the collection with our own purchases, once every two months.)

23.8.67 Another unexpected visit from the International Red Cross man, Senn, with two welcome surprises. The first, a slab of chocolate for each of us. The second, a hint that there would soon be changes in the official attitude about upgrading us.

(A good night: chewing through a whole slab of chocolate, saving none of it on the basis that one slab in the stomach is worth more than any number in a boer's pocket – and wondering whether, at last, there might be a breakthrough for us on grouping, at last letting us have some of the rudimentary privileges given as a matter of course to all criminal bandiete.)

24.8.67 Yes, indeed: C group for three former D's, B group for four former C's, and – most remarkable – after serving more than two thirds of their sentences, Baker and Levy get to the top, A group. A group, with two half-hour visits a month, five letters a month (reduced later to three), and the right to buy groceries from the canteen with the monthly order – but, warns du Preez: A group for us does *not* mean what it means for ordinary bandiete: for us, *no* newspapers, *no* radio, *no* contact visits, *never*!

But still, A group – and when the two privileged

gents got their first grocery order (maximum allowance R3 – £1.50, including tobacco and toiletries) they made an illicit share-out of instant coffee, and some cocoa, and we sat in our cells and mixed our first mugs of our own coffee, thinking back through more than two or three years to the time when we began there in Local, when the psychos had laughed and said we'd never get A group, never be allowed to smoke, never never never.

We thought back to those early times and, with mugs of cold coffee, offered a preliminary toast to Jock Strachan, whose articles in the *Rand Daily Mail* first broke open the prison system, and to Helen Suzman and the others who continued to push and keep watch. We'd come quite a way – in what was, for me, my first 1,000 days inside. But that was only a preliminary toast. We had a long way to go yet. We were still, for instance, sleeping on mats on the floor, in cells which contained neither toilets nor running water.

All that would change, we heard mid-way through 1967, when we moved into the new prison being built for us, just over the wall. By November 1967 we could even see it, just rising above the far wall when you stood at the opposite end of the yard. It would, they said, be a real five-star prison. Wait and see. We waited, till the end of 1968, a long year.

There was never much, in our day-to-day lives, to entertain us and you cannot, like at school, be expelled from jail. You can never get away from the routine, except very occasionally, like the once I was taken into town in Pretoria to a dentist because the equipment in the prison was too archaic. I was in full prison uniform, with corduroy jacket and khaki longs, plus handcuffs – 'bangles' – and two armed warders to watch me. I stepped out of the prison van with my bangles and all, out on to a pavement full of people, full of life. Beautiful. We walked through a passage full of people, strangers in strange beautiful colours, short dresses and long legs, walking easily and unconcerned, where they liked, and we waited, my two attendant boere and me in my bangles, at the lift – and there was a young mother with her kid, and others there too, and they all looked down at my bangles as we approached and they all, with my boere, seemed embarrassed, shy of the young bandiet in his bangles. But the kid wasn't, and the bandiet wasn't, and the kid danced in front of his mother in front of the lift, laughing up at her, and laughing when I rattled the bangles for him as we jived for a few brief seconds together outside the lift, living a brief full life in front of the lift, dancing to the tinkling rattle of the bangles. Then the lift-doors opened and the boere, awkwardly, held me back to avoid our sharing the lift with the kid and his mother and the other shy silent strangers whom I could not tell how good it was to see them, and the dancing child.

But outings like that were rare and the distractions, inside, were few. Our work, sewing mailbags, was a meaningless drudge and we built our lives instead around various horizons: our studies, with short-term horizons for each university assignment due, each corrected script returned; and the occasional contacts with the outside, letters and visits, which provided most important long-term horizons. So during 1965, we thought we would try to provide some sort of a horizon for ourselves to coincide with the inevitable horizon of Christmas.

9 The Courtyard Players

Our first Christmas together – in 1964, within a month of sentence for most of us – had been especially hellish. There had been nothing to mark it as special except that we were locked up for even longer than at a normal weekend – and, during the morning exercise, the chief had produced a packet of old, very dry, very dark tobacco with which we had rolled some large inelegant zolls in brown paper. Still newly abstinent at that early stage of our sentences, we had grabbed the opportunity of temporary official goodwill, had smoked hard for an hour or so and been soundly sick. By Christmas 1965 we had had a long nasty year in which to dream up something more worth-while to mark the occasion. (It was an indication of the background of most of us that Christmas was regarded as a time of celebration, albeit secular, particularly a time when people remember their families.) The Regulations listed, mysteriously, 'a concert' as one of the possible diversions offered to prisoners, of which we had been offered none. May we, we asked, hold a concert over Christmas? What concert? asked the O.C. We drew up a tentative programme: songs, carols and one or two turns, all revolving around a play-reading. OK, said the O.C., but remember that the play cannot contain women: you are forbidden, in a male prison, to represent women, in any shape or form.

Dave Evans (thirty, ex-journalist from Durban, doing the Sabotage Act's five-year minimum) directed the play-reading. What play? Not easy, with only a few study texts available, even fewer potential actors – and no women. The solution that year was to choose extracts from Eliot's *Murder in the Cathedral*: the Archbishop's early 'Now is my way clear' speech, his murder and the final justification by the knights. Short, fairly stark, no women, and not unsuited to the courtyard at Local: black slate floor, concrete gutters, brown brick walls, watched by barred windows.

It began as a play-reading. Dave allotted the parts and then each of us borrowed the one copy of the play during a week of nights, writing out our own parts, with cues, ready for the first reading – in the yard, as far away from the others as possible in a 15 ft × 40 ft space, huddled into a corner during Saturday morning exercise. (No mailbags at weekends, so we had a Saturday morning exercise of a couple of hours, sometimes more.) First a read through the parts individually, then once together. Try, said Dave, without scripts next Saturday. Impossible, objected Marius Schoon – one of the knights. Try, said Dave.

We tried and it worked. We'll do the play, said Dave, without scripts, as if in performance. Maybe with a couple of props too.

Props? How to create any semblance of props, or costumes, when you've nothing: no tools, no access to any materials, or shops, and no desire to approach the authorities for anything. Props – with nothing except rudimentary cleaning equipment and clothing in the section, and mailbags, mailbag needles and rags. Denis Goldberg said he'd handle it – what did we want? (Denis, then thirty-three, former engineer, one of the Rivonia trialists, doing life.)

From nothing, the play and its props grew. We could rehearse only in exercise times: the short half-hours during the week, the longer times at weekends. But we'd decided to try the play only in mid-November and there wasn't much time – nor was it possible to rehearse every day, in between the normal prison routines of cleaning pots, washing clothes and, all day every day of the week, sewing mailbags. Some stolen times, like when you write your part out on a small piece of paper and slip it into the mouth of the mailbag on your knee – time to learn lines between stitches.

It was a focus, involving not only those of us actually acting but virtually the entire community. A focus for everybody on something definite, something there ahead, for Christmas, that would be happening, that might even be entertaining. Exciting times.

Which du Preez, unerringly, managed to spoil. Dave had asked – and been granted – permission for the 'Christmas concert' to be in two parts: a short business of songs and carols on Christmas Day (a Saturday, that year 1965) with the main part of the concert on the Boxing Day holiday, the following Monday. Christmas Day itself went well, with the carols and songs and small Goldberg-made gifts for everybody. We did a final run-through of the play on the Sunday, tensed in dramatic anticipation for the following morning's Big Night and the launching of the play for its one performance, Grand Opening, Grand Finale, all for the exclusive entertainment of a highly exclusive audience. We invited the O.C., but didn't expect him to come. He didn't.

Du Preez came. 'Mailbags,' he said. 'Prisoners don't get Boxing Day as a holiday,' he said. 'No play today – mailbags. The play can wait till Saturday. Today, mailbags.'

It was one of those moments, common with du Preez, of extreme, very tight, ready-to-burst, ready-to-scream anger. Du Preez, leaning in the doorway, smiling with closed eyes – mailbags. And us, already keyed up and going, already thinking through the parts, going beyond the small petty structures which enclosed us, ready for a moment's release in something done by us, for us. Mailbags, he says. Ready to burst and scream and let loose, ready to spit scream kick scratch tear into the grinning flat face of scorn and try to mark it, try to break its sneering calm. But that perhaps would wreck the chance of the play next Saturday, perhaps stop the chance of possible Christmases ahead, so many Christmases ahead. Therefore calm, calm, sore hard calm – leaving Evans, his nose white with the anger we suppress, to re-negotiate, seek again permission from the O.C., and give us another horizon, Saturday next.

The delay gave Denis time to add to his assembled props and produce a programme: the Courtyard Players present excerpts from T. S. Eliot's *Murder in the Cathedral* – Priest: Costa Gazides; Knights: Dave Kitson, Alan Brooks, Paul Trewhela, Marius Schoon; Beckett: Hugh Lewin – with scurrilous biographies of each of the players, and the final credit to 'the Special Branch and Prisons Department, without whose efforts these actors could not have been brought together'. One copy only of the programme, hand-written, and illustrated (by Paul Trewhela), and later lost (to du Preez) in a cell-search.

There was no stage – just the far corner of the yard, in the sun beneath the walls with their barred windows, and the black slate floor – and the short line of a dozen stools, the audience, all those not actually acting. No visitors. No guests. In the corner, two small cell-tables, covered with a sheet, made the altar. (The sheet was the only outside prop, borrowed for the morning from the hospital. We had no sheets in our section.) On the altar, a white crucifix: made, by Denis, of cardboard from the carton in which came the section's toilet rolls, and white because there was only white paint in the section, a little left over from the time du Preez wanted spots painted on the yard floor to mark where we had to sit, five yards apart, while sewing mailbags. The knights each carried short (white) daggers (toilet-roll carton) and were dressed, under Denis's direction, in tights and jerkins. The jerkins were short-sleeved jerseys turned back-to-front, the tights were long-sleeved jerseys worn as trousers, with a leg through each arm, and made decent by a pair of P.T. shorts. The priest wore a monk's habit of cassock and cowl: a dark cell-blanket, cunningly stitched on to him with mailbag needle and thread; and sandals – of mailbag string wound round the toes and up round the ankles.

My robes as archbishop were grandest of all: the same blanket-habit, set off with red and white edging (white rags, dyed with red ink) and the same sandals, made into boots by continuing the criss-crossed string up the calves. Plus embroidered stole – bits of white rag sewn together and scribbled on with red and blue ball-point. Plus episcopal ring – plaited mailbag string, adorned with ruby, cardboard dyed red. Plus magnificent eighteen-inch mitre (cardboard, with glued-on rag overlay), embroidered, with embossed cross and tassels (stripped rags).

We dressed in one of the cells while the audience in the yard was kept entertained to a concert, compèred by Dave Kitson in raucous music-hall grandeur with boater and bow-tie (cardboard) and striped jacket (prison- issue pyjama jacket). No curtain, just the line of wooden stools and the people we saw every day, sitting waiting in the clothes they wore every day. Murder, in the courtyard, on New Year's Day 1966.

Beckett talked, the priest warned and pleaded, the knights arrived and did their deed, leaving Beckett slumped on the slate (very hot) under his blanket with the altar sheet added (very sweaty) so that the tables could be moved forward to become the lectern for their justification speeches. At the end, a short ripple of applause, no curtain, and a brief gathering around while the audience came forward to examine the costumes more closely. That was that. Only two boere had watched, from a distance, du Preez and another, leaning against the door. Soon after the play finished, he called the usual 'Time' – lunch-time lock-up, and the end of the festivities for a year.

It did not seem likely, the next year – 1966 – that we would do anything at all for Christmas: that was the year of our stay at Central and we returned to Local half-way through November, hardly a month before Christmas. The initial shock and flurry of being back absorbed most time and thoughts, until Dave again agreed to get something going. Again the problems: few available texts, few props, dwindling actors (Costa and Alan of the previous cast, both gone) – and no women.

In the event, the choice for the second play was more ambitious, and the production itself far more spectacular than the first. We did excerpts from Shakespeare's *Henry IV* – the Gadshill robbery and the scenes in the Boar's Head after the robbery, with much cutting and arranging, making it something of a cameo-piece between Hal and Falstaff – and we smuggled Mistress Quickly into Local by making her a landlord.

Because of the lack of time available, we planned a small production, with simple costumes, no props. But we planned without considering the ingenuity of Jock Strachan – artist by trade, remarkably practical and (fortunately for us) not allowed to study during his second stretch of a year (a mean deprivation imposed by a sulking Prisons Department still obviously angry about the revolution that Jock's revelations had caused within South African prisons). Barred from studying and barred, by du Preez, from borrowing books from the rest of us, Jock used to disappear into his cell at evening lock-up (barred also, by du Preez, from the possibility of sharing a cell) and produce, next morning, a glittering piece of makeshift beauty: swords with bejewelled handles (putting sweet papers to good use), scabbards in different colours (glued-on rags, with ink dyes), belts and huge buckles (cardboard), rings for fingers (sweet papers) and bells for edging Falstaff's cloak (bells from silver paper, the cloak from a number of floor rags, carefully washed and sewn together).

My costume (as Hal) was typical. I had a pair of boots – real, calf-high boots, designed by Jock and made by John Matthews from mailbag rags: with pointed, curving-up toes; and a set of spurs (cardboard, covered with silver paper) with rowels that rotated; and scalloped edging (of white rag, trimmed with red ball-point). I had a jerkin (reversed jersey) neatly laced across with cord (dyed string, plaited) and embossed with gold buttons (chocolate paper). My tights were the now-usual long-sleeved jersey worn upside-down, but improved by the addition of a pair of pantaloons: to make pantaloons you draw on a pair of pyjama trousers, upside-down, pulling the legs right up into your crutch, then pull up the top of the trousers and fasten. And a short cloak (coloured floor rags, washed and sewn together); a sword with cloth scabbard; a regal ring; all topped off with a jaunty hat: the hat was a pair of rugby shorts, worn with the elastic round my forehead and the rest tossed into shape by a few deft movements from Jock, then fastened with a large red feather nicked from the section duster and dyed in red ink.

Paul Trewhela did a marvellous Falstaff – made complete, by Jock, with bulging belly, boots, cloak, sword, and an almost successful wig and moustache (ruffled-out scraps of mailbag string) which transformed Paul's regulation clean-shaven, short-hair locks into boozy exuberance. Similar variations of costume for the rest too: John Laredo and Baruch Hirson, briefly making their stage debut as muttering, robbed travellers, in blanket-cloaks and silly hats; Lewis Baker as Master Quickly in landlord's apron, offering wine from an impressive flagon (milk bottle, dangerous weapon, borrowed briefly for the day and covered with silver paper); and Jock himself and Marius

Schoon as Poins and Gadshill, colourfully completing the cast.

That was the startling effect Jock produced: colour, where there was no colour; colour, briefly, in the dull sameness of the yard's gloom. We had something of a stage too: in our absence at Central, a clothes line, with several strands, had been built at the end of the yard. Jock draped blankets over the line, some forward, some back, making a backdrop and battens from behind which we could enter. But we first had to get behind the blankets by walking into the yard through the only door – and thus in front of the assembled audience, seated as before on its short line of stools. We marched in from the section and, I remember, they gasped: the less-than-a-dozen members of our audience, none of whom had been allowed to see the costumes beforehand, gasped as we flaunted past in our colours and finery, gasped and clapped spontaneously as we disappeared behind the blanket battens. After that sort of opening, you can't lose: Norman Levy, readily on hand as Prompt (there'd not been long for preparation), wasn't needed. The show was a wow.

It was over in about half an hour. The audience spent about five minutes investigating the costumes. And that was that. (Except that I managed to keep my mailbag boots which, minus their spurs, were the most comfortable shoes I'd worn in jail. I lined the soles with rags and wore them, warmly, as slippers through all the winters ahead.)

By the end of the next year – 1967 – Jock Strachan had been released, so had Paul Trewhela and Lewis Baker of the Shakespeare cast. The prospects of putting on something to match the Boar's Head seemed remote. We needed, we thought, something smaller – so Dave Evans, rightly established now as producer/director, chose something which might have seemed smaller but which was, under the circumstances, far more ambitious and more difficult to stage than either of our earlier productions: Harold Pinter's *Dumb Waiter*, a modern black comedy, with only two actors in a full-length play. Dave thought it might be possible because he thought Dave Ernst and myself could do Ben and Gus, two gangsters waiting in a basement for instructions to rub out their next victim – and because the three of us shared a cell and thus had an ideal set-up for rehearsing.

But besides the obvious and considerable difficulties involved in staging a play which has only two characters (and makes great demands on one's line-learning capacity), *Dumb Waiter* had additional problems for us, inside. It required the presence on the stage of an actual dumb waiter – one that worked, capable of being shot up and down, carrying plates with a variety of goodies on. Could we make it? And the set required two beds. We had no beds. And the gangsters, to look at all authentic, had to be dressed in ordinary outside clothes. We had only prison khaki and corduroy. The script required a number of fairly ordinary items which, inside, were impossible: revolvers, shoulder holsters, a packet of crisps, an Eccles cake (*what* is an Eccles cake?), and, at one crucial stage, the sound of a toilet flushing. How could we do even half of it?

Dave Evans consulted the two engineers, Denis Goldberg and Dave Kitson. Could we do it? Denis read the script – you'll also need two doors, he said. Of course we'll do it, we said. And costumes? Producer Evans asked Issy Heymann, whose background included everything from watch-maker to concession store-keeper, and tailor: ordinary clothes for two spivs? Sure thing, says Issy, and John Matthews'll make the Eccles cake. What, asks John, is an Eccles cake? Nobody knew what's an Eccles cake.

But John made an Eccles cake: using paper and cardboard and a fluff of cotton-wool from the medical orderly, John produced a delicious-looking cream-puff cookie in a cake-çup (weighted down, inside, by a chunk of soap). That was our Eccles cake. Together with (cardboard) crisps in a (plastic) packet. And a slab of chocolate, also in cardboard, with each portion of chocolate actually shaped. And two shoulder holsters, made from finely-worked cardboard, boned with floor-polish and looking like expensive chamois-leather holsters – to which was added the final touch: the straps of each holster were expandable, having built-in elastic adjusters, and covered in rag-cloth dyed in coffee.

Issy produced two suits of clothes, from floor rags. He saved his beetroot from lunch and concocted himself a beetroot brew. From this he extracted two sorts of dyes: a strong dye for the material that made one puce-fronted waistcoat, and a weaker dye used for tinting some strips of rag which became two evil-looking ties. The waistcoats were gems: mine of puce was fastened with startling red buttons (red ink, cardboard) and had a plush velvet appearance; Dave's was faced with rag normally used for cleaning the brass, from an old bedspread, with a woven effect – washed and shaped by Issy, it appeared to be an expensive piece of brocade. Our ties were large and hideous, neatly nestling into starched collars (cardboard, with glued-on paper fronting) and white shirts (a front bib only). Dave's prison jacket – heavy brown corduroy – was converted into a jazzy blazer with red and white (rag) piping, which contrasted well with my suit: new issue pyjamas (dark dirty blue), made to look heavier with extra pockets and a large belt, and 'ironed' under a sleeping mat. With our hair slicked down and our sloppy brown prison hats stiff with Issy's sugar water, we looked, said the audience, truly awful.

Dave Kitson did the guns – layer on layer of cut-out cardboard, steeled with shoe polish and looking very real: they had working magazines. (Du Preez nicked them straight after the show.) Dave also did the dumb waiter, so effectively that he had to become the third member of the cast, hidden back stage, working his toy. It was a beautifully constructed toy, made solely from cardboard and gummed paper: a six-foot shaft with pulleys which lowered and raised the inner tray (just large enough to take a dixie-plate) and which could also do several cunning things like close the front opening of the waiter, invisibly from the back. It came complete with speaking-tube and whistle. Dave worked it throughout the show, raising and lowering, whistling and stamping – and finally, with two buckets, making like a toilet flushing. The dumb waiter was seemingly built into the set by blankets suspended from the washing-line. Accompanying the blankets, Denis produced, amazingly, two full-scale doors: both constructed from cardboard cartons, they came complete with frames and handles – and they opened and shut as needed. The old stage-end of the yard was transformed that year – December 1967 – because Denis, with usual thoroughness, insisted on trying to construct a curtain. Some curtain: it had to stretch some thirteen yards across the width of the yard and Denis made it with an elaborate cantilever pattern of string, stretched between the bars of the cells overlooking the yard, which was (just) strong enough to hold up half-a-dozen blankets.

When the curtains opened (no chance of dimming the lights in our broad morning daylight Courtyard Theatre) there were Ben and Gus, sprawled in their basement, waiting – on beds. The one bed had been brought into the section some time before to cater for Denis, just back from hospital and a knee operation – and in time for us to borrow it for the play. We couldn't borrow any other beds, so constructed one: somewhat divan-like, with a series of rolled mats laid next to each other and covered by the other bed's mattress. As before, the show seemed to go well, and was quickly through. Ben shot Gus dead, the curtains closed for the first and last time, and that was that. End of Courtyard Theatre.

We hadn't planned that *Dumb Waiter* should be the last of our courtyard productions. Quite a while before Christmas of the next year, 1968, Dave Evans had worried about what we could do and had finally opted for safety, so he thought, in Shakespeare again: taking scenes from *The Tempest*, we traced what amounted to the Caliban story. No women were allowed to be represented, so out went Miranda, and we were left with interesting potential: the slave Caliban's revolt, using the drunken Stephano and Trinculo, against Prospero, the benevolent tyrant, watched over and guarded by his noisome security man, Ariel.

There were, by then, only fifteen of us left at Local, which meant problems for casting, but Dave finally managed to twist the arms of two people who had previously had no parts in the Courtyard Theatre and who, through the rehearsals, developed well: Fred Carneson, who made an eloquently boozed-up Stephano; and Eli Weinberg, short, round and sixty, who confounded everybody by making a light and tripping Ariel. John Laredo was Prospero, Dave Ernst was Trinculo, myself Caliban. We prepared and rehearsed through November and when suddenly, on 3 December 1968, we were moved across to the new section, Dave immediately got permission to continue the rehearsals. Moreover, the new O.C. actually gave us time off from the workshop for some rehearsals: down at the end of the huge new yard where I remember crouching in the mud of a newly laid lawn, simulating Caliban under his gaberdine. Issy Heymann had already begun making the costumes, Denis Goldberg had begun sizing up the stage. Everything was ready for the production to roll.

Then, two days before Christmas, Headquarters banned the play: 'permission withdrawn, no concert allowed'. And no explanations given (neither then, nor later). Perhaps they'd been listening to the rehearsals after all, to Caliban's song:

> No more dams I'll make for fish,
> nor fetch in firing
> at requiring
> nor scrape trenchering, nor wash dish,
> Ban, ban, Ca-Caliban . . .

They did, and banned Caliban, Shakespeare and all future Christmas concerts. Their way of saying – Happy Christmas 1968.

10 Life for Lifers

Every morning at Local Prison – at 6 a.m. or 7 a.m., opening-up time – they perform a short pantomime called Inspection. This consists of the duty officer marching through each section of the prison, accompanied by a duty warder and preceded into each section by the section warder. It is the section warder's duty to greet the Inspection Team by vigorously stamping his feet at the entrance to the section, then to proceed down the section screaming Staan reg!/Stand straight! as he flings open and flings closed each cell door. The startled bandiet behind each door sees remarkably little of the performance but hears remarkably much.

But one does see enough of the spectacle over the years to differentiate two distinct types of duty officer. The first is of the here-comes-my-head/here-comes-my-bum sort. These march past, leaning forward on their swagger-sticks with their large backsides pushed far behind, their faces seeming solemnly to declare that they are suffering severely from constipation. The second type is of the 'pens en pootjies' variety – 'pens' for stomach, 'pootjies' for comparatively little feet. Here the swagger-stick surrenders pride of place to the huge round belly beneath it. Atten-shun! – somewhat ponderously.

Captain Schnepel is of the second sort, pens en pootjies, belly predominant. I first saw him when I was a detainee, soon after I had arrived at Local in July 1964. At one early morning inspection, with du Preez doing his stamping screaming act, there appeared an extra performer alongside the duty officer. The duty officer (Mr Breedt) was distinctly of the backside-backwards breed. His new companion was distinctly pens en pootjies, with very big pens, and a remarkably opulent handlebar moustache. He looked like an ad for Kaiser Wilhelm cigarette-sweets. I thought perhaps it was a joke, a sort of make-the-detainees-laugh exercise. It wasn't a joke. It was Mr Schnepel.

Mr Schnepel became our commanding officer when, at the end of 1968, we moved into the New Section, the new 'five-star' accommodation which had been built specially for us white politicals, just over the wall from our old section in Local, replacing what used to be a store, and the Local morgue. We had not, in the early years at Local, seen much of Schnepel. He was around in the prison but seemed to have nothing specific to do with us. Apart from the occasional sortie into our section, snorting through his moustache and touting his belly, we saw him only once, at Christmas 1965, when he brought through a welcome packet of dry tobacco and helped us roll some inexpert zolls. He had the reputation, among the younger warders, of being good-natured and friendly. Then he became an officer and disappeared to Head Office to become assistant to Aucamp, boss-man of the political prisoners. His apprenticeship with Aucamp (clearly a bosom friend, and fellow belly-touter) was rewarding: before then, he had served some fifteen years as a warder but had gone up only one rank in all that time, to head-warder (equivalent to sergeant). When he became O.C. of our new section in December 1968, he was already up a rung at chief-warder, and within two years had progressed to lieutenant, then captain.

Captain Schnepel is a fine example of white South African authority. He prays, he says, to God every morning, asking for guidance in the decisions he might take during the day. He is not, he says, necessarily a Christian but the Bible is his Bible. If he is given an instruction by his superiors, he will carry it out, he says, to the letter, and God is his witness. On the walls of his office he has framed pictures of old General Hertzog, of Dr Verwoerd, and of the Nationalist Cabinet. He once said he thought Hitler was a fine leader. He also, for our first Christmas in his new prison, gave us a huge hamper of fruit. And he had a cooker installed in our new dining-room – but ruled that it could not be used as a cooker, only to warm things with. Mr Schnepel wept openly when one of the young warders, Erasmus, died suddenly of a heart attack, two days after playing volleyball with us. But when Bram Fischer went to him to ask for some extra minutes on a visit from Bram's sister Ada (who both Schnepel and Bram knew was dying of cancer) Schnepel brusquely said: 'No – why should you have extra time? People are dying every day.' Ada died shortly after *not* being given a few extra minutes on her last visit to her brother.

Mr Schnepel means well. He thinks that he is right and that his actions are virtuous. There can be nothing quite so tormenting as a well-meaning man who thinks he is blessed with virtue and who, at the same time, has the means of arbitrary power at his disposal. Like that of a commanding officer of political prisoners. Schnepel, at the start, seemed so much better than du Preez. Moving into our new quarters, we seemed at last to have a man in charge who could be approached with reason and who was not motivated by a seemingly implacable and blind antagonism. One of du Preez's last actions in the old section had been to refuse permission for the issue of some new towels – larger than the old miniature dish-cloths which went for towels, and with towelling texture. Schnepel allowed a complete new issue, to everyone – a small and gracious act which promised changes. They came. Schnepel encouraged the development of a garden in the larger yard; he brought fruit for Christmas, and plants for the garden; and he was clearly proud of the new jail and concerned to keep it neat and respectably tidy. The jail was certainly something, especially after those years at Local and Central, a 'five-star' place by comparison with the old. There are fifty-two cells, all single, on two floors of an L-shaped building: each cell has a bunk-bed, with mattress (and pillow, and sheets); a toilet (that works); a basin, with hot and cold running water; and a fixed cupboard with a table-leaf that slides out. And a window-casement, overlooking the yard downstairs, at a height that one can see out when standing at it, and with narrow windows that can be opened and shut. (There is not, as some had hoped, a light switch inside the cell. Each door, as at Central, is made doubly secure with both grille and outside door.)

Downstairs there is a dining-room. No more meals, said

Schnepel, in the cells: all meals to be taken in the dining-room, seated at large smart tables, using (which I found strangest – stranger even than having a bed to sleep on, a bed with sheets, after four-and-a-half years on the floor between only blankets) using a knife and fork. So silly, it seemed, when a spoon had done for everything. So little you can do with a fork. Forks and knives, it was to be – and no meals in the cells. None at all, said Schnepel. Which started the first major row, our first confrontation with the New Regime.

Schnepel's ruling on the food meant that we would be locked in our cells without food from supper-time until open-up the next morning. Supper, at the New Section, was at 4.00 in the afternoon – making it a long hungry night, usually of some fifteen hours, longer at weekends when supper was soon after 3 p.m.

We fought him on his food ban for four months, and won, but only after a long stupid battle. In our beautiful new quarters, beds and all, we had to revert to practices we'd almost forgotten: smuggling bits of bread tucked beneath our shirts, sugar smuggled in folded envelopes, or grains of tea-leaves scattered in the bottom of pockets. Amid the new luxury of beds and forks, we found it hard to break the habits of the old life, where supper had always been served in the cells at lock-up, so there was always the chance of saving half a kattie of bread for an eight o'clock nibble or nine o'clock nosh. Without this break, the evenings were long and empty.

So we smuggled, and Schnepel stayed stubborn. Erasmus (the one who died of a heart-attack) laid traps for us just round the corner of the dining-room door to catch us smuggling our little bits of bread and sugar. Ivan Schermbrucker, aged fifty-three, one-time company secretary, and Eli Weinberg, aged fifty-nine, professional photographer, were caught by Erasmus carrying a load of contraband beneath their shirts: two bits of bread, and oh dear, the bread was buttered. Schnepel stormed the following day: No Food in the Cells, or he would remove *all* privileges, from everybody. He put a notice up in the dining-room, in both official languages, signed and stamped with the official Gevangenis Department/Prisons Department stamp:

> No Smoking in the Dining Room
> No Food in the Cells
> Trespassers will be Prosecuted.

Then, in mid-battle, Ivan Schermbrucker and Eli Weinberg both within a year of the end of their five-year sentences for being members of the banned Communist Party got promoted to A group. A group: with permission to buy groceries from the canteen with their monthly order. Groceries – food. Monthly orders are kept in cells: tobacco, soap, shaving cream, writing paper, ... and now food. The notice downstairs still said No Smoking/No Food/Trespassers will be Prosecuted. Mr Erasmus pounced on us all again in March as we walked innocently back to our cells after our 4.30 p.m. supper – and discovered two more bits of (prosecutable) bread. The next morning, while we were still hungrily eating our breakfast at 7.30 a.m., fifteen hours since the last bread was discovered and confiscated, Schnepel came into the dining-room and stormed: the Last Warning, for Everybody, No More Warnings, No Food in Cells, Trespassers, Trespassers ... and no more tea at tea-break. 'Tea-break': another of Schnepel's happy innovations at New Section. Unexpectedly, right in amongst the Trespassers business, we were stopped in mid-morning and mid-afternoon for a ten-minute break from the workshop. Yes, said Schnepel, we could have tea – tea, from the A group groceries, while most of us were still not A groupers.

But now Schnepel stormed and warned: No more Tea. Crisis. Confrontation.

With du Preez in the old days, crisis meant a blank wall of sullen silence, days on days of hateful confrontation, smouldering wrath. We wondered what it would mean with Schnepel, the man who could be jovial and approachable, or unpredictably petty and mean. We discussed it at tea-break in the morning (our last tea-break?) and wondered whether a new approach would work, trying decency, sense, where neither had been possible before. In the afternoon, Ivan Schermbrucker and John Laredo asked permission to talk, urgently, to Schnepel.

Yes. They presented our case: hungry stomachs, long hours. Schnepel listened, then called a remarkable meeting: between him and us, all of us, gathered around him (and Erasmus, now dead) in the sun in the yard. It was polite, very genial – and quite exceptional in terms of anything else we had ever experienced in prison before. It seemed, too, eminently workable and pleasant, both for us and for Schnepel. We got sanity, at last, after four months, on the question of food in the cells – OK, he said, as long as there aren't any crumbs. From us, he got a promise of cooperation: no crumbs, no untidy section.

There was never again quite such a meeting as that one in the yard. It was the most reasonable moment of my time inside. Which is probably why it was never repeated. No boer – even Schnepel, friend of boss-man Aucamp – could afford to act too reasonably towards the politicals. It might make us appear normal. It might give us a reasonably normal time, inside. The Branch wouldn't like that. The Branch – as made clear by the intransigence of Aucamp – want a bad time for the politicals and when the Branch barks, the prison officials dance. When the dancing official is someone like pens-en-pootjies Schnepel, the whole performance becomes distinctly obscene.

I liked Schnepel. And sometimes I hated him. Now I pity him. He is so much the complete white South African. When he felt himself in control, he could be so charming. Like the first time he got permission (so he claimed – quite without notification, so I now learn) for the young children of some of the prisoners to see their fathers. Marius Schoon hadn't seen his Jane for five years. She came in, aged nine, hand-in-hand with Schnepel to see the father she knew only as a name mentioned in letters. She sat on Marius's lap in an inside office (not the cramped visiting-room), chatting and telling him about her school and friends and paintings – but when she went out afterwards, back to the car outside where her grandparents waited, she wanted to know more about the fat smiling man with the big moustache who had held her hand walking down the passage and who had been so nice to her.

A good father to his children, Mr Schnepel, so he thought. An Old Testament father. And dangerous when he felt not completely in control, with the Branch obviously breathing down his neck – or when he, in his righteousness, tried to carry out the responsibilities of the Branch himself. When, for instance, he felt the security of the State threatened. Like by a letter from a happy hippy friend of mine, a letter written on brown paper. Fifi came on one of my monthly visits in April 1970; I wrote to her in May, asking her to reply in June (you organize your life carefully when you have only three lots of 500 words allowed, monthly). At a visit late in June I was told by a mutual friend that she had written. But no letter inside. I went to see Schnepel at his interview time on Wednesday morning (by then he was well established as commanding officer and you could ask to see him on Wednesdays only, outside emergencies).

Had there, I asked, been a letter to me from a Miss Fifi? No, he said, he would tell me if there was. He always told us when there were letters. That warned me to expect a lie. I had once before been through a similar episode with him, early in 1969, when he lied about a letter from a friend giving me advice about my Honours exam. I had asked for a replacement letter for the one that apparently hadn't come, but Schnepel said No, wait, maybe it would come. It came, from him, just *after* I had written the exams, and clearly dated a month before.

So I knew he lied about letters and was warned about Fifi's letter. When the end of the month passed and I had received only two of my three-letter quota, I went again to see him. His ruling always was that letters not received within the month couldn't be 'carried over'. Within the month, or nothing. Would he please allow the letter if perhaps it came late, I asked.

What letter? (Looking stern, puffing through his moustache.) From Miss Fifi, Sir.

Suddenly Schnepel exploded. That letter, he shouted, that woman! She wrote a letter on brown paper, *brown* paper! Ordinary brown paper you get at a butcher's to wrap up meat in. Brown paper, one big sheet, written to a prisoner in jail. Dis 'n skande/It's a scandal. And all that nonsense she wrote about too.

Can I have the letter please, Sir? She was probably only joking.

No. It's been sent to Head Office. Dis 'n skande. Brown paper.

Two days later I was told that the letter had been returned from H.Q. and I could *not* receive it. But as it had arrived within the month, I could write a note to Miss Fifi saying she could write another letter – but NOT on *brown* paper.

I wrote a note to Fifi, explaining these matters of state – and waited. Still no letter. Any letter yet, I asked Schnepel. No – sniffing through moustache – I always tell you when there's a letter.

So I knew there *had* been another letter, but not for me yet, it seemed. Not for two weeks, not for three weeks, then a sudden summons one afternoon, into the inside office: Schnepel, with a young Security man in civvies, embarrassed. Did I know a Miss Fifi? Yes, of course, I was actually expecting a letter from her. Yes, yes, he had it there – the letter, on white paper, transcribed in triplicate. Would I please read it? Yes gladly. A delightful letter, full of easy wit and happy discussion about some of the friends we knew when she was secretary to my editor, and some thoughts about how changed I would find the world after all these years . . .

Yes, I said, so? Would I please, uh (embarrassed – with Schnepel watching, dipping his legs every few minutes to cool his crutch) please interpret it?

Interpret? You mean translate to Afrikaans?

No, he spoke English. Interpret the meanings of passages he couldn't understand. They seemed to mean other things. I hesitated, reluctant to cooperate in any Branch nonsense, particularly when watched by a snuffling, lying, knee-bending Schnepel. But if I refused I automatically condemned as subversive a purely innocent letter from an innocent friend. So I 'interpreted'. I forget all the contents now but there was an obviously straightforward reference to an air-hostess's comments to a friend travelling by plane, which excited the Branch, much to my puzzlement (I had then heard nothing of the things called 'hijacks'). Fifi talked of a 'new movement' among young people, questioning and gentle, agreeing with many of the things I had believed in. What was that all about, asked the man, didn't that indicate some new underground organization, some subversive group she was training on my instructions? I laughed, and eventually he laughed too. He left, taking the letter and the three transcriptions with him. So you see, said Schnepel as I left, you got to see the letter after all.

It would be funny, say, in a circus: Captain Schnepel as ringmaster, bedecked with baubles and swagger-stick, benevolent boss of happy animals. But not so funny when the cage is closed off from the audience, who can't see in, with animals who can't see out. And a prancing ringmaster acting God. His finest hour was also his worst, and well demonstrated the true nature of his paternalism. When we arrived at the New Section (December 1968) Dave Ernst was the only A group bandiet, the only bandiet allowed to buy groceries. Three months later, four others were promoted to the heights of privilege – but that left some dozen others, some of them still in C group, an arbitrary distinction between us that rankled. Schnepel repeatedly promised to see what he could do about getting everybody upgraded and he repeatedly boasted that it might be possible – and that it would be his doing, his benevolence.

The A group Promise became the focus of everybody's hope. At the beginning of 1970, the promise of the Promise brightened when three more of us were upgraded to A, with the remainder to B. Schnepel made some comments during the early part of the year which suggested that he was still pressing for everybody's upgrading and that he might be successful. Then, in October 1970, he dropped one of his Deliberate Hints, telling somebody that it wouldn't be long before it was A's for everybody. How long is 'long'? The futile debate raged, aided by further dropped snippets from the Master's table suggesting that there might be a Surprise Announcement at Christmas. Everybody waited for Christmas, and the underprivileged non-A groupers began planning their first grocery orders and working out to whom they could write the expected extra letter. On Christmas Day, Schnepel passed through the section briefly, gave permission for us to stay unlocked over lunch – and left, with a cheery Happy Christmas/Sorry-you're-here greeting, but nothing else. No A group Announcement. People began to murmur and wonder, more so when, early in January 1971, he again leaked the fact that he was strenuously pressing for A group for all and might succeed soon. By now, patience was being strained by a year's over-expectancy. Perhaps it would be all right after all: he would come in some time in February and announce that everybody had been A group from the beginning of the month.

He came in some time in February – and announced that everybody had been promoted to A group, from the beginning of the next month, March. Not noticing the obvious disappointment around him, he then proceeded to lay down the Branch law about what A group for politicals means: no radio, no news, no newspapers, no contact visits – and *no* applications for any of these things would be passed on to Head Office. And no more trouble, thank you.

I suppose he expected to be thanked with vast shows of gratitude. He was thanked, but the mood was muted: the delay and the insistent qualifications had turned the whole thing sour and he, the one man who should have been able to anticipate our disappointment, was hurt by it. He sulked. A year later, when I left, he was still sulking. He stomped around like a great big wounded elephant, surly and unresponsive, wont to mutter angrily about 'you people . . . you reds . . . you're all the same . . .' and No No No to most requests.

I think he thought that, once every bandiet had A group, we'd shut up. A group would end all complaints. It didn't, so he felt hurt, so sulked. And he muttered, to Fred Carneson: 'If I had my way, you people would be allowed *no* letters and *no* visits either.'

His decisions thereafter were marked even more than before by his pettiness. Like when Issy Heymann went to him with the Jimi Hendrix problem. This arose from our efforts somehow to keep abreast with what was happening in the world outside. Denied all news, and without radio or newspapers, we tried to get from our visitors at least some indications of changing fashions and ideas outside. So, for instance, we tried to keep up with changing musical tastes through the records we were allowed to buy every other month.

Issy Heymann's young son mentioned one Sunday that we must, but *must*, get Jimi Hendrix – so dutiful 58-year-old Issy ordered Jimi Hendrix. Our records were played for a couple of hours each evening by the night staff; but only full sides of records were allowed. The night Issy Heymann's order arrived, the entire section of white politicals – most of whom had been in prison since 1964 and many of whose musical appreciation stopped at Strauss, if not Beethoven – was subjected to an uninterrupted full side of the Best of Jimi Hendrix, played at full volume.

The following morning, with concerted prompting from several of the older members of the section, Issy asked to see Schnepel and begged him, as a special favour, to let him return the Jimi Hendrix record to the record shop and swap it for something else, less noisy. Schnepel snorted. 'If you want to buy kaffir music,' he said, 'you must listen to kaffir music. No swapping.'

At times like that, when Ringmaster Schnepel revealed his prejudices, it was easy to hate him, hate him as the ample embodiment of the system which made him and which he reflected so well, hate him for his stupidity and arrogance, hate him for his hatred and his power. Yet possible to pity him, for being, at times, such an amiable fool, so laughably a fat pawn in the game of his masters.

There would be room for pity – if it were a circus. It is not a circus. It is life, It is life, for instance, for Denis Goldberg and Bram Fischer. They are serving life sentences which – because South African political prisoners get no remission, no amnesty, no parole – means life. Denis Goldberg was thirty-one when he was sentenced at the Rivonia Trial in 1964 together with the leaders of Umkhonto we Sizwe, the military wing of the African National Congress. They all got life, on four counts under the Sabotage Act. They could have got the rope. Leader of the defence team at the trial was Bram Fischer, Q.C. Two years later, in 1966, Bram himself was charged under the same act and also sentenced to life. He was then fifty-eight.

Bram Fischer has always been a very special sort of bandiet for the boere. His father was Judge President of the Orange Free State, where his grandfather had once been prime minister. His could not have been of a more eminent South African, Afrikaans family. Bram himself, a Rhodes scholar, was justly well-known as a leading advocate, as a communist, and as an Afrikaner. The boere tend to regard him as the leading Black Sheep of the Afrikaner Nation: they view him with distinct fascination, sometimes with veiled respect, sometimes open admiration. And sometimes they derive malicious pleasure from tormenting him, rather as if tormenting *him* gives them social status.

Proud men, dressed in their petty brief authority. Like head-warder du Preez, who set out to make Bram's life hell. Bram was sentenced in May 1966 when the rest of us were at Central. He was kept at Local, in du Preez's section, first on his own, then joined in isolation by Issy Heymann and Jock Strachan. These three politicals were kept alone at Local until we all returned in November. (Their only other companion in our absence was a convicted counterfeit expert who was put, briefly, with them because the authorities were terrified of putting him even momentarily amongst ordinary criminals. They felt sure, it seemed, that the politicals posed no threat counterfeit-wise.) Having so few prisoners in his section, du Preez had plenty of time to do what he wanted. He set out to break Bram – using every little trick available – and Bram, puzzled, lost as a bandiet, and always, even with du Preez, irrevocably polite and courteous, was slowly ground down. Du Preez issued him with outsize clothes: a ridiculously large jacket which hung far below his hands, and trousers he had to roll up. Du Preez took Bram straight after sentence and snipped off most of his hair. He kept Bram in isolation longer than any of us had ever been. One day he peeped in through the judas after lunch and saw Bram reading – in he stormed: 'You can't read now. This is rest time. If I catch you again, I'll confiscate your books.' And left, saying over his shoulder: 'Read the Bible if you must read.' Bram complained that he was hungry – could he have another piece of bread? Du Preez raged again, No! Issy Heymann made a small waste-bin for Bram out of a paper bag; du Preez saw it in Bram's cell, trampled on it and kicked it away: 'Don't keep collecting rubbish!' And he loved to watch Bram cleaning the yard, particularly the latrines. Du Preez made Bram clean the toilets, with a brush and a rag, down on his knees in front of the bowl. I suppose that was du Preez's finest moment: standing command over Bram Fischer, Q.C., as he scrubbed the shit-house with a brush and rag.

Bram says his life was saved in those first six months before the rest of us returned from Central by Jock Strachan and Issy Heymann, helping him and protecting him where they could. But when we returned in November 1966 Bram looked old, haggard, and it was quite a few months before he was well again.

Unlike du Preez (who always called Bram 'Fischer! Fischer!') the other boere liked to call him 'Bram'. The younger warders liked calling him Bram as a way of proving *their* authority (some of them had been special guards during the Rivonia trial, when Bram led the defence team). More senior officers made a point of being shown to him, looking him up and down, the prize exhibit – hello, Bram, they say, Hoe gaan dit?/How goes it? Bram, always polite, nods and answers, and asks about their health.

Except Mr Thys Nel. Mr Thys Nel, Brigadier Thys Nel, was Deputy Commissioner of Prisons, second-in-charge to God in Prisons. Six foot six and fairly presentable – known amongst bandiete at Central as a smoothy – he visited us one day in our new quarters behind Local, strolling across the yard in civvies, hands in pockets, drawling down at Schnepel puffing at his elbow. They strolled purposefully across the yard towards where Bram and Ivan Schermbrucker were gardening. The bandiete saw them coming and Bram, trained by du Preez never to address a senior officer until spoken to, stood politely aside, hat in hand. Brigadier Thys Nel stopped, looked down at Bram, paused, then began cursing him for being disrespectful, for not greeting him, who did he think he was to act like that to a senior officer? Bram, amazed, apologized – which started Nel off on another bout of vituperation.

Thys Nel's second visit to the New Section was at the end of that year, 1969. He came into the section one evening – drunk. It appeared he had been to a dinner party with friends and decided to bring a friend along to Local – to bait the animals, it seemed. The inner windows of the cells in the New Section open directly into the passage, at about shoulder height, so that anybody walking past the cells can look straight in and, with the windows open, carry on an easy conversation. Thys Nel and Friend, acompanied by a suitably terrified night warder, strolled down the section, stopping at each window and addressing the bandiete.

From inside the cells it's possible to hear what's going on in the passage and it's always a diversion when there are visitors. Usually they don't stop. But on this occasion they did: the Deputy Commissioner of Prisons, with friend, out for an evening's entertainment. Jew-baiting, with the normal inhibitions of protocol removed by a good dinner and the absence of anyone besides a row of red bandiete. I heard the talking down the passage, then could recognize Nel's voice, raised angrily against Rowley Arenstein, just down the row – and Rowley's patient, persistent replies. 'Jood,' said Nel, 'Jew – you're a communist because you're a Jew – you're a Jew so you must be a communist.' And similar pleasantries. Then a slouch further along the corridor, to Bram's window, next to mine. 'You're a fool,' said Nel, 'a lawyer and they all say you're so clever – but I know you're a fool, and you'll sit here forever.' And similar conciliatory offerings.

Nel's companion, distinguished only by a good whiff of brandy (my first whiff for many years) and his rugby blazer, came to my window. Name, he demanded. Sentence? What for? Like the rest. What's that? Politics. Ha! he says, with brandy – and passed on, following Nel up the passage to Laredo's cell where Nel, beginning to repeat himself, was becoming angrier and more uninhibitedly rude and obscene.

It was a shoddy business. Its aftermath, looked at now, gives a fair indication of the sort of pressures bandiete are subject to, not least of them being their own reticence and politeness. Nel had been grossly abusive to at least four prisoners. Within a day of the visitation, four letters of protest were handed in to the commanding officer, addressed to the commissioner – which meant, as with all our affairs, that they went first to Brigadier Aucamp. Within two days, Aucamp visited the prison himself and asked to speak to Bram Fischer, one of the complainants. He would prefer, he said, not to pass the letters on to the commissioner. *He* would prefer, said Bram, that Aucamp did pass them on. Would you reconsider, asked Aucamp – it was a regrettable incident and he, Brigadier Aucamp, would ensure that it never happened again. Bram reported back to the other three – it was argued endlessly for three days, and finally agreed that the matter would not be pressed, on condition that the letters were not withdrawn but left to stand, as legitimate complaints. It seemed churlish to press for anything more. So Aucamp was happy. And Brigadier Thys Nel, Deputy Commissioner of Prisons (and Aucamp's senior), has never again set foot in the New Section, Pretoria Local.

Whether he visits Local again or not, the lives of the Local bandiete won't be much affected – whoever visits, whoever's in command, the routine will remain largely unchanged. This is the routine that is life at Local:

5·30 a.m. Lights switched on by the night warder – the second night warder, who begins his shift at midnight. You have from now until open-up to wash, shave, make the bed, sweep and tidy the cell, and get dressed. Long enough, in fact, once you're used to it, to sleep on a while, make a cup of coffee from the tap, and read in bed a while, before a well-ordered rush and . . .

7·00 a.m. Open-up, accompanied by the old inspection business, standing at your grille to be counted. Thereafter, each to his appointed early-morning chores: some to sweep the passage, some to dust, one to collect the letters/study assignments/ requests for doctor, some to prepare the dining-hall downstairs for arrival of breakfast. (Each chore is appointed according to monthly list drawn up by the bandiete, signed by the O.C.)

7·20 a.m. Breakfast arrives: one canister with mielie-pap, one with coffee, plus small katkop (bread) for each, and sufficient milk for two ounces each. Sugar and butter and jam from what you've saved of the two-ounce ration from supper the night before.

7·45 a.m. Workshop call. Those who are fit enough, into the carpentry workshop: small, but sufficient, with four well-equipped benches in the shop next to the dining-room. Initially, there was a fully-qualified workshop-warder in charge, Snyman, but he vanished suddenly one day in 1971 – removed, said the rumours, because he had become too nice towards us. (He'd been fair, certainly, but strenuously correct – and a good craftsman who taught me a lot about carpentry.) Since then, one of the ordinary boere takes charge, with occasional assistance from a junior workshop-warder from Central. The work: constructing kits (e.g. tables, cupboards, builders' floats, pelmets, kit-boxes) – all of wood, cut and roughly prepared in the machine shops at Central Prison; or (tediously) having to renovate office furniture (tables, correspondence racks) wrecked by years of bored civil servants. Everything is either for the Prisons Dept (e.g. cupboards for cells) or the Public Works Department. Political prisoners – unlike others – receive no gratuity, no payment for any work completed. Those who aren't fit for the 'shop' are cleaners (wash up and tidy the dining-room and section); thereafter gardeners – in the yard, tending the grass and the lines of flower-beds developed over the years. They've developed many flowers, interspersed, when allowed, with some fruit (e.g. a fine grenadilla trellis) and vegetables (mielies, green peppers and tomatoes).

9·30 a.m. Ten-minute tea break. Tea brewed by the cleaners in an urn and tea-pot – always black, always weak, to conserve rations. Tea usually drunk sprawled on the grass in conversational clusters.

11·30 a.m. Lunch. Main meal of the day: usually some sort of meat, with two or three vegetables. Meat-pies on Wednesday, fish on Thursday, cold sliced roast on Sunday, sometimes with roast potatoes. One large katkop each . . . No coffee. No pudding, except, occasionally, as Sunday treat.

12·00 Lock-up, in individual cells, originally. Then (about 1970) allowed to have only the grilles at the end of the section locked, leaving free movement within the section between the cells. An opportunity to chat and socialize – or, the major weekday occupation at lunch-hour, sleep – or a bridge four in one of the cells. This has now changed again, with all cells being locked, all of lunch-time.

1·00 p.m. Open-up, weekdays. Straight to 'shop' and garden and wash-up of lunch things, preparing dining-room for supper.

2·30 p.m. Ten-minute tea-break.

3·30 p.m. Stop shop: sweep, clean tools, lay them out on bench for counting, and lock up in cupboard. Then showers for everybody – two cubicles, with two showers each, in centre of section. *4·00* p.m. Supper. Two canisters: one of soup, one of coffee (always black) and a tray with bread (one large katkop each), and small two-ounce dishes for sugar, butter and jam. The only variation is, very occasionally and more recently, on Sunday nights when there might be a piece of cheese, or some pastry, or fruit, even an egg. (An egg! I went six-and-a-half years before the first egg. Seven-and-a-half without a mixed grill. I craved a grill and a coke, or some fizzy drink.)

After supper, the critical time: waiting for the chief-warder to issue letters/study material/library books/magazines, or nothing at all. With three letters a month and sometimes a fortnightly magazine, there's often nothing at all. Watching for the pile of books to come from his office, knowing exactly the shape of the letter-book, waiting, expecting, and then nothing. You shrug – nothing means another horizon established for tomorrow night, and another wait then, for nothing, or something.

Often something cut, censored. The *Financial Mail* (Johannesburg – no overseas magazines allowed) arrived with the front cover removed, which'll mean a sizeable slice of pages removed from inside too. Or the *Huisgenoot* (Afrikaans family magazine) with pages out, and a single line of type painstakingly removed from the Contents section. Sometimes a snip even from *Fair Lady* – women's magazine. (We traced a whole social revolution simply by following the coloured ads: who'd ever heard of 'panti-hose' in 1964? Or mini's? Or seen men in long hair? We had to discover from visitors what 'psychedelic' meant.)

The letters, personal letters, often arrive cut – or with sentences blacked out, indelibly – or with a note from the Commanding Officer: 'This letter is 556 words long. Next time it will be chopped. Pas op!–Watch out!' A gracious warning, when compared with the times they come chopped without explanation. A critical time this, balancing the fury produced by the insult (imagine it: a busy prisons warrant officer, sitting down to count, word by word, each word of each letter that

arrives. 'This letter is 556 words long . . .') – balancing the fury
with the relief that the letter's come at last, the joy of being able
to read, re-read, put away, then re-read, drawing in the whole
world of pictures, impressions, colours, conversations, a whole
world from a few hurried lines. Even the obvious hurry tells a
story. To read, then re-read of the alive world outside there,
peopled with those who can write as many letters as they like,
when they like, who can afford to waste words, to expand
thoughts, to digress, and who in one morning may get, say
casually, half-a-dozen letters. Half-a-dozen letters – two
months' ration, for a bandiet in A group.

4·45 p.m. Lock-up. In cells for the night, till 7 the following
morning. At 5 p.m. the day staff goes off, replaced by the night
warder, who sits downstairs in the offices, coming upstairs to
check every hour. Outside, in the yard with its lights blazing all
night (no curtains in cell-windows), there is always the dog-
handler and his dog: an alsatian always, locked into the yard
until midnight when he's replaced by the second shift and
another dog, till dawn. Surprisingly, you can learn to sleep
through the midnight racket when the dogs change over, barking,
tearing at each other as they cross over. There are two sorts of
dogs used in the service: 'vangers/catchers', who are trained to
hold you – and 'killers', trained only to be as nasty as possible, to
everybody. The dogs outside our windows, making a mess of the
garden every night, are killers. From 5 till 8, music via the loudspeakers in the passage opposite each cell, played on the machine
downstairs by the night-staff disc-jockey according to a list
provided each day by Bram Fischer, Chief Record Programmer.
A time to be lazy, lying on the bunk dozing, or listening, or
reading. Always reading. Or working at university assignments.

8·00 p.m. The silence bell ends music – and all the lights across
the way in Old Local go out, the singing stops. Late lights only
for students. Silence, and a time to study or write letters – or
read, always read.

11·00 p.m. Lights out – if you've made it, awake still, reading.
Not long, through the brief remission of the night, until morning,
and . . .

5·30 a.m. Lights on.

This basic routine seldom varies, except there's more time locked up at weekends. Mondays to Fridays, the times remain the same: upwards of fourteen hours in the cell every night, with an extra hour over lunch. At weekends, it's worse: lunch at 10.30 a.m., then lock-up for three hours, till 2 p.m., then supper an hour early at 3.15 – so lock-up an hour early by 4 p.m. Fifteen hours locked up every night, plus three during the day. The weekend routine applies every public holiday. Weekends, and holidays, are bad times inside.

The daily routine, out of the cells, persists through Monday to Thursday. Then on Friday mornings, it changes: cleaning time – scrubbing the floors of the corridors and the dining-room, then of the individual cells, and the windows, and dusting everywhere. Once a fortnight (beginning mid-day through 1969, shortly before another visit from the International Red Cross) on Friday afternoons, it's movie time. Excitement! The dining-room is transformed with long, dark floral curtains – the only curtains in our part of the jail – tables moved aside, chairs ready for fortnightly goodies, movies ordered from approved distributors in Johannesburg. Full-length 16 mm. features, apparently about three or four years behind the current movies, well-stocked with many oldies.

Saturdays and Sundays – and the afternoons of the non-movie Fridays – are 'free': free, in the yard, once the washing-up's completed and everything's tidy – and excluding Sunday morning when you have, aimlessly, to sit around ready to spring into full regalia for a two-second, always disinterested inspection. Time, at last, for exercise. We couldn't, because of the way the yard in the New Section was built, continue our 'boop-squash' against the wall. But it was arranged that a concrete strip be laid in the new yard, large enough for a volleyball court. The poles for the court were designed by Denis Goldberg so that they could accommodate both a volleyball and a tennis net – and we hadn't been at the new place more than a couple of weeks before we were using the volleyball court as a tennis court, using wooden bats as racquets. The bats are restrictive, necessarily so on the shortened court, but so much an improvement on the original hands-only games that the mini-tennis has thrived, producing some remarkably proficient tennis.

Volleyball thrived too, while numbers lasted: a great game for involving everybody, of whatever standard, but impossible with less than eight players – and our numbers were dwindling, happily, by mid-1970. Our enthusiasm for volleyball was infectious: the boere first watched with interest, then wanted to join in. The young ones made a point of it. Even commanding officer Schnepel joined at first, huffing and snorting round the court, bull elephant at play, pleasantly participating in a few moments of sporting equality. But then he was promoted – or perhaps reprimanded for over-friendliness with the enemy. He stopped playing, then stopped watching, then forbade the young warders to play either. So now they're waiting for volleyball recruits in Pretoria, New Section.

They're waiting for a lot else too. Mainly two things – available, as a matter of course, to all other prisoners in South Africa but consistently denied to the politicals, in Pretoria and on Robben Island: the chance to earn remission of sentence, or be given amnesty; and news. The ban on news is totally mean. Prison officials who are prepared to discuss the matter agree that it is an awkward order for them to carry out, but they insist that they have no option: the Special Branch insist that any news, for a political, would be a threat to security. This is nonsense. We had news, briefly, at Central in 1966, when we were treated like other prisoners. *That* hardly shattered the State. The security arrangements, particularly at a maximum security prison like New Section, provide ample control over every single aspect of one's life, all the time. The effect of the ban – and this is known to them – is to aggravate and embitter every aspect of life in prison.

I saw this, for instance, in my dealings with the young warder we called Duckpond. Duckpond had arrived at Local about the same time as I did, in 1964. During the years that followed, he was often on duty in our section and we inevitably got to know each other fairly well and, as we didn't quarrel, established a relationship which was respectfully friendly. Inevitably too, I pumped him for news – with absolute failure, for the simple reason that he knew none, never reading a paper nor listening to news broadcasts. Except about rugby. Rugby was Duckpond's life. His heaven was a galaxy of rugby players: large invincible Springboks, about each of whom he knew the minutest detail of performance, family, education, origins, the lot. We couldn't, because of the news ban and his own limitations, talk about much else, so endlessly, comprehensively, exhaustively, we talked about every rugby player under the immortal sun, and particularly about the rising stars of the 1970 season, the stars of the clubs, of the provinces, of the final selection trials for the tour of Britain. Duckpond described them all and I tried to remember them all so that I could join the feverish debate about form and performance and national pride.

The team, at last, was chosen (my predicted team wasn't too far off – I'd been well briefed) and they left on tour. Let's see, I said conversationally to Duckpond, how we do against the Brits – we should do OK, yes? Of course we will, he said. Then, suddenly, silence. Duckpond, who had previously spent considerable time in the workshop standing by me, talking, talking about rugby – suddenly Duckpond avoided me, hiding in the office. Our routine being what it was, it was difficult for me to nail him alone. He refused to answer my pointed inquiries: surely the first game of the tour was over? It's usually an easy game – against Oxford, wasn't it? – so what was the score? He shot off, embarrassed. I waited, and finally got him about three days later. What's what?

He couldn't tell me, he said. They'd been given specific instructions not to say anything to any of us about the rugby tour. He couldn't tell me. About what, I asked? What's wrong? Nothing's wrong, he said. So why can't you tell me? He ran off again. I got him the following week. And slowly extracted the story of the disaster: we'd lost the first game of the tour and were losing others. Not our fault, of course. The fault of 'betogers, lang-harige betogers'/demonstrators, long-haired demonstrators, who were buggering up the tour with smoke-bombs and whistles and demos and everything. Our boys wanted to come home. 'It's those verdomde Engelse again, those

damned English – and that vark/pig who used to be in Pretoria
and who we let go with his parents.'

Who's that, I asked – entranced by the revelations. Duckpond
shut up, looked worried, and shot off in hurried silence. But I
got the name eventually, and laughed: the son of the parents who,
daily, through my 90-days at Local, had organized my food
parcels, organized my washing, kept me going and whose son,
then, was hardly fifteen – and now even Duckpond, the boer who
didn't read newspapers, knew him: Peter Hain.

Those were gloomy weeks for Duckpond and the boere. We
judged the progress of the world situation – i.e. the rugby tour –
by the expressions on their faces when they arrived each morning:
the longer the expressions, the better we felt, judging that things
were going badly on the tour. It didn't matter to us when the
boere seemed more cheerful because that, in immediate terms,
meant that they would be more relaxed and tolerable for that day.
Sometimes, as a bandiet, you can't lose.

But ordinarily, you can't win, and the news-ban aggravation
has far more serious effects on personal lives, driving the warders
into actions which even they must regret. Like when Bram
Fischer's son died in February 1971. We had just showered one
afternoon and were going downstairs for supper when Bram was
called – a visit, trek aan/get dressed. It was unexpected, un-
planned, and I remember saying to Marius Schoon that, being
prison, it meant either something bad or something good. In
prison you always wait for and hope for the unexpected, because
it might mean something good – yet you always dread the unexpected, because it might mean something bad. You have no
control, either way. You wait. And, like Bram, hurriedly get
dressed and go down, across the yard, to the door in the wall that
leads into the box with its four cubicles, four wooden partitions:
the visiting room, with the long four-inch-wide perspex strip
through which you peer to see your visitor, in his box on the
other side. And all around the wooden partitions, and the
deadening sounding-board which panels the whole box, trapping
the sounds so that there's no interference on the tape-recorder in
the little (ostensibly secret) room next door. Always one-at-a-
time for visits (to keep the tape clear?). Always a warder next to

you on your side, and a warder next to your visitor on the other side, everyone attentive to ensure that the security of the State is not shattered by an inadvertent slip about what's happening outside. Family news only, they insist.

Bram's brother came with family news only, unexpectedly in the afternoon, at our supper-time. A special visit, with two warders on Bram's side of the box, and at least two on the other, next to Bram's brother, attentively standing by while he passed on the news.

Paul died this morning. He went into hospital for an ordinary check-up and his lungs suddenly collapsed. He died, early this morning.

Paul Fischer had been ill since birth, with cystic fibrosis, the child-killer which his parents had managed to fend off through years of constant patient care, knowing always that Paul might die suddenly, unexpectedly. But foreknowledge doesn't prepare you, particularly when the latest news of Paul had been that he had just got through his Honours course at university, and he had looked so well when he flew up from Cape Town to see his father for the January monthly visit. He had been so well, and happy with his results. The hospital check-up was quite regular, nothing unusual. Then the collapse.

Bram's brother had to come to Pretoria to tell him about it. They wouldn't give permission for a contact visit. They wouldn't let brother meet brother, at a time like that, in one of the offices. That would threaten the security of the State. They stood, two on the one side of the partition with Bram and at least two on the other side with Bram's brother.

Paul died this morning.

They couldn't touch each other.

Bram came out of the box-room just as we were being locked up for the night. There was no chance to talk to any of us. He was locked up as usual – then briefly opened for Schnepel to come up and say he was sorry to hear the news – then locked up, alone, in his cell for the next fourteen hours, alone. Fourteen hours, through the usual prison night, alone with the news of his son's death.

They refused him permission to attend the funeral. Aucamp

came and offered sympathy, and offered as many special visits as he wanted in connection with the funeral arrangements. Bram's two daughters came, and another close friend. But when, after the funeral, the daughters returned with his other brother and asked that the brother be allowed in with them, the commanding officer, on behalf of Aucamp, said No, no special visits, no more.

In order, they say, to maintain the security of the State.

That is life in the New Section, Pretoria Local Prison. I left it at the end of November 1971.

It was more difficult to leave than I had thought it might be. The last six months took *so* long. I had watched, in the earlier years, how others reacted when their time began to draw close: some became edgy, irritable; others seemed light-headed, silly. I wondered how I would feel and dreamt of it, dreamt of it endlessly, for years dreaming of it and wondering what it would be like. But only in the last two years was it possible really to imagine that it would happen at all. Before then, Out was just the distant blissful unseen horizon. Then, after five years inside, Dave Evans and John Laredo left. That was my trigger: two years to go and it seemed possible. Then Ivan and Eli left: eighteen months to go. Then Issy: one year, one month. Just next year. Then, incredibly, this year. *This* year – just eleven months and a bit, ten months and a bit. I worked out the days: 200, 150, 120, 110, 100.

I got bored with it all. I found that I didn't really feel any different. I remembered how Ivan Schermbrucker had been before he went: embarrassed almost, concerned to think that he was going and us others not. I didn't feel that. I felt glad I was going. It was wrong, arbitrary, that I should go and the others stay – but I was glad. Myself, I felt unchanged – changed only in relation to the others, that I could no longer regard things in the same light. At the end, the pettiness and meanness seemed contemptible. The boere and their behaviour didn't touch me as in the past. I was in limbo. Out but not Out. Bored, bored, bored with the whole stupid mean façade, the whole ridiculous circus with its ringmasters and clowns in their petty finery, strutting machines that barked and snapped, twitched in mechanical unison – who would soon be unable to touch or menace me any further. They had never tried to reach me, never got through to me. I had been just another performing flea, absorbed into their invisible ring, held invisibly in an empty box for a fixed time, then spewed out invisibly, leaving behind not even a slight mess.

I waited, wondering what it would be like. How would they do it? Shortly before my trial in 1964, I had taken out a British passport on the strength of my father having been born in England (my own South African passport was withdrawn while I was a student). Some time before my release date, I informed the authorities that I wished to remain in the country for about three weeks to clear up my affairs and then leave for England where my mother was living, unwell since the death of my father in 1963. Brigadier Aucamp came to see me: Why three weeks? Why so long? He implied that I would be placed under twenty-four-hour house arrest until I left, so what was the point of staying so long? I explained about wanting to clear up my affairs, left in disarray when I was detained seven-and-a-half years before. Could I have, say, fourteen days?

What, he said, can you do in fourteen days under permanent house arrest? Could I have a week then? Why a week? What'll you do for a week?

Etc., etc., etc. In the end he gave me four days. I thought it significant that he, Aucamp, brigadier in the Prisons Department, should clearly have such authority, authority in effect to tell the Minister of Justice what was what.

I was due for release on Tuesday, 30 November, the full seven-year sentence, to the last minute. Aucamp said he'd pick me up on the Monday and run me round, doing some of the things I wanted to do, like visit my father's grave in Irene, our home village near Pretoria. I slept hardly at all on the Sunday night, pacing the hours off as the night warder did his rounds, expecting a call before dawn. It came only at breakfast, giving me a second chance to shake hands all around, before leaving to join Aucamp, and Schnepel in civvies, in a chauffeured car with such a comfortable back seat. Almost like an armchair it seemed. I'd not sat in an armchair for years.

It all seemed so easy. Walking out of the front door of the prison, into the car, driving around Pretoria to Irene, to Johannesburg, chatting pleasantly about cars and rugby and the changes in the road – a whole vast new road complex, built in what had been veld when I last saw it. Pleasantly chatting, as we drove into Johannesburg where they would drop me at the Fort for my last night. All so easy and harmless – why not for the others too?

Could I, I asked Aucamp, could I please borrow five cents? He began putting his hand into his pocket. What for? For a newspaper, please. I won't be returning to Local now and I've got nothing to read for the rest of the day and night. He took his hand out of his pocket: 'You're not allowed papers. You've been without papers for the last seven years. Another night's not going to make any difference. No newspapers.' That was Aucamp, the sort of man in charge of political prisoners.

We drove into the Fort and they dropped me, stopping only to give instructions about keeping me in solitary. I did not see Aucamp again. I wasn't sorry. Schnepel paused briefly and said Good-bye and don't get into trouble again. I was locked in a small cold isolation cell for the rest of the day, and the night. I was taken for one exercise in the afternoon and chatted to a young boer, until he was called to the grille and muttered at, after which he didn't talk any more. The cell was like the Old Local: empty, mats on the floor, pot in the corner. It was a useful reminder, ending up as I'd begun.

I was called early the next morning – Tuesday, Out-day. Was it true? They wanted me in front: sign here please, fingerprints here, please, here's your money, thank you. Early still, an hour before the usual time of release, 9 a.m. A chief-warder asked me to accompany him, first to the commanding officer's office – any complaints, Mr Lewin? I'd prefer not to waste time now, thank you, Sir. Good-bye. Good-bye. Then, instead of taking me to the front entrance as I thought likely, he took me down round to the bottom, a long way round inside the grounds of the Fort, vaguely stopping at flower-beds, watching his watch. Then he turned to me: Do you know this town at all? Yes, I lived here. Oh, good, says the boer – and opens a small side door in the wall, and pushes me through. You can go now, God bless.

I laughed. Seven-and-a-half years before, a car-load of

Branchmen had picked me up at my office and taken me off for 90-day detention, for trial, for seven years' hard. Now, at 8 a.m. on a nice summer's day in Jo'burg, they smuggle me out of prison, through the back door, without a ban or a restriction, and nobody around at all. Just an embarrassed boer who says 'OK, you can go now, God bless.'

The door led into a side street in Braamfontein, an empty side-street leading towards the morning traffic. I had on shirt and trousers sent in by friends and I was carrying a small case. I walked round to the traffic, then up the hill on the outside of the wall I'd just before been inside, then around to the front gates they wouldn't let me out of. A lovely feeling, just me and the traffic. I suppose the Branch were around too, but I didn't see them then – not like later, during the next three hectic days, tearing along always behind me everywhere, right up to the plane as I left for London. I saw nobody but the traffic, fast impersonal traffic with so many unknown faces, none of whom took any interest in me and I needed to take no interest in them if I didn't want to. Nobody to stop me. Nothing between me and wherever I wanted to go.

I walked past the Fort's front gates, across the road and into a cafe. There they were: newspapers, piles of newspapers, today's newspapers, English papers and Afrikaans papers, and maga-zines, uncut magazines, and books for sale. I bought my first newspaper and held out my hand, like a foreigner with strange coins. My first personal purchase, using coins already five years old which I had never seen before. How much to phone, please? The man behind the counter glared and mumbled. His phone didn't work anyway. I went next door into a greengrocer who let me use the phone behind the counter. The first phone-call I'd made. It worked just as before. Dave sounded sleepy, surprised I was out so soon, and said he'd come and fetch me.

I walked out into Hillbrow's early morning rush-hour and sat down on the pavement to watch the world go to work. Colours, everywhere colours, flashing, moving, changing – so many different beautiful colours of people passing. To the left, I could look right down the hill, far down to the skyline, and on the right, right down to where the road disappeared into the clustered buildings, and above, past my lamp-post, a vast open sky. Even the buildings were differently coloured. And so many people, so many unknown faces, a world of anonymous faces, all moving changing rushing past to their own worlds, oblivious, uncaring, me on the pavement against the lamp-post, watching, breathing in deep welcome gulps of anonymity. I hadn't opened the paper. Dave's car arrived from among the many and I recognized him, unchanged, as if it had been yesterday.

Hello, bandiet, he said.

Hello – and good to see you.